Getting Started With
Microsoft Office Starter 2010
(Word & Excel)

By Dr. Indera E. Murphy

Tolana Publishing
Teaneck, New Jersey

Getting Started With Microsoft Office Starter 2010 (Word & Excel)

Published By:
Tolana Publishing
PO Box 719
Teaneck, NJ 07666 USA

Find us online at www.tolanapublishing.com
Inquiries may be sent to the publisher: tolanapub@yahoo.com

Our books are available online at www.barnesandnoble.com.
They can also be ordered from Ingram and Baker & Taylor.

Quantity discounts are available for corporations, non-profit organizations and educational institutions
for educational purposes, fundraising or resale. www.tolana.com/wholesale.html

ISBN-13: 978-1-935208-14-3
ISBN-10: 1-935208-14-4

Library of Congress Control Number: 2010930627

Printed and bound in the United States Of America

Notice of Liability
Every effort has been made to ensure that this book contains accurate and current information.
However, the publisher and author shall not be liable to any person or entity with respect to any
loss or damage caused or alleged to be caused directly or indirectly, as a result of any information
contained herein or by the computer software and hardware products described in it.

Trademarks
All companies and product names are trademarks or registered trademarks of their respective
companies. They are used in this book in an editorial fashion only. No use of any trademark is
intended to convey endorsement or other affiliation with this book.

Cover by Mary Kramer, owner of Milkweed Graphics, www.milkweedgraphics.com

About The Series

Getting Started With Microsoft Office Starter 2010 (Word & Excel), is part of the growing series of computer software books that are designed to be used in a classroom setting, an online class or as a self-paced learning tool. The books contain an abundance of step-by-step instructions and screen shots to help reduce the "stress" often associated with learning new software.

Titles In The Series

	ISBN
ACT! 2007	978-0-9773912-5-7
ACT! 2009	978-1-935208-07-5
ACT! 2010	978-1-935208-09-9
Using Crystal Reports 2008 With ACT! 2010 Databases	978-1-935208-10-5
Crystal Reports For Visual Studio 2005	978-0-9773912-6-4
Crystal Reports Basic For Visual Studio 2008	978-0-9773912-8-8
Crystal Reports for Visual Studio 2010	978-1-935208-12-9
Crystal Reports XI For Beginners (2nd Edition)	978-1-935208-00-6
What's New In Crystal Reports 2008	978-1-935208-01-3
Crystal Reports 2008 For Beginners	978-0-9773912-9-5
Crystal Xcelsius 4.5	978-1-935208-02-0
Xcelsius 2008	978-1-935208-05-1
OpenOffice.org 2 Writer	978-0-9773912-4-0
OpenOffice.org 3 Writer	978-1-935208-08-2
Microsoft Office Starter 2010 (Word & Excel)	978-1-935208-14-3
Microsoft Works 7	978-0-9773912-2-6
Microsoft Works 8 & 8.5	978-0-9773912-1-9
Microsoft Works 9	978-0-9773912-7-1
Windows XP	978-0-9773912-0-2

Why A Book Specifically For Microsoft Office Starter 2010?

There are a few reasons that I decided to write a book for Microsoft Office Starter 2010. They are listed below.

⇒ It has been reported that a lot of people did not upgrade to Office 2007. If that is the case, many people that are upgrading to any version of Office 2010 may be in for a shock when they open Office 2010 because the interface is completely different then Office 2003.

⇒ The Starter edition of Office 2010 will come installed on a large percent of new computers because it replaces Microsoft Works.

⇒ Until now, no matter what edition of Office (Student, Standard or Professional, etc) that you used, Word and Excel had all of the same features. The versions of Word and Excel in the Starter edition of Office 2010 has less functionality then all of the other editions of Office 2010. This means that some features that you used in a previous version may not be in the Starter version of Word or Excel.

Who This Book Is For

This book is primarily for people that have never used Microsoft Word or Excel. The second audience is people that have used a previous version of Microsoft Word or Excel or another word processor or spreadsheet package and want to learn about the versions of Word or Excel in the Starter edition of Microsoft Office.

Over the years, I have come to realize that many people only use a small percent of the features that software has to offer. One of my goals in all of the books that I write is to point out as many features as possible. My theory is that if more people knew about more than 10% of the features that a software package has, at the very least, they would try a few of them.

I know that many books claim to have "step-by-step instructions". If you have tried to follow books that make this claim and you got lost or could not complete a task as instructed, it may not have been your fault. When I decided to write computer books, I vowed to really have step-by-step instructions that actually included every step. This includes steps like which file to open, which option to select, when to save a file and more. In my opinion, it is this level of detail that makes a computer book easy to follow. I hope that you feel the same way.

About The Author

Dr. Indera E. Murphy is an author, educator and IT professional that has over 20 years of experience in the Information Technology field. She has held a variety of positions including technical writer, programmer, consultant, web designer, course developer and project leader. Indera has designed and developed software applications and web sites, as well as, manage technology driven projects in several industries. In addition to being an Executive Director and consultant, as an online adjunct professor, she has taught courses in a variety of areas including project management, technical writing, information processing, Access, HTML, Windows, Excel, Dreamweaver and critical thinking.

CONTENTS

SECTION 2 EXCEL STARTER 2010

MICROSOFT OFFICE STARTER 2010

Overview

Welcome to Microsoft Office Starter 2010!

Whether you just want to see if the Starter edition of Word and Excel can handle your word processing and spreadsheet needs or if you are a college student, a senior citizen or for whatever reason that you are going to use Office Starter, I hope that you find this book helpful. I am not a genius, but I suspect that the price of Microsoft Office Starter is one thing that prompted you to give it a try.

The goal of this book is to be by your side every step of the way through learning how to use Microsoft Office Starter 2010. This book is a visual guide that has over 600 illustrations that practically eliminate the guess work. There is more to Office Starter than knowing how to open and print a document or spreadsheet. Office Starter is robust and has a lot of features.

It is my sincere hope that whatever your current skill level is with word processing and spreadsheet software, that you will learn more about features that you are already familiar with as you go through this book and that you learn about features that you did not know existed. While you can jump to the section that covers something that you need to know right now, I hope that you go through the entire book because you will get more from the book that way.

Learning new tips and shortcuts will let you work faster and smarter. The more that you know about Office Starter, the easier your day to day word processing and spreadsheet experiences will be, which will make you more productive.

So sit back and lets get started.

Thank you for purchasing this book!

CHAPTER 1

What Is Microsoft Office Starter 2010?

Microsoft Office Starter 2010 is the free version of Microsoft Office 2010. It comes pre-installed on new computers. It is **NOT** a trial version that expires. The Starter edition of Word and Excel (which you will see referred to as Word Starter and Excel Starter) are scaled down in terms of features, compared to the versions of Microsoft Office (like Professional or Home and Business) that you pay for. When I first heard about this version of Office, I couldn't figure out why this version only came with Word and Excel. Then I remembered that they are the two most used packages in the Microsoft Office suite.

If you have used another word processing or spreadsheet software package, many of the features in Office Starter 2010 will be familiar. One thing that you will notice is that the interface has changed, especially if the last version of Microsoft Office that you used was the 2003 version or older.

The interface (sometimes referred to as the "look and feel") differences may take a little getting use to, but the more that you use the software, the faster you will feel comfortable with the interface. Overall, you will find that the features in this version of Word and Excel produce the same results that they did in prior versions of Office. The major difference in my opinion, is that the options are easier to get to because a larger percent of the options are visible on the interface, instead of only being on a dialog box.

How This Book Is Organized

To get the most out of this book, it is not advised that you skip around unless you have used Word and Excel 2007. The main reason is that a topic or option may have been covered in more detail earlier in the book. If you decide to skip around and discover that there is something that you do not understand, you will have to go back and find the section that covers the topic in detail. If you purchased this book just to learn Excel, you should read the first three Word chapters because a lot of the information also applies to Excel. While Word and Excel have different purposes, many of the options are the same. These options are covered in detail in the Word chapters. In the Excel chapters, you will see a reference to the option in the appropriate Word chapter.

If you have used Word 2007 or Excel 2007, you know that the menus and toolbars are gone and have been replaced with the Ribbon. I realized that the order of the tabs is often the order that you will use the options, from the most used to the least used. The first few chapters on Word cover common features. The remaining chapters in each section cover the options on each tab. I tried to stick to this format as much as possible to help make learning where the options are easier, but there are a few exceptions. For example, in Word, the Home and Page Layout tabs on the Ribbon both have paragraph options. I cover all of the paragraph options in the same chapter.

This book is really two books in one because it covers both Word and Excel. Chapters 1 to 10 cover Word and Chapters 11 to 15 cover Excel. Below is an overview of what is covered in each chapter.

Section 1 Word Starter 2010

Chapter 1 provides an overview of Word Starter. It covers the conventions used in this book, so that you will know what certain things mean. The primary focus of this chapter is to help you feel more comfortable using the options in Word.

Chapter 2 covers the Ribbon, which includes the tabs, groups and commands. You will also learn about the options on the File tab, status bar and keyboard shortcuts.

Chapter 3 covers creating and saving different types of documents. You will also learn about the file formats that Word supports.

Chapter 4 covers the editing options on the Home tab, which includes some of the most used options like text effects, the Format Painter and spell checking.

Chapter 5 covers the formatting options on the Home tab, which includes paragraph alignment and styles.

Chapter 6 covers the Insert tab options, including adding images, headers and footers.

Chapter 7 covers the Page Layout tab options, including themes, watermarks and wrapping text around images.

Chapter 8 covers the Mailings tab options, which includes creating mail merge documents, envelopes and labels.

Chapter 9 covers creating and editing tables.

Chapter 10 covers creating and editing charts.

Section 2 Excel Starter 2010

Chapter 11 covers what's new in Excel, as well as, the Excel workspace, options on the File tab and file formats that Excel supports.

Chapter 12 covers the Home tab options, including number formatting and styles.

Chapter 13 covers the Insert tab options, including chart types and sparklines.

Chapter 14 covers the Page Layout tab options, including scale to fit and worksheet options.

Chapter 15 covers the Formulas tab options, including the Function Library and calculation options.

What's New In Word Starter 2010

What you will notice that's new, depends on the previous version of Word that you used, if any. The older the version that you are upgrading from, the more new features you will notice. The following list does not include all of the new features in the full version of Word 2010, just some of those that are available in Word Starter.

Backstage View This feature contains options to save, open and print documents. You can also share documents and access templates from this view.

The ability to add **visual text effects** like glow, gradient glow and shadow to text.

Improved tools for Tablet PC's This option is used to add handwriting to a document.

Recover documents This feature is used to restore files, even if you did not save the file.

Share and access documents online This option is used to place documents online. Once online, you can view and edit the documents from almost any computer or Windows based Smart Phone.

The **Accessibility checker** is used to find and fix content that could be difficult for people with disabilities to read.

The **Navigation task pane** is mainly used to search long documents for specific content.

Conventions Used In This Book

I designed the following conventions to make it easier for you to follow the instructions in this book.

- ☑ The Courier font is used to indicate what you should type.
- ☑ **Drag** means to press and hold down the left mouse button while moving the mouse.
- ☑ **Click** means to press the left mouse button once, then release it immediately.
- ☑ **Double-click** means to quickly press the left mouse button twice, then release the mouse button.
- ☑ **Right-click** means to press the right mouse button once, which will open a shortcut menu.
- ☑ Press **CTRL+SHIFT** means to press and hold down the CTRL (Control) key, then press the Shift key.
- ☑ Click **OK** means to click the OK button on the dialog box.
- ☑ Press **Enter** means to press the Enter key on your keyboard.
- ☑ Press **Tab** means to press the Tab key on your keyboard.
- ☑ **SMALL CAPS** are used to indicate an option to click on or to bring something to your attention.
- ☑ 🔆 This icon indicates a shortcut or another way to complete the task that is being discussed. It can also indicate a tip or additional information about the topic being discussed.
- ☑ 💣 This icon indicates a warning, like a feature that has been removed or information that you need to be aware of.
- ☑ [See Chapter 3, Selecting Text] refers to a section in a chapter that you can use as a reference for the topic that is currently being discussed.
- ☑ [See Chapter 6, Figure 6-8] refers to an illustration (screen shot) that you can use as a reference for the topic that is currently being discussed.
- ☑ Clear the (name of option) means to remove the check mark from the option specified in the instruction.
- ☑ **PAGE LAYOUT TAB** ⟹ **PAGE SETUP GROUP** ⟹ **ORIENTATION**, means to click on the **PAGE LAYOUT** tab, look in the **PAGE SETUP** group to select the **ORIENTATION** option, as shown in Figure 1-1.

Figure 1-1 Ribbon navigation technique

 Minor changes were made to Officer Starter 2010 after this book was published. Changes that I noticed are listed on the errata page on our website for this book.

Assumptions

Yes, I know one should never assume anything, but the following assumptions have been made. It is assumed that . . . .

☑ You have Microsoft Office Starter 2010 installed on your computer and understand that there are differences between Office Starter 2010 and all of the other Office 2010 versions. While you can use this book to learn about the full version of Word 2010 and Excel 2010, there are differences including options being on different tabs on the Ribbon.

☑ You know that the operating system used to write this book is Windows Vista. If you are using a different version of Windows, some of the screen shots may have a slightly different look.

☑ You are familiar with the Windows environment including Windows Explorer and are comfortable using a mouse.

☑ You know the difference between the **INSERTION POINT** (the blinking vertical line in the document), which indicates where what you type or insert into the document will be placed and the **MOUSE POINTER** (when not in use, it looks like an I-beam), which is used to select content or commands. The mouse pointers symbol changes, based on the task being performed.

☑ You have access to the Internet to download the practice files that come with this book and to download any updates to Office Starter that are available.

☑ When you see <smile>, that signifies my attempt of adding humor to the learning process.

☑ Optional: That you have access to a printer, if you want to print any of the documents or spreadsheets that you create while using this book.

Learning To Create Great Documents And Spreadsheets

For some, learning to create documents longer than one page or spreadsheets with formulas can be intimidating. **LEARNING TO CREATE DOCUMENTS OR SPREADSHEETS REQUIRES TIME, PATIENCE, DEDICATION, PRACTICE AND ATTENTION TO DETAIL**. As you go through this book, take your time and try to understand how the concepts that you are learning can be applied to documents or spreadsheets that you will create on your own. It is possible to go through this entire book in a few days if you already have above average experience using Word and Excel.

The reality is that we all will make some mistakes along the way. If you have a fear of making mistakes, this is the time to let go of that fear, because the fear will prevent you from learning. It is also normal to initially get confused on what to do next. Even though you may not understand why you are being instructed to do something, the steps in this book will allow you to achieve the expected result. This is how you will begin to build a foundation for creating great documents and spreadsheets.

Getting Started With Word Starter

If you have used Word 2007, the look and feel of Word Starter will not be that much different and this chapter will be a refresher. If the last version of Word that you used was version 2003 or if you have never used Word, you need to read this chapter. The majority of the options that you have used in prior versions are still in Word Starter, they are just in a different place.

Word Starter 2010 vs Word 2010

Below are some of the features that are not in Word Starter that are available in the full version of Word. If you open a document that has any of the options listed below, you may be able to view the content, but you will not be able to edit or create it.

① The Reference, Review and View tabs are not available. However, some of the options on these tabs are in Word Starter.
② There are no options to customize the Ribbon or Quick Access toolbar.
③ Cannot create SmartArt graphics.
④ Macros cannot be created.
⑤ The ability to track changes, protect documents or create comments is not available.
⑥ There is no option to create an automated table of contents, index, bookmark, footnotes or endnotes.
⑦ Cannot create screen shots (like the figures in this book) or create a signature line.

Opening Word For The First Time

The first time that you open Word, you will see the dialog box shown in Figure 1-2.

As indicated, enter your name and initials, then click OK. The information that you enter is used to keep track of documents that you create or edit. It is also used for options like mail merge.

Figure 1-2 User Name dialog box

This information may have been filled in for you if you had set it up previously in another Microsoft software package. If you did not fill in this information when you first opened Word, you will find out how to add it in Chapter 2.

Word Starter Workspace

Figure 1-3 shows the Word Starter 2010 workspace. Table 1-1 provides an overview of the workspace. The majority of the rest of this chapter explains the workspace, which will start to give you an idea of where to look for the options that you want to use.

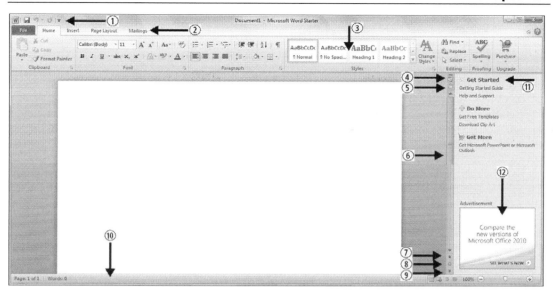

Figure 1-3 Word Starter workspace (in Print Layout view)

Option	Description
1	The Quick Access toolbar. The options are explained in Table 1-4.
2	The **TABS** are used to navigate the Ribbon to display the options.
3	The **RIBBON** is the navigation tool in Word.
4	**VIEW RULER** Clicking this button displays the rulers, as illustrated in Figure 1-4.
5	Turns the **PANNING HAND** option on. When clicked, this option is used to move the document around in the workspace by dragging the document with the left mouse button.
6	**SCROLL BAR** Right-clicking on the vertical scroll bar displays the shortcut menu shown in Figure 1-5.
7	**PREVIOUS PAGE BUTTON** Clicking this button displays the previous page in the document based on the location of the insertion point.
8	**SELECT BROWSE OBJECT BUTTON** Clicking this button displays the options shown in Figure 1-7.
9	**NEXT PAGE BUTTON** Clicking this button displays the next page in the document based on the location of the insertion point.
10	The **STATUS BAR** contains information about the document. The document view and zoom percent can also be changed in the status bar.
11	**HELP AND SUPPORT** opens the Microsoft Office support page on Microsoft's web site.
12	**ADVERTISEMENT SECTION** This section displays ads, which is how Microsoft makes money from giving Office Starter away for free. The ads are interactive, meaning that if your computer is connected to the Internet and you click on an ad, a web page will be displayed in your browser for the product or service.

Table 1-1 Word Starter workspace options explained

The rulers that you see depend on the view that is selected, as explained below.

The Print Layout view displays both rulers.

The Web Layout and Draft views display the horizontal ruler.

The Outline view does not display rulers.

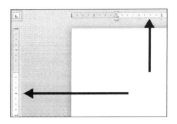

Figure 1-4 Horizontal and vertical rulers illustrated

Vertical Scroll Bar Shortcut Menu

The options on the shortcut menu shown in Figure 1-5 provide additional functionality for the vertical scroll bar, as explained in Table 1-2.

Figure 1-5 Vertical scroll bar shortcut menu

Vertical Scroll Bar Shortcut Menu Options

Option	Description
Scroll Here	Displays part of the document based on where you click on the scroll bar. This is the same as dragging the scroll bar up or down.
Top	Displays the top of the document.
Bottom	Displays the bottom of the document.
Page Up	Displays the previous page, based on the location of the insertion point.
Page Down	Displays the next page, based on the location of the insertion point.
Scroll Up	Moves up one line, based on the location of the insertion point.
Scroll Down	Moves down one line, based on the location of the insertion point.

Table 1-2 Vertical scroll bar shortcut menu options explained

Horizontal Scroll Bar Shortcut Menu

Right-clicking on the horizontal scroll bar at the bottom of the workspace displays the shortcut menu shown in Figure 1-6.

The options are similar to the ones shown above in Figure 1-5.

Figure 1-6 Horizontal scroll bar shortcut menu

Empty t1

Horizontal Scroll Bar
The horizontal scroll bar is available in the Draft and Outline views by default. It is available in the Print Layout view if the Zoom Percent is greater than 100%.

Select Browse Object Button

Clicking on this button on the vertical scroll bar displays the options shown in Figure 1-7. Hold the mouse pointer over a button to see the browse option. These options are used to customize the Previous and Next Page buttons (options 7 and 9 in Figure 1-3 shown earlier on the vertical scrollbar).

Figure 1-7 Select Browse Object button options

The options that you select in Figure 1-7 will change the functionality of Previous and Next Page buttons. For example, if you select the Browse By Heading option and then click the Previous button, the previous text with a heading style will be displayed. The default is Browse by Page. If you select a different option, it will only be available until you close Word.

Status Bar

Figure 1-8 shows the status bar, which is at the bottom of the workspace. The options are explained in Table 1-3.

Figure 1-8 Status bar

Option	Description
1	**PAGE NUMBER** Displays the page number that the insertion point is on and the total number of pages in the document. Clicking in this section displays the Go To tab on the Find and Replace dialog box. The options on this tab are used to navigate to different parts of the document.
2	**WORD COUNT** Displays the total word count of the document. If a portion of the document is selected, the number of words that is selected is displayed first, as shown above in Figure 1-8, then the total number of words in the document is displayed. Clicking in this section displays the dialog box shown in Figure 1-9.
3	**SPELL CHECK** Displays whether or not the document has spelling or grammar errors. If the check mark in this section is blue, the document does not have any spelling or grammar errors. If the check mark is red, the document has spelling or grammar errors. Clicking in this section displays the shortcut menu shown in Figure 1-10 if the document has grammar errors. Clicking in this section will display the shortcut menu shown in Figure 1-11 if the document has spelling errors. The options on these menus will help you fix the errors.

Table 1-3 Status bar options explained

Option	Description
4	**VIEWS** The four options in this section are used to select how the document is displayed in the workspace. The options are explained later in this chapter.
5	**ZOOM** The options in this section are used to change the size of the text displayed on the screen. The default is 100%. Sliding the button to the left will reduce the size of the text on the screen to a minimum of 10%. Sliding the button to the right will increase the size of the text to a maximum of 500%. Clicking on the zoom level (the percent) opens the dialog box shown in Figure 1-13.

Table 1-3 Status bar options explained (Continued)

Word Count Options

If you only want to display statistics for specific sections of the document, select the sections before opening the Word Count dialog box.

By default, the words in text boxes, footnotes and endnotes are counted. If you do not want these sections included in the count, clear the check mark at the bottom of the dialog box.

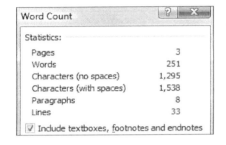

Figure 1-9 Word Count dialog box

Grammar And Spell Check Shortcut Menu

Figure 1-10 Grammar shortcut menu

Figure 1-11 Spelling shortcut menu

View Options

There are several ways to view documents, as explained below.

① **PRINT LAYOUT** Displays the document as it will look when printed. This view displays the header and footer sections if the document has them.

② **WEB LAYOUT** Displays the document as it will look when displayed as a web page. Any formatting that is not web friendly in the document will not be displayed in this view.

③ **OUTLINE** Displays the document as an outline, as shown in Figure 1-12.

④ **DRAFT** Displays the document without showing images and the header and footer sections. (In Word 2003, this was called the **NORMAL VIEW** and it displayed images.)

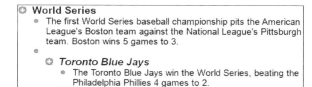

○ **World Series**
  ● The first World Series baseball championship pits the American League's Boston team against the National League's Pittsburgh team. Boston wins 5 games to 3.
  ●
      ○ *Toronto Blue Jays*
          ● The Toronto Blue Jays win the World Series, beating the Philadelphia Phillies 4 games to 2.

Figure 1-12 Outline view

Zoom Dialog Box Options

The options in the **ZOOM TO** section shown in Figure 1-13 are used to select a pre-defined percent.

The **PERCENT** option works the same as the slider on the status bar.

The **PAGE WIDTH** option displays the page so that the borders of the page are visible.

The **TEXT WIDTH** option is used to enlarge the text so that it fills the page between the left and right margins.

The **WHOLE PAGE** option displays the entire page on the screen whether or not the text is large enough to read, as shown in Figure 1-14.

The **MANY PAGES** option is used to select how many pages of the document to display on the screen at the same time. Click the button below this option to select the number of pages to display, as illustrated in Figure 1-13. When you select the number of pages, the layout that you select will be displayed in the **PREVIEW** section of the dialog box, as shown in Figure 1-13.

Saving Zoom Settings
If you select zoom options and make changes to the content of the document, the zoom options that you selected will be saved when you save the document. If you only make zoom changes and save the document, the zoom settings will not be saved.

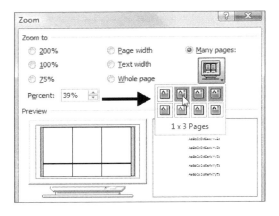

Figure 1-13 Zoom dialog box

Figure 1-14 Whole Page zoom option

Status Bar Customization Options

The status bar can be customized by right-clicking in an empty space on it and adding or removing the options shown in Figure 1-15.

The items that are checked are enabled and will appear on the status bar as needed.

Customize Status Bar		
	Formatted Page Number	4
	Section	1
✓	Page Number	4 of 6
	Vertical Page Position	
✓	Line Number	
	Column	
✓	Word Count	399
✓	Spelling and Grammar Check	Errors
✓	Language	
	Signatures	Off
✓	Information Management Policy	Off
	Caps Lock	Off
	Overtype	Insert
✓	Selection Mode	
✓	Upload Status	
✓	View Shortcuts	
✓	Zoom	100%
✓	Zoom Slider	

Figure 1-15 Status bar customization options

Quick Access Toolbar

This toolbar is shown in Figure 1-16. It is in the upper left corner of the workspace. It displays the options that the developers of Word think that you will use most.
The options are explained in Table 1-4.

Figure 1-16 Quick Access toolbar

Button	Description
1	Opens the menu shown in Figure 1-17. These options are used to resize or close the workspace. In reality, this button is not part of the Quick Access toolbar, it is part of the workspace.
2	Is used to save the document.
3	Is used to undo (remove) the last action or undo several actions. If you want to undo the last action, click the button. If you want to see previous actions, click the arrow on the button.
4	This button repeats your last action. The F4 key and CTRL+Y provides the same functionality.
5	Clicking this button and selecting the **SHOW BELOW THE RIBBON** option will move the Quick Access toolbar below the Ribbon.

Table 1-4 Quick Access toolbar buttons explained

Figure 1-17 Window menu

The Ribbon

The Ribbon, as shown in Figure 1-18 is the heart of Word. It is the navigation system. The Ribbon replaces the menu and toolbars in Word 2003. The purpose of the Ribbon is to make it easier to find options because more options are visible by default.

Figure 1-18 The Ribbon

Displaying Missing Options On The Ribbon
If you do not see all of the options on the Ribbon that are shown above in Figure 1-18, check the following:

① The workspace window must be maximized. To maximize the window, click the middle button in the upper right corner of the workspace shown earlier in Figure 1-3.
② The screen resolution must be set to at least 1024x768. To check the resolution (in Windows Vista), open the Control Panel. Double-click on the Personalization option, then click on the Display Settings option. You will see the dialog box shown in Figure 1-19. Change the resolution option illustrated to at least 1024x768.

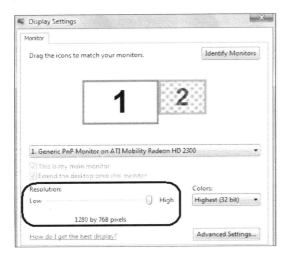

Figure 1-19 Display Settings dialog box

Minimize And Maximize The Ribbon

If you find that the Ribbon takes up too much space on the computer screen for your liking, you can minimize the Ribbon by following the steps below.

1. Double-click on a tab on the Ribbon, other then the File tab. The Ribbon will look like the one shown in Figure 1-20.

Figure 1-20 Minimized Ribbon

2. To restore the Ribbon, double-click on a tab other then the File tab.

Getting Help With Word Starter

The section on the right side of the workspace shown earlier in Figure 1-3 has links to different types of help. This section of the workspace cannot be changed, moved or closed. There are five primary ways to get help if you have a question on how to use a feature or option in Word, as discussed below.

① Read this book from cover to cover. Many of the questions that you may have are probably covered in this book.

② Getting Started Guide. The guide has articles on features and tasks in Word 2010. Keep in mind that this guide is for the full version of Word 2010, meaning that some features discussed in the guide are not available in Word Starter. (1)

③ The Online Help file. It is helpful for the definition of features and options in Word. (1)

④ Microsoft Word forums. (www.microsoft.com/communities/forums/default.mspx) Click on the Office forum link on this web page. In the Word section on the next page, click on the link for the subject area that is closest to the question that you have. You can post questions and learn how other people are using the software. The forums are also a great way to get ideas on how to enhance the documents that you create. (1)

⑤ Hire a Microsoft Word consultant. Need I say that this is the most expensive option and you probably will not get an answer to your question as fast as you would like.

(1) Your computer must be connected to the Internet to use this option.

Help File

When you open the Help file, it opens in a new window instead of opening on the right side of the workspace, like it does in other software packages.

There are two ways to open the Help file, as discussed below. Figure 1-21 illustrates the first option. Figure 1-22 shows the help file.

Figure 1-21 Option to open the Help file

① Click the question mark button in the upper right corner of the workspace.
② Press the F1 key.

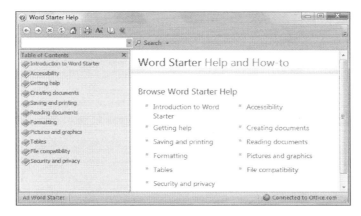

Figure 1-22 Word Starter Help file

Keyboard Shortcuts

As you read earlier in this chapter, the menus and toolbars have been removed from Word. If you used keyboard shortcuts to access commands, most of them are still available.

Click on the **ACCESSIBILITY** link shown above in Figure 1-22, then click on the Keyboard shortcuts for Microsoft Word link.

Help Toolbar

Figure 1-23 shows the Help toolbar buttons and search options. The options are explained in Table 1-5.

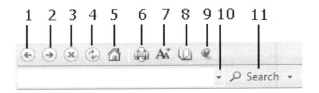

Figure 1-23 Help toolbar options

Button	Description
1	**BACK** Displays the previous help topic that you viewed. This option is only available after you have viewed at least two help topics.
2	**FORWARD** Works similar to the Back button. This button will also display topics that you have already viewed.
3	**STOP** Is used to stop the search from continuing.
4	**REFRESH** Redisplays the content in the Table of Contents section of the Help file.
5	**HOME** Displays the first page of the Help file, shown earlier in Figure 1-22.
6	**PRINT** Opens the Print dialog box so that you can select the printer and print options to print the Help topic that is displayed on the right side of the Help window.
7	**CHANGE FONT SIZE** Displays the options shown in Figure 1-24. The options are used to change the size of the text displayed in the help window.
8	**HIDE TABLE OF CONTENTS** Displays or hides the Table of Contents section (the left side) of the help window.
9	**KEEP ON TOP/NOT ON TOP** When enabled, the help window will stay open. When you click the Help button on a dialog box, the help window will appear and display the help topic associated with the dialog box.
10	**SEARCH FIELD** This field is used to type in the keyword to find the help topic that you are looking for. If you have searched for other topics, the keywords or phrases that you entered are in the drop-down list, as shown in Figure 1-25.
11	**SEARCH BUTTON** The options shown in Figure 1-26 are used to select where the search tool should look for information. The **CONTENT FROM OFFICE.COM** option will only search the web site www.office.com. The **ALL WORD STARTER** option will search online and will search the help file that is on your computers hard drive. The **CONTENT FROM THIS COMPUTER** option will only search the help file on your computers hard drive.

Table 1-5 Help toolbar options explained

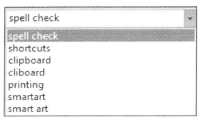

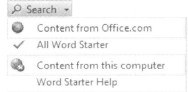

Figure 1-26 Search button options

Figure 1-24 Font size options

Figure 1-25 Search field

Connection Status

As shown in Figure 1-27, there is another way to select and know what search option is selected.

To display the options, click on the button in the lower right corner of the help window.

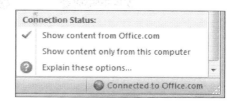

Figure 1-27 Connection options

Create A Folder For Your Files

Many of the topics discussed in this book have step-by-step instructions. If you want to follow along, there are practice files that you can download and use. The files for this book are in a zip file named starter2010.zip.

Throughout the book I will refer to the folder that you will create as "your folder". This is the folder that you will put the practice files in, as well as, any files that you create or save when using this book.

To obtain the files, send an email to starter2010@tolanapublishing.com. If you do not receive an email in a few minutes with the subject line Starter 2010 Book Files, check the spam folder in your email software. When you receive the email, follow the steps below.

1. Open Windows Explorer, then click on the C drive or the primary drive that you save files on.

2. File ⇒ New ⇒ Folder.

3. Type `Office Starter Files` as the folder name, then press Enter.

4. Go to the web page listed in the email that you received and download the zip file into the folder that you just created.

5. In Windows Explorer, click on the folder that you just created.

   Right-click on the zip file and select **EXTRACT TO HERE**, as illustrated in Figure 1-28.

   The files will be extracted (copied) to your folder.

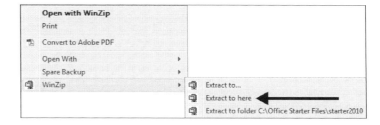

Figure 1-28 How to extract the files

Word Starter Tabs Overview

Below is a brief description of the options on each tab.

Home Tab

The options shown in Figure 1-29 are used to edit and format documents.

Figure 1-29 Home tab

Insert Tab

The options shown in Figure 1-30 are used to enhance documents by adding additional features.

Figure 1-30 Insert tab

Page Layout Tab

The options shown in Figure 1-31 are used to change how text, images and other objects are displayed in the document. As the name of the tab suggests, options to change the layout of pages are also on this tab.

Figure 1-31 Page Layout tab

Mailings Tab

The options shown in Figure 1-32 are used to create envelopes, labels or a mail merge document.

Figure 1-32 Mailings tab

THE RIBBON AND FILE TAB

Overview

In this chapter you will learn about the Ribbon. You will also learn about the options on the File tab and the features listed below.

- ☑ Contextual tabs
- ☑ Access keys
- ☑ Galleries
- ☑ Task panes
- ☑ Using Live Preview
- ☑ Templates
- ☑ Customization options

CHAPTER 2

Overview

In this chapter, the Ribbon and options on the File tab are covered in detail. The Ribbon first appeared in Office 2007. Because of its radical change from the menus and toolbars in all previous versions of Office, the reviews ran the gamut, from "loved it" to "hated it". Many people did not know what to make the radical change. At the time, people like yours truly, did not want to invest the time to learn about the Ribbon and how it worked.

Because of the wide variety of documents that I create, I did not have the time to figure out how to set up or move all of the customizations that I have in Word 2003 to Word 2007. So, for the first time since I started using Office, at least 15 years ago, I passed on upgrading to Office 2007. And if the introduction of such a radical interface facelift was not enough, new file formats were also introduced. I say all of this to let you know that if this is your first time using the Ribbon and the new file formats, you are not alone because it is my first time also <smile>.

Welcome To The Word Ribbon

As you read in Chapter 1, the Ribbon is how you access the options that were on the menu and toolbars in Word 2003 and earlier. One benefit in my opinion, that the Ribbon has over the menu and toolbars, is that the majority of the most used options are visible on a tab, instead of having to open a dialog box to select the option that you need. The Ribbon has three sections: tabs, groups and commands, as illustrated in Figure 2-1. The sections of the Ribbon are explained below.

Figure 2-1 Sections of the Word Ribbon illustrated

Sections Of The Ribbon

Tabs

Word has the following tabs: File, Home, Insert, Page Layout and Mailings, as shown above in Figure 2-1. These tabs are always available. Clicking on each tab will display a related set of commands.

Groups

Groups are a collection of related commands. The Home tab shown earlier in Figure 2-1 has the following groups: Clipboard, Font, Paragraph, Styles, Editing, Proofing and Upgrade. Each tab except the File tab has several groups of commands that generally relate to the tab name.

Commands

Commands are the options on a tab that cause something to happen, like change the font size or add a chart to the document.

Screen Tips
If you are thinking that you do not want to memorize the icons that are used for the commands, you can hold the mouse pointer over a command, as shown in Figure 2-2 and see the name of the command in bold and a description of the command.

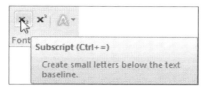

Figure 2-2 Screen tip

Additional Ribbon Features

In addition to the three sections of the Ribbon, the Ribbon has the following features, which are explained below:

① Contextual tabs
② Access keys
③ Galleries
④ Dialog box launcher

Using The Mouse To Navigate The Ribbon
If your mouse has a scroll wheel, you can switch between tabs by placing the mouse pointer over the ribbon and rolling the scroll wheel.

Contextual Tabs

The five tabs shown earlier in Figure 2-1 are always available. Some of the options on the tabs have their own tabs, which are called contextual tabs. These tabs automatically appear based on the task that you are working on. When you start working on a different task that does not require a contextual tab, the contextual tabs are automatically hidden.

For example, if you use the Draw Table option on the Borders and Shading drop-down list or select a table already in the document, you will see the Table Tools contextual tabs (Design and Layout), as illustrated in Figure 2-3.

These tabs have more options for creating and customizing tables. Throughout this book you will learn about the contextual tabs.

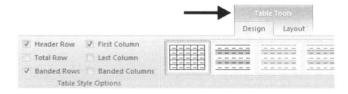

Figure 2-3 Table Tools contextual tabs

Access Keys

In addition to the keyboard shortcuts that you read about in Chapter 1, Word has access keys. Access keys are keyboard shortcuts that you can use to access commands, instead of clicking on the command to use it. Each tab and group has an access key shortcut. To use these shortcuts, press the ALT key. You will see buttons called **BADGES**, as illustrated in Figure 2-4.

The badges are the keys that you press to display the tab. The badges that you see in the figure are for the tabs. Press the key that corresponds to the tab that you want to use. You will then see the tab.

The commands also have badges. Press the access key combination for the command that you want to use.

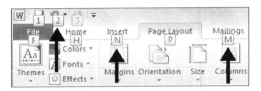

Figure 2-4 Access keys illustrated

Galleries

To the right of many command buttons you will see a down arrow. This arrow indicates that the command has additional options in a gallery, as shown in Figure 2-5, or a drop-down list, as shown in Figure 2-6.

A gallery is a collection of related visual effects that can be applied to text, as shown in Figure 2-5.

Commands that have an **ELLIPSIS** (three dots), like the More Colors option shown in Figure 2-6, will open a dialog box that has more options.

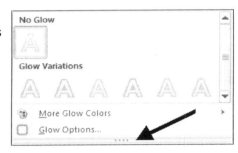

Figure 2-5 Gallery

Commands that have a right arrow, have a submenu that has additional options, as shown in Figure 2-7.

 Galleries that have an **ELLIPSIS** at the bottom, as illustrated above in Figure 2-5 can be resized by clicking on the bottom border and dragging it up or down.

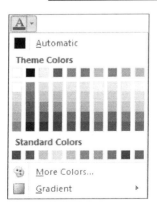

Figure 2-6 Command with an arrow

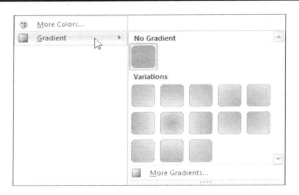

Figure 2-7 Gradient submenu options

> **Drop-Down Lists**
> What may not be obvious about drop-down lists is that there are two places to click on it. One is any place except the arrow on the right and the arrow. Clicking on the arrow displays the list. Clicking any place else, often applies the default command for the option.

> **Drop-Down Lists vs Dialog Boxes**
> Many commands are available through both of these options. The commands on drop-down lists provide easy access to the most used options. The dialog box provides more options and provides greater control of the options. One advantage that many of the drop-down lists provides is that there are icons on the left border that provide a visual representation of what the option will do.

Dialog Box Launcher

This button is in the bottom right corner of some groups on the Ribbon. For example, on the Home tab, the Clipboard, Font, Paragraph and Styles groups have this button. When you click on this button, a dialog box or task pane will open, which provides more options for the group.

Task Panes

As you just read, some Dialog box launcher buttons will display a task pane. As shown in the upper right corner of Figure 2-8, there are three options that can be used to make the task pane better meet your needs. The options are explained below.

The **MOVE** option is used to dock the task pane any place in the workspace, except on top of the advertisement section. The steps below show you how to move a task pane.

The **SIZE** option is used to resize the task pane. After selecting this option, the mouse pointer will appear in the lower right corner of the task pane. Move, but don't click, the mouse pointer in the direction that you want to resize the task pane to. Click the mouse button when the task pane is the size that you want.

Figure 2-8 Task pane

The **CLOSE** option, as well as, the X in the upper right corner of the task pane will close it.

How To Move A Task Pane

1. Home tab ⇒ Styles group ⇒ Dialog box launcher button.

2. You will see the Styles task pane. Click the down arrow button and select Move. The mouse pointer will change to four arrows.

3. Hold, but don't click, the mouse pointer over the task pane and move it to where it will work best for you, then release the left mouse button.

If you do not want the task pane in the body of the document, you can move it to the right of the vertical scroll bar, as shown in Figure 2-9.

From now until you use the Move option to change the location of the task pane, this is where it will automatically be displayed, when you open it, even in other documents.

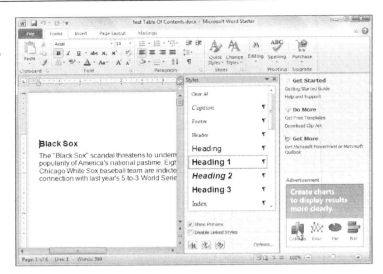

Figure 2-9 Task pane moved

Using Live Preview

This feature will display what the text will look like when a command is selected. This will save time because you do not have to apply the command to see what it will look like, then undo it if you do not like it. To use this feature, follow the steps below.

1. Select the text that you want to apply a different font to.

2. Open the font drop-down list, then hold the mouse pointer over the font that you want to use. You will see the font applied to the text, as shown on the right of Figure 2-10.

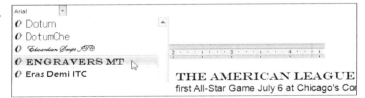

Figure 2-10 Live Preview option

3. If you want to use the font, click on it in the drop-down list, otherwise, move the mouse pointer away from the font drop-down list.

Using The Live Preview Option With Styles

If you click in a section of the document and then hold the mouse pointer over a style, the style will temporarily be displayed on the text. Figure 2-11 shows the mouse pointer on the Intense Quote style and it being applied to the text. When you move the mouse pointer away from a style, the text in the document will be displayed in its original format. Other options like the text effects also have the Live Preview feature.

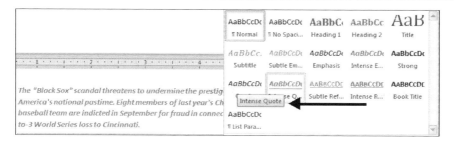

Figure 2-11 Style live preview option demonstrated

File Tab

The File tab (which is also called the **BACKSTAGE VIEW**) is new and replaces the File menu in Word 2003 and the Microsoft Office Button in Word 2007. The File tab reminds me of a "File Manager", meaning that everything external to creating, editing and formatting documents, is on this tab. I personally do not understand the significance of the alternate name, Backstage View for the File tab, but it is, what it is.

When you click on the File tab you will see the window shown in Figure 2-12. The options on this tab are used to manage the files that you use. Unlike the other tabs which have groups, the File tab has what I call "Panels", which are the options below the commands down the left side of the window. I call them panels because I could not find an official name for them. The commands and panels are explained below.

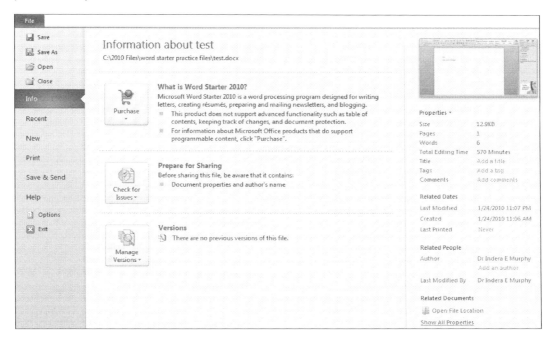

Figure 2-12 File tab (Info panel)

File Tab Commands

The File tab has the commands explained below.

The **SAVE** option saves the current document. If the document has not been saved before, you will be prompted to select a location (a folder) to store the file in and to enter a file name.

The **SAVE AS** option is used to save a document that has already been saved, with a new file name or in a different folder with the same file name or a different file name. A different file type can also be selected.

The **OPEN** command is used to open existing documents.

The **CLOSE** command is used to close the current document.

> **Closing Documents**
> If you get tired of having to select the Close option on the File tab to close files, you can right-click on the icon of the file that you want to close on the Windows taskbar and select Close. You can also click the X in the upper right corner of the workspace to close the file.

The **EXIT** command is used to close Word and all open documents.

File Tab Panels

The File tab has six panels: Info, Recent, New, Print, Save & Send and Help. They are explained below.

Info Panel

This is the panel that is automatically displayed when you click on the File tab. The content on the right side of Figure 2-12 shown above is the Info panel. The information shown is for the document that was selected before the File tab was clicked on. The **PURCHASE** button is used to buy a full version of Office 2010.

The **CHECK FOR ISSUES** button displays the options shown in Figure 2-13. Use these options when you want to share the document with someone and want to make sure that they can open the document.

The **CHECK COMPATIBILITY** option is covered in detail in Chapter 3.

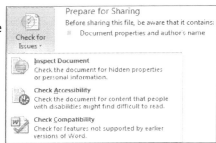

Figure 2-13 Check for Issues options

Selecting the **INSPECT DOCUMENT** option shown above in Figure 2-13 will display the dialog box shown in Figure 2-14. The options selected on the Document Inspector are what the document will be checked for in terms of content that you can select to be removed from the document before you share the document with other people. For example, you may not want other people to know who created the document, how many times the document was revised or when the document was created. Figure 2-15 shows the results of the inspection. You would click the "Remove All" button in the section that has content that you do not want to share.

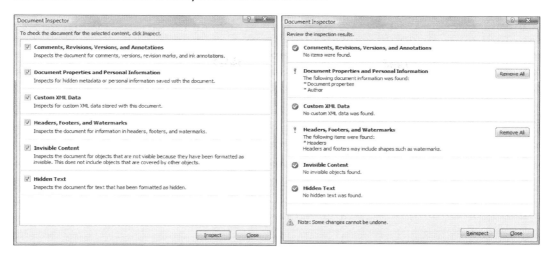

Figure 2-14 Document Inspector   **Figure 2-15** Document Inspector results

The **MANAGE VERSIONS** button displays the options shown in Figure 2-16. The options are used to view, recover or delete previous versions of the document that is currently open.

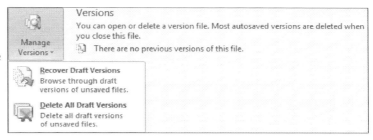

Figure 2-16 Manage Versions button options

If you open a document that you did not save before closing it, but the document was auto saved, you will see the **AUTO SAVED VERSION** button and options shown in Figure 2-17 instead of the Manage Versions button shown above.

Figure 2-17 Autosaved Version options

PROPERTIES This section is on the right side of the Info panel shown earlier in Figure 2-12. The options are a summary of statistics and information about the creation and editing of the document.

Recent Panel

This options shown on the right of Figure 2-18 are the files that you opened. By default, the maximum number of files that will be displayed is four. You can change this to a maximum of 20 by changing the option at the bottom of the figure, as shown. Later in this chapter you will learn how to increase the maximum to 50.

Figure 2-18 Recent panel

RECOVER UNSAVED DOCUMENTS This option is used to find documents that were created and not saved. This can happen if your computer loses power or if you close Word and have documents open that were created or edited, but not saved.

New Panel

The options shown in Figure 2-19 are the types of new documents that you can create. The non template options are explained in detail in Chapter 3. The template options are discussed below.

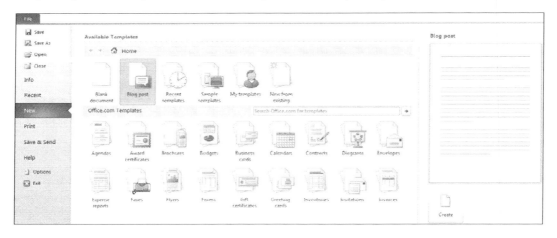

Figure 2-19 New panel

Clicking the **HOME BUTTON** displays the panel shown above in Figure 2-19, regardless of the template screen that is currently displayed.

The **RECENT TEMPLATES** option displays the templates that you have opened last.

The **SAMPLE TEMPLATES** option displays more templates that you can use. These are the templates that come with Word and are on your computers hard drive.

The **MY TEMPLATES** option is used to select a template that you have created or to create a template.

What Are Templates?

Templates are a collection of styles and other formatting options that are saved in a document. Templates are used as the basis for creating documents. When you open a template file, you are really opening a copy of it. Every document that you create is based on a template. If you find yourself creating several documents that require the same styles or page layouts, you should save these settings in a template. Doing this would save you time and the documents that you create would have a consistent look.

The most used template that comes with Word is the **BLANK DOCUMENT** template. Unless you have created a template and set it as the default template, every time that you create a new document in Word, you are using the Blank Document template. Templates should only contain text, formatting and objects that you want included in the majority of documents that will be created from the template.

Using Templates

There are a variety of templates that you can use, as shown above in Figure 2-19. Initially, many of them are on www.office.com. The templates are in categories, like brochures, forms and newsletters. To view the templates in a category, click on the category. To select a template click on it. On the right you will see a larger view on the template.

When you view the template on the right side of the panel, you will see a **CREATE** or **DOWNLOAD** button below it. The download button means that the template is not on your computers hard drive. When you double-click on the template, it will automatically be downloaded if your computer is connected to the Internet. If you are like me and don't care where the template is, but want to use it, double-click on it. In the next chapter, you will learn how to use a template and how to save a document as a template.

If you scroll down to the bottom of the categories you will see the **MORE TEMPLATES** category. Clicking on this category will display another window of template categories that you can use.

Print Panel

The options shown in Figure 2-20 are used to select a printer and the print options for the current document. The options are explained in Table 2-1.

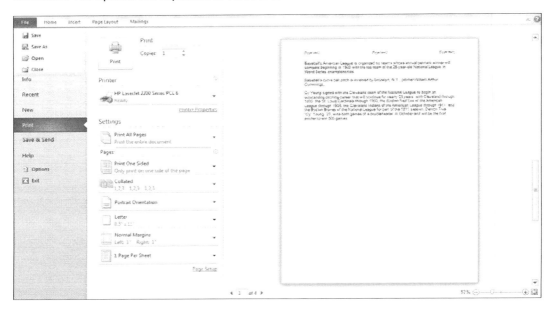

Figure 2-20 Print panel

Option	Description
Print button	Clicking this button will print the document using whatever options are already selected on this panel.
Copies	Is used to select the number of copies that you want to print.
Printer	Is used to select the printer that you want to use. You can also add a printer or create a PDF file with this option, as shown in Figure 2-21.
Print	This option defaults to **ALL PAGES**. It is used to select what pages of the document or document properties that you want to print, as shown in Figure 2-23.
Pages	If you do not want to print all of the pages in the document, type in the page numbers that you want to print in this field.
Print one sided	The options in this list are used to select whether or not you want to print the document on both sides of the paper. This is for printers that do not have built-in support for duplex printing.
Collated	Is used to select how you want a multi page document to print each page if you are printing more than one copy. **COLLATED** means that all of the pages in the document will print consecutively for each copy. **UNCOLLATED** means that the first page will be printed X number of times, where X equals the number of copies that you selected, then the second page will print X copies.

Table 2-1 Print panel options explained

Option	Description
Orientation	This option defaults to the orientation set on the Page Layout tab. If you need to print the document in the other orientation, select it here. If you want to keep the orientation that you select here, save the document after selecting the orientation.
Page Size	Is used to select a different paper size then the one saved with the document.
Margins	Is used to select different margins then the ones saved with the document.
Pages per sheet	Is used to select the number of pages in the document that you want to print on each side of the paper.
Page Setup link	Opens the Page Setup dialog box, which has many of the options discussed in this table.

Table 2-1 Print panel options explained (Continued)

Print Preview
The **PRINT PREVIEW** window in previous versions of Word has been removed. The only way to preview a document is on the right side of the Print panel shown above in Figure 2-20. The problem that I have with this is that you cannot edit the document in this panel like you could in the Print Preview window.

Printer Options

Figure 2-21 shows some of the printers that I have set up.

If you do not see the printer that you want to use in your drop-down list, select the **ADD PRINTER** option at the bottom of the drop-down list to set up the printer.

The **PRINT TO FILE** option is used to save the document in .prn file format, which can be used by a different printer. If this option is selected, the Print to File dialog box will open so that you can type in the name for the .prn file that you will create.

Figure 2-21 Printer options

Printer Properties

The options on this dialog box are specific to the printer. For example, if your printer has duplex printing built in, you would select the option on this dialog box.

Figure 2-22 shows the printer properties for the printer that I use most.

To open this dialog box, click the **PRINTER PROPERTIES** link on the Print panel.

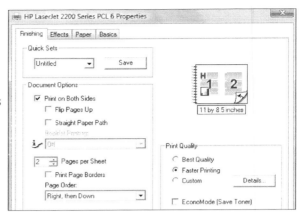

Figure 2-22 Printer Properties dialog box

Settings

In addition to printing the document, the options shown in Figure 2-23 are used to print a specific part of the document. You can also print some of the document properties.

If selected, the **PRINT CURRENT PAGE** option will print the page shown on the right side of the Print panel.

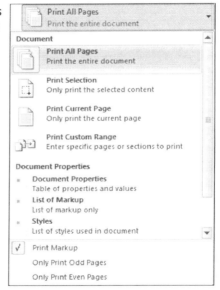

Figure 2-23 Print options

Selecting A Default Printer

The default printer is set up in Windows. It is the printer that all of the software installed on the computer will use. Some software like the full version of Adobe Acrobat (not the free reader) will install a print driver, which Windows will treat as a printer, as shown earlier in Figure 2-21. The default printer has a check mark. To select or change your default printer, follow the steps below.

1. Click the Start button on the Windows taskbar, then Control Panel ⇒ Printers. You will see a list of printers and fax machines.

2. Right-click on the printer that that you want to make your default printer and select **SET AS DEFAULT PRINTER**, as illustrated in Figure 2-24.

You can also click on the printer that you want to set as the default, then click the **SET AS DEFAULT** link shown at the top of the figure.

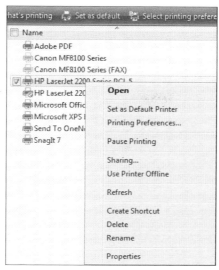

Figure 2-24 Set as default printer options

Printing Tips And Shortcuts

Below are other ways that you can print a document and additional printing techniques.

Print Range Options

There may be times when you only need to print certain pages of a document. Table 2-2 describes the types of print range options that are available on the Print dialog box. You can also print sections of the document, as described in Table 2-3.

If you want to print pages	Type this in the Pages field
1, 2, 3, 4 of a 6 page document	1-4
2, 4, 6, 8	2, 4, 6, 8
2, 3, 4, 10, 11, 88	2-4, 10-11, 88

Table 2-2 Print range options

If you want to print section	Type this in the Pages field
Section 2	S2
Sections 4, 5, 6	S4-S6

Table 2-3 Section range options

 You can also print pages and sections at the same time. Typing S1, 42-50 in the Pages field will print section 1 and pages 42-50.

Print A Document From Windows Explorer

You can print a document without opening it, Word or Excel, by following the steps below.

1. Open Windows Explorer.

2. Click on the icon in front of the folder that has the file that you want to print. On the right you should see all of the files in the folder. If not, click the **FOLDERS** button shown in Figure 2-25.

Figure 2-25 Windows Explorer toolbar

3. Right-click on the document that you want to print, then select **PRINT**, as shown in Figure 2-26. The document will now print.

    Close Windows Explorer.

Figure 2-26 Print option in Windows Explorer

Print A Document From The Open Or Save As Dialog Box

You can print a document from either of these dialog boxes in Word or Excel without opening the document that you want to print, by following the steps below.

1. In Word, File tab ⇒ Open or File tab ⇒ Save As.

2. Right-click on the document that you want to print and select **PRINT**, as shown in Figure 2-27.

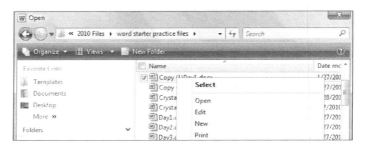

Figure 2-27 Print option in the Open (or Save As) dialog box

You can also print files from other software packages, as long as you can see the file that you want to print in the dialog box. For example, you can use the Open dialog box in Excel to print a Word document.

Printing Booklets

This option is used to convert regular documents into booklets. When this option is selected, Word will shrink each page. The only downside to this feature is that you cannot preview the booklet before it is printed. You can test it by only sending one or two pages to the printer instead of the entire document. The other way to test it is to create a PDF file to view. To create a booklet, follow the steps below.

Not all printers support printing booklets.

1. Open the document that you want to print as a booklet.

2. File tab ⇒ Print panel. Click the Printer Properties link. Change the **PAGES PER SHEET** option to 2.

3. If your printer supports duplex printing, you may also want to check the option, **PRINT ON BOTH SIDES**. Your options should look similar to the ones shown earlier in Figure 2-22.

4. Click OK, then click the Print button to print the booklet.

Zoom Options

The zoom options in the lower right corner of the Print panel work the same as the ones on the status bar. [See Chapter 1, Zoom Dialog Box Options]

Save & Send Panel

The options shown in Figure 2-28 are used to accomplish the following tasks.

  ① Send the document via email.
  ② Publish the document as a blog post.
  ③ Change the document file type.
  ④ Create a PDF or XPS file of the document.

Figure 2-28 Save & Send panel

Sharing Documents

Sharing documents with people that do not have the same software that you do and sending documents via email have become very popular. Word provides several ways to share and email documents, as explained below.

①   **SEND USING EMAIL** This option is used to send the document via email. As shown in Figure 2-29, the document can be sent as an attachment, a link, as a PDF or XPS file. Click the button on the right that corresponds to how you want to email the file.

②   **SAVE TO WEB** The options shown in Figure 2-30 are used to save the document on the web. This allows you to access to the file via the Internet or people that you want to share the file with can access it on the web.

③   **PUBLISH AS BLOG POST** The option shown in Figure 2-31 is used to post your document as a post on a blog. Some of the blogging web sites that you can post to are shown on the right of the figure.

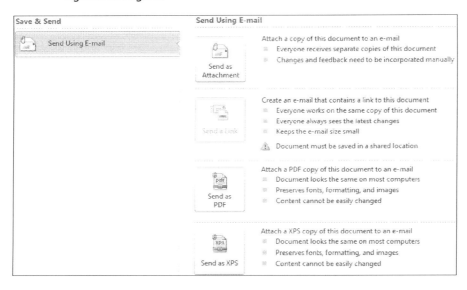

Figure 2-29 Send using e-mail options

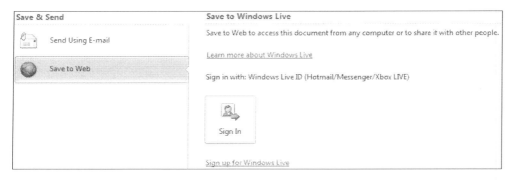

Figure 2-30 Save to web options

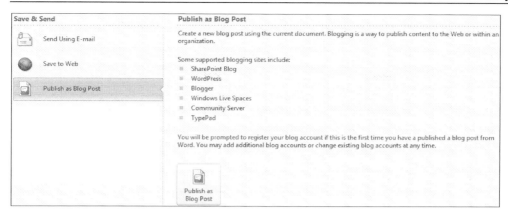

Figure 2-31 Publish as Blog Post options

Share File Types

If the document that you want to share is not in the format that you need it to be in, you can change the file type by selecting one of the options in the File Types section shown above in Figure 2-31. The options are explained below.

CHANGE FILE TYPE Selecting this file type option displays the file types shown on the right of Figure 2-32. When you click on the file type that you want to save the document as, the Save As dialog box will open with that file type selected in the Save As type field. You can use the same file name or type in a different file name.

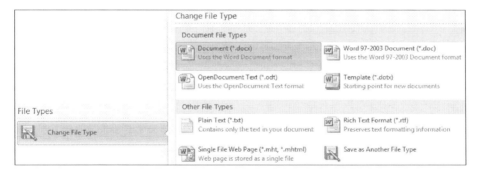

Figure 2-32 Change File Type options

CREATE PDF/XPS DOCUMENT [See Chapter 3, How To Create PDF And XPS Files]

Help Panel

The options shown in Figure 2-33 provide help and tools for Office Starter. The options are explained below.

Figure 2-33 Help panel

Support Options

The options in this section provide ways for you to get help with Office Starter.

MICROSOFT OFFICE HELP [See Chapter 1, Help File]

GETTING STARTED Clicking this button opens the Getting Started With Office Starter web page.

CONTACT US Displays a support page on Microsoft's web site that is used to ask a question or find the answer to a question.

Tools For Working With Office

The options in this section provide additional functionality for Microsoft Office.

OPTIONS Opens the Word Options dialog box, which is covered later in this chapter.

TAKE OFFICE WITH YOU Is used to install Office Starter on a USB drive, which you can use on another Windows based computer. It does not allow you to install Office Starter on another computer. To be on the safe side, the USB drive should have at least 500 MB of free space.

CHECK FOR UPDATES Will check Microsoft's web site to see if there are any updates for Office Starter.

ABOUT MICROSOFT WORD STARTER Previous versions of Office had an "About" option on the Help menu. This option would display a dialog box that contained information about the software, like the version that is currently installed. In Word Starter, this information is in the lower right corner of the Help panel shown above in Figure 2-33.

Word Options Dialog Box

Selecting the **OPTIONS** option on the File tab displays the dialog box shown in Figure 2-34. The options on this dialog box are used to customize the options that are set for Word when Office Starter was installed. The majority of options on this dialog box are explained in the rest of this chapter. If you encounter a feature that is not working the way that you think it should, this would be a good place to look for a solution.

While it is tempting to start changing several options, unless you have an above average understanding of what each option controls, you may want to come back and read this section again after you are more familiar with Word Starter.

 If selected, some of the options on the Word Options dialog box can cause your computer to run slow, especially if your computer does not have enough RAM. The options where I know that this is the case are indicated with a (1).

 Many of the options on this dialog box are explained in detail in another chapter in the book. When this is the case, the chapter reference and section is in brackets.

General Panel

The options shown in Figure 2-34 are used throughout Word. They are explained below.

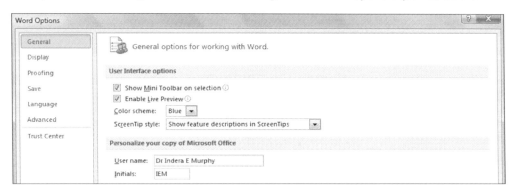

Figure 2-34 General panel

SHOW MINI TOOLBAR ON SELECTION Displays a toolbar that has formatting options. [See Chapter 3, The Mini Toolbar]

ENABLE LIVE PREVIEW [See Using Live Preview, earlier in this chapter] (1)

COLOR SCHEME The options in this drop-down list are used to change the color of the interface. The choices are limited and you cannot create your own color scheme.

SCREEN TIP STYLE The options in this drop-down list are used to enable or disable screen tips (which you may know as tool tips) that are displayed when the mouse pointer hovers over an option. [See Figure 2-2 earlier in this chapter]

PERSONALIZE YOUR COPY OF MICROSOFT OFFICE [See Chapter 1, Figure 1-2]

Display Panel

The options shown in Figure 2-35 are used to select how documents are displayed on the screen and how they are printed.

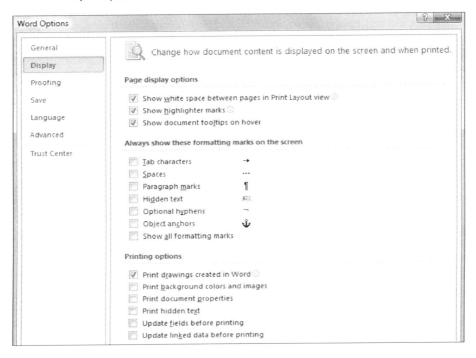

Figure 2-35 Display panel

Page Display Options

SHOW WHITE SPACE BETWEEN PAGES IN PRINT LAYOUT VIEW [See Chapter 3, Hiding White Space]

SHOW HIGHLIGHTER MARKS Is used to keep the text highlighting from appearing on the screen or printed. [See Chapter 5, Table 5-1 Text Highlight Color]

SHOW DOCUMENT TOOLTIPS ON HOVER Displays tool tips (like hyperlinks) that are hidden in the document when the mouse pointer hovers over an item.

Always Show These Formatting Marks On The Screen Options

The options in this section are non printable characters that can be displayed. The symbols after the option is what is displayed in the document. [See Chapter 5, Nonprinting Characters]

Printing Options

PRINT DRAWINGS CREATED IN WORD Clearing the check mark will print a box instead of the actual image file in the document. Text boxes are not printed. This will allow the document to be printed faster (and save toner).

PRINT BACKGROUND COLORS AND IMAGES Will keep objects like watermarks and background colors that are in the background of the document from printing.

PRINT DOCUMENT PROPERTIES [See Chapter 3, Using Document Properties]

PRINT HIDDEN TEXT If you want to print text that is hidden in the document, select this option.

UPDATE FIELDS BEFORE PRINTING Documents like those created via a mail merge or a template can have data fields that may need to be updated (refreshed) to display the most current data. Check this option if you use a lot of documents that fit this criteria. (2)

UPDATE LINKED DATA BEFORE PRINTING Select this option if you use documents that have fields that get data from an external data source. (2)

(2) Checking this option will keep you from having to remember to check to see if the fields have been updated.

Proofing Panel

The options shown in Figure 2-36 are used to select default spell check, grammar and formatting options.

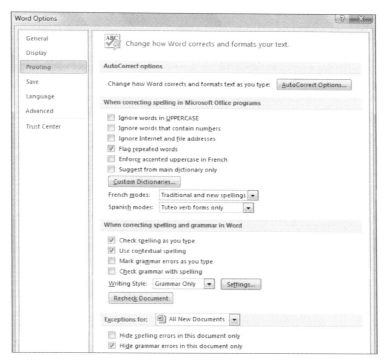

Figure 2-36 Proofing panel

Auto Correct Options [See Chapter 6, Using The Auto Correct Dialog Box]

When Correcting Spelling In Microsoft Office Programs Options

IGNORE WORDS IN UPPERCASE If checked, any words that are in all capital letters will not be spell checked.

IGNORE WORDS THAT CONTAIN NUMBERS If checked, words that have numeric values as part of the word will not be spell checked.

IGNORE INTERNET AND FILE ADDRESSES If checked, web site addresses will not be spell checked.

FLAG REPEATED WORDS When a word appears twice in a row, the second instance of the word will be marked as misspelled.

SUGGEST FROM MAIN DICTIONARY ONLY If checked, all dictionaries except the main one (the one that comes with Office) will not be used.

CUSTOM DICTIONARIES BUTTON [See Chapter 4, Custom Dictionaries]

When Correcting Spelling And Grammar In Word Options

CHECK SPELLING AS YOU TYPE If checked, spell check is enabled and will display red squiggly lines under misspelled words. If the squiggly lines get on your nerves, clear this option. You can spell check documents manually. [See Chapter 4, Using The Spell Checker] (1)

USE CONTEXTUAL SPELLING This option is used to catch most words that you use out of context. For example, you type "their", but it should be "there", based on the words around it. If your computer has less than 1 GB of RAM, this option is not enabled during the installation of Office Starter. (1)

MARK GRAMMAR ERRORS AS YOU TYPE If checked, the grammar checker is enabled and will display green squiggly lines for grammar mistakes.

CHECK GRAMMAR WITH SPELLING If checked, spell check and grammar check will happen at the same time.

WRITING STYLE Is used to select the grammar style options for the grammar checker.

SETTINGS This button opens the Grammar Settings dialog box, which is used to select the grammar options to use when the grammar checker is run.

RECHECK DOCUMENT The text that you previously clicked the Ignore button for during spelling or grammar checking will be checked again.

EXCEPTIONS FOR By design, you cannot save the option selected in this drop-down list or any other drop-down list on this dialog box that is like this one.

The **HIDE OPTIONS** are for all new documents, if that is what is selected in the Exceptions for field.

Save Panel

The options shown in Figure 2-37 are used to select options for saving documents and embedding fonts.

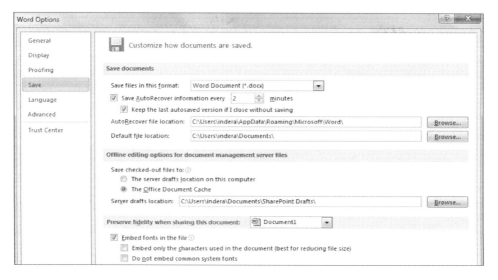

Figure 2-37 Save panel

Save Documents Options

SAVE FILES IN THIS FORMAT The options in this drop-down list are the file formats that you can save Word documents in. The default is shown in Figure 2-37 above. You can override the option that you select on the Save As dialog box when saving a document. If you know that the majority of documents that you create need to be edited by people that have Word 2003, select the Word 97-2003 Document (*.doc) option. [See Chapter 3, File Format Options]

SAVE AUTO RECOVER INFORMATION EVERY X MINUTES This option will automatically save open documents at the time interval that you select. This option is helpful if your system locks up or crashes because you will not lose all of your changes.

KEEP THE LAST AUTO RECOVERED FILE IF I CLOSE WITHOUT SAVING If checked, the last version of the file that was auto recovered will be kept.

AUTO RECOVER FILE LOCATION The path shown above in Figure 2-37 is the default location where auto recovered files are saved. Clicking the Browse button at the end of the field will let you select a different location to save these files in.

DEFAULT FILE LOCATION The path shown above in Figure 2-37 is used to select the location that Word displays on the Open and Save As dialog boxes. You should change this to the folder that you use most. For example, every time that I start writing a new book, I change this option to point to the main folder for the book that I am working on. To help make it easier to access the practice files for this book, you could change this option to the folder that you created in Chapter 1.

How The Default Location Option Works
If you click the Open option on the File tab, the contents of the folder that you selected in the Default File Location field will be displayed. The default folder that you select will always open when you first click the Open or Save As button. If the next document that you open or save a file to, is in a different folder then the default folder, the default folder temporarily changes to the one of the document that was opened or saved last, until you use the default folder again. When you reopen Word and open the Open or Save As dialog box, the default folder that you selected will be displayed.

Offline Editing Options For Document Management Server Files Options

The options in this section are for documents that you save on a Share Point server that other people will use.

PRESERVE FIDELITY WHEN SHARING THIS DOCUMENT This option makes sure that the document looks the same on other computers as it does on yours.

EMBED FONTS IN THE FILE Select this option if you will create PDF files or if you want anyone that opens the file to view and use the fonts in the document, even if the fonts are not installed on their computer. [See Chapter 3, Embedding Fonts]

EMBED ONLY THE CHARACTERS USED IN THE DOCUMENT Select this option if there is a concern about the file size because the document has a lot of fonts. If the document will be shared, it is best not to select this option.

DO NOT EMBED COMMON SYSTEM FONTS If checked, the fonts that come with Windows will not be embedded in the document. This means that if you use a Windows font in the document and someone opens the document and does not have the Windows font that you used, a different font will automatically be used. This could alter the layout of the document.

Language Panel

The options shown in Figure 2-38 are used to select the languages that you need to use in Word. To add another language, open the **ADD ADDITIONAL EDITING LANGUAGES** drop-down list and select the language that you need to add, then click the Add button.

Figure 2-38 Language panel

Advanced Panel

The Advanced panel options are shown in Figures 2-39 to 2-41 and 2-43. They are used to set defaults for options that you may use and are not aware that they can be changed.

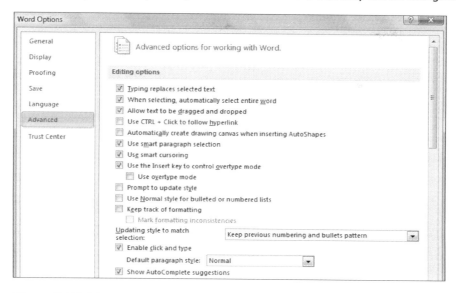

Figure 2-39 Advanced panel

Editing Options

TYPING REPLACES SELECTED TEXT If you select text to type over it, select this option.

WHEN SELECTING, AUTOMATICALLY SELECT ENTIRE WORD If checked and you select part of a word, the entire word will automatically be selected. This may or may not be what you want.

ALLOW TEXT TO BE DRAGGED AND DROPPED [See Chapter 4, How To Move (Drop And Drag) Text]

USE CTRL + CLICK TO FOLLOW HYPERLINK If checked, this option requires you to hold down the CTRL key while clicking on a link. This is not the norm. Can you imagine having to do this each time that you click on a link on a web page?

AUTOMATICALLY CREATE DRAWING CANVAS WHEN INSERTING AUTO SHAPES If you primarily only add an image file here and there, you do not need to have the drawing canvas enabled. I do not need this option enabled for all of the images in this book because I do not need to have them grouped, which is the benefit of using the drawing canvas.

USE SMART PARAGRAPH SELECTION If checked, this option will automatically select the paragraph mark, which contains all of the formatting for the paragraph. This is helpful if you move paragraphs around and want the formatting to stay with the paragraph. [See the Display Panel, Always Show These Formatting Marks On The Screen option, earlier in this chapter]

USE SMART CURSORING If checked, the insertion point is automatically moved to the page that you are viewing. This may be helpful if you scroll a lot to modify a document.

USE THE INSERT KEY TO CONTROL OVERTYPE MODE and **USE OVERTYPE MODE** [See Chapter 3, Insert And Over Type Modes]

PROMPT TO UPDATE STYLE If checked, when you apply a style and then change the style, Word will prompt you to save the style changes.

USE NORMAL STYLE FOR BULLETED OR NUMBERED LISTS If checked, the default style for bulleted and numbered lists will be the normal style instead of the Paragraph List style.

KEEP TRACK OF FORMATTING and **MARK FORMATTING INCONSISTENCIES** These options are used to keep track of the formatting styles that you create and use. You will see a blue squiggly line under text, which lets you know when there are formatting inconsistencies.

UPDATING STYLE TO MATCH SELECTION Is used to select whether or not you want the style that you are using to update the bullet and numbering style based on your current selections.

ENABLE CLICK AND TYPE and **DEFAULT PARAGRAPH STYLE** [See Chapter 3, Using Click And Type]

SHOW AUTO COMPLETE SUGGESTIONS If checked, suggestions from the Auto Complete list will be displayed while you are typing. If you do not use Auto Complete, you do not have to select this option.

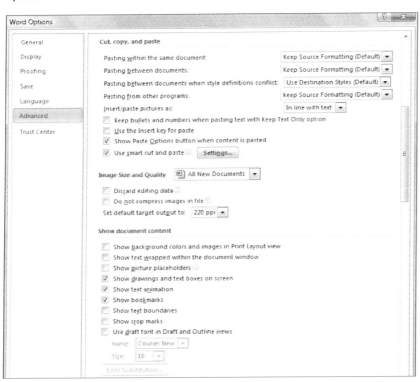

Figure 2-40 Advanced panel (Continued)

Cut, Copy And Paste Options The options in this section are used to select how you want the Paste feature to work. [See Chapter 4, Clipboard Group]

The four paste options are used to select the formatting for the content that will be pasted. The options in the Paste drop-down list are explained below.

The **KEEP SOURCE FORMATTING** option pastes the content using its current formatting.

The **MERGE FORMATTING** option uses some formatting from the surrounding content and some formatting from the content that is being pasted.

The **USE DESTINATION STYLES** option uses the styles surrounding the location that the content is pasted into.

The **KEEP TEXT ONLY** option does not paste an image file if it is not part of what was selected to be pasted. Text in a table will be pasted in paragraph format if this option is selected.

Image Size And Quality Options The options in this section are used to select image options. If the majority of documents that you print have images, you should select the highest output in the **SET DEFAULT TARGET OUTPUT TO** field.

Show Document Content Options The options in this section are used to select which features of a document are displayed.

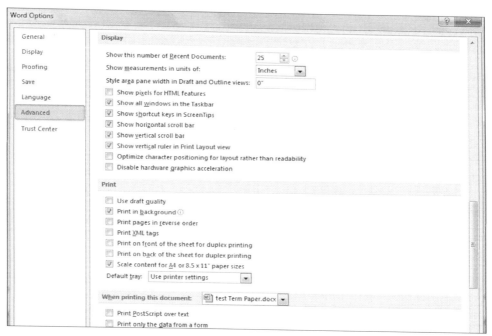

Figure 2-41 Advanced panel (Continued)

Display Options

The options in this section are used to select the non document items that are displayed in the workspace.

SHOW THIS NUMBER OF RECENT DOCUMENTS This option controls how many documents are displayed on the Recent panel. The maximum is 50. [See Recent Panel, earlier in this chapter]

STYLE AREA PANE WIDTH IN DRAFT AND OUTLINE VIEWS
This option creates a pane on the left side of documents and displays the style that is applied to the text, as illustrated in Figure 2-42.

I use this feature to help make sure that I have applied styles correctly. The number that you enter in this field uses the same unit of measurement as the option that you selected in the **SHOW MEASUREMENTS IN UNITS OF** option above it.

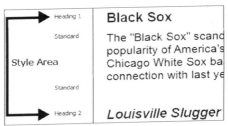

Figure 2-42 Style area pane illustrated

If you want to set paragraph indent, margins or tab stops using the ruler, you should select the unit of measurement option that you want to use on the ruler.

SHOW ALL WINDOWS IN THE TASKBAR This option will add an icon to the taskbar for each document that you have open.

OPTIMIZE CHARACTER POSITIONING FOR LAYOUT RATHER THAN READABILITY This option is used to display text as it will look when printed. If checked, the text may be repositioned on the screen, which may make it a little harder to read on the screen.

Print Options

PRINT IN BACKGROUND Selecting this option allows you to print a document and work on something else at the same time. (1)

SCALE CONTENT FOR A4 OR 8.5 X 11 PAPER SIZES This option is for documents that are not using either or these paper sizes. If checked and the document does not have one of these paper sizes, the text will automatically be enlarged or reduced to fill up an 8.5 x 11 piece of paper. For example, the paper size of this book is 7.5 x 9.25. I print out draft copies on 8.5 x 11 paper. If this option is selected, the text is enlarged to fill the 8.5 x 11 sheet of paper, which makes the book look like a large print book, which is not what I need.

When Printing This Document Options

The options in this section are used to select additional printing options.

PRINT POST SCRIPT OVER TEXT Is used when a Word Macintosh document that has print fields is converted to Windows format.

PRINT ONLY THE DATA FROM A FORM Is used for documents that have form fields. If checked, the actual form (a document) will not be printed, just the data.

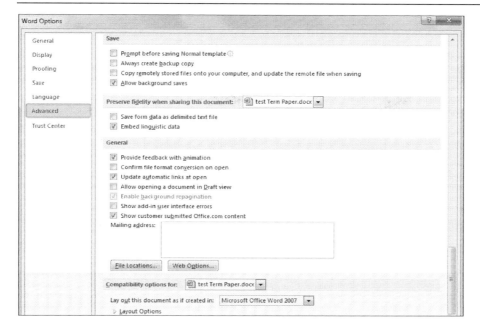

Figure 2-43 Advanced panel (Continued)

Save Options
PROMPT BEFORE SAVING NORMAL TEMPLATE If you knowingly or unknowingly make a change to the normal template file (aka Blank Document template), you will be prompted to save the change or disregard it if this option is checked. If this option is not checked, the change to the template will be saved without your knowledge.

ALLOW BACKGROUND SAVES If checked, while a document is being saved, you will be able to work on other documents. This is helpful if you regularly work on long documents or documents that have a lot of images or shapes.

Preserve Fidelity When Sharing This Document Options The options in this section are used to save form and linguistic data in the document that is selected in the drop-down list.

General Options
CONFIRM FILE FORMAT CONVERSION ON OPEN If you have the need to open a lot of documents that are in the old file format, check this option.

UPDATE AUTOMATIC LINKS AT OPEN If you open a lot of files that have links to data or to other files, check this option so that the links will be checked automatically.

ALLOW OPENING A DOCUMENT IN DRAFT VIEW If checked, the page view that was used before Word was closed is the one that will be used when Word is reopened.

ENABLE BACKGROUND REPAGINATION This option cannot be changed because it is needed to properly display items on the screen.

MAILING ADDRESS This box is used to enter your return address information. This is helpful if you are going to print envelopes and want your return address information to print on the envelope.

FILE LOCATIONS BUTTON Opens the dialog box shown in Figure 2-44. You can select folders for the file types based on where you store files of that file type.

As shown, I changed the Documents and Clipart pictures file types to folders that I created and use for these file types.

To change the location of a file type, click on the file type, then click the **MODIFY** button and double-click on the folder that you want to use for the file type.

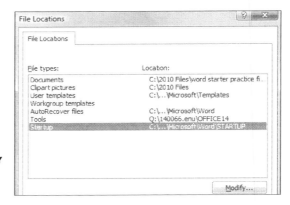

Figure 2-44 File Locations dialog box

Compatibility Options For Options

LAY OUT THIS DOCUMENT AS IF CREATED IN The file format that you select in this drop-down list determines which of the layout options are automatically selected in the Layout Options section below this option. You can select other options as needed.

Trust Center Panel

The **TRUST CENTER SETTINGS BUTTON** on the Trust Center panel opens the dialog box shown in Figure 2-45. These options are used to set security. Microsoft recommends not to change any of these options, but if you see one that is preventing you from creating the document that you need, change the option.

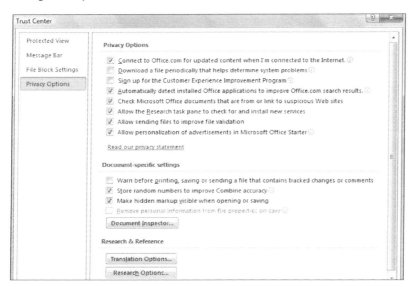

Figure 2-45 Trust Center dialog box

CREATING AND SAVING DOCUMENTS

In addition to learning the basics of creating and saving documents, you will also learn the following:

- ☑ How to open an existing document
- ☑ How to recover unsaved documents
- ☑ Save As dialog box options
- ☑ Insert and Overtype modes
- ☑ Hiding white space
- ☑ Converting documents to the new file format
- ☑ How to use the Click and Type feature
- ☑ Document properties
- ☑ Selecting text
- ☑ Mini toolbar
- ☑ Outline view
- ☑ Create a PDF file
- ☑ Create an XPS file

Overview

As the title of this chapter indicates, you will learn about the available options for creating and saving documents. In Word, the options to create a new document and open an existing document were always visible because they were on the Standard toolbar. As you read in Chapter 2, these options are now on a tab. This seems like a step in the wrong direction to me.

Yes, I did put in a request to have the Open and New Document options, as well as, the Print button placed on the Quick Access toolbar because the toolbar cannot be customized in Office Starter. I received a reply saying that my request had been denied, but hopefully, if enough other people complain about this, at some point these options will be added to the Quick Access toolbar in Starter. In all of the other versions of Office 2010, the Quick Access toolbar can be customized. It would really help if everyone that reads this book would also request these changes. Until then, the File tab will be used a lot to create, open and print documents <smile>.

File Format Options

When Word 2007 was released, so were new file formats. The main benefit of the new file formats are file security. The new format .docx does not allow macros to be saved in it. As you will learn in Table 3-1, there is a format specifically for documents that have macros. If a document has a macro or VBA code, it is automatically saved with the macro extension. Knowing this should bring some relief to opening files in the .docx format and cause you to start looking at the file extension before opening files, especially from people that you do not know well or know at all.

Other benefits are that the new format decreases the file size of documents and are designed to make repairing and recovering files easier. The only downside that comes to mind about the new file formats is that some of the functionality in a document will not be available on a computer that has Office 2003.

The way to know if a document was saved in one of the new file formats, is that the last letter of the extension is an X for basic documents and an M for documents that have macros, as shown in Figure 3-1. Table 3-1 explains the Word file formats.

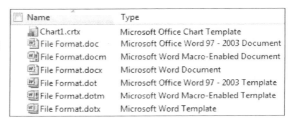

Figure 3-1 File type extensions

Word File Format Options

Format	Description
.docx	This is the format used for most documents. It replaces the **.DOC** format in Word 2003.
.dotx	This format is for templates. It replaces the **.DOT** format in Word 2003.
.docm	This format is for documents that have macros.
.crtx	This format is for chart templates that you create.

Table 3-1 Word file formats explained

File Extensions

In Figure 3-1 above, at the end of the file name you see the file extension (which is the same as the file format). It is possible that you may not see the extension in Word or Windows Explorer. This depends on how the **HIDE EXTENSIONS FOR KNOWN FILE TYPES** option in Windows is set. If the option is selected, extensions that Windows recognizes will not be displayed like they are in the figure. If you currently cannot see the extensions but want to, follow the steps below to enable the option.

1. Open Windows Explorer.
2. Tools $\Rightarrow$ Folder Options $\Rightarrow$ View tab.
3. Scroll down the list of options, then clear the check mark for the Hide extensions for known file types.
4. Click the Apply button, then click OK.

Other File Formats

In addition to the Word file formats discussed above in Table 3-1, there are other file formats that you can save documents in, as explained in Table 3-2.

Format	Description
.xps	This format is known as the XML Paper Specification. It is used to create a file that cannot be modified, similar to PDF files.
.pdf	This file format will create an Adobe PDF file which can be opened on any computer that has the free Adobe reader or the full version of Adobe Acrobat, regardless of the operating system installed on the computer.
.mht & .mhtml	This is known as the **SINGLE FILE WEB PAGE** file format. This format saves everything for the web page in one file, including images. (1)
.htm & .html	This is the standard web page file format. This format does not save everything for the web page in the same file. Instead, links are created that point to objects like images. These objects are saved as individual files. (1)
.rtf	(Stands for Rich Text Format) Select this file format when the document needs to be opened or edited in other word processors. (1)
.txt	This file format is known as a plain text file because this file format does not save any formatting. (1)
.odt	This is an open document file format. OpenOffice.org's word processor uses this file format. (1)
.wps	This is the file format for Microsoft Works, which will be discontinued. (1)

Table 3-2 Other file formats explained

(1)

All Word 2010 features or functionality may not be saved in this file format.

Creating New Documents

Believe it or not, Word provides three ways to create a new document, as discussed below. The options are illustrated in Figure 3-2.

Figure 3-2 Ways to create a new document

① **BLANK DOCUMENT** Select this option when you need to create a new document. This is the most used option for creating new documents.

② **FROM A TEMPLATE** This option often has a lot of the formatting saved in the template that will be applied to the document that you create.

③ **NEW FROM EXISTING** Select this option when there is a document that has a lot of text, page layout or formatting that you need for the new document that you will create.

Using The Blank Document Option

The steps below show you how to create a blank document.

1. File tab ⇒ New panel ⇒ Blank Document.

2. Add the text, images and formatting that the document needs.

Using The Template Option

As you read in Chapter 2, Word comes with a lot of templates that you can use. You will learn how to use two of the templates in the next two sections.

Use A Template To Create A Document

The steps below show you how to download a template and use it to create a newsletter.

1. File tab ⇒ New panel.

2. Click on the Newsletters category, then double-click on the Newsletter (Executive design template). If you look in the Title bar, you will see the words [Compatibility Mode]. This means that the template is in the old template file format.

3. If you click on different parts of the template, you will see that the text that you can change is in a text box. Highlight the text that you want to change and delete it, then type in your information. Any part of the template that you do not need, you can delete it.

4. When you are finished making the changes, click the Save button. You will see the option **MAINTAIN COMPATIBILITY WITH PREVIOUS VERSIONS OF WORD** on the Save As dialog box. Select this option if you need to save your document in a format that can be opened by Word 2003 and earlier, otherwise, save the document in the new file format.

Create A Blog Post Document

Blogs have become very popular in the last few years. There is a blog or two (and that is being very conservative) for just about any topic that you can think of. Word has a template that can be used to create a blog post, which you can upload to a blog.

Some of the free blog services that have built in support for blog posts created in Word are WordPress (www.wordpress.com), Windows Live Spaces (www.spaces.live.com) and Blogger (www.blogger.com). If the blog service that you want to use is not listed on www.office.com, you can set up your blog provider on the New Blog Account dialog box. The steps below provide an overview of how to use the Blog post template.

1. File tab ⇒ New panel ⇒ Double-click on the Blog Post option.

2. You will see the dialog box shown in Figure 3-3 unless you have already set up a blog account.

    For now, click the Register Later button.

Figure 3-3 Register a Blog Account dialog box

3. You will see the document shown in Figure 3-4.

    Create the content for the blog post, then upload the document.

Figure 3-4 Blog post document

Blog Post Tools

Blog Post documents have their own tabs. Because a blog post document must meet HTML standards, many of the options for documents are not supported with blog templates. The supported options are explained below.

Blog Post Tab

The options on the tab shown in Figure 3-5 used to create and edit blog post documents. The options are explained below.

Figure 3-5 Blog Post tab

Blog Group

The options in this group are just for blog post documents. They are explained in Table 3-3.

Option	Description
Publish	Is used to upload (publish) the blog post to the blogs web site.
Home Page	Is used to display the Home page of the blog in a web browser.
Insert Category	Is used to put the blog post in an existing category that the blog has or create a new category for the blog post.
Open Existing	Is used to edit an existing blog post.
Manage Accounts	Displays the dialog box shown in Figure 3-6, which is used to create, change or remove blog host accounts.

Table 3-3 Blog group options explained

Figure 3-6 Blog Accounts dialog box

Clipboard Group

[See Chapter 4, Clipboard Group]

Basic Text Group

The options in this group are used to format text. The options are a combination of two groups on other tabs. [See Chapter 5, Font Group and Chapter 5, Paragraph Group]

Styles Group

Only displays styles that can be displayed on web pages. [See Chapter 5, Styles Group]

Proofing Group

[See Chapter 4, Proofing Group]

Insert Tab

The options on this tab are shown in Figure 3-7 and are used to add objects to the blog post.

The Tables group option is covered in Chapter 9. Charts are covered in Chapter 10. All of the other groups are covered in Chapter 6.

Figure 3-7 Insert tab for blog posts

Using The New From Existing Option

This option is helpful when making minor changes to an existing document will give you the new document that you need. The steps below show you how to access this option.

1. File tab ⇒ New panel ⇒ New from existing. You will see the dialog box shown in Figure 3-8.

   This dialog box has the same functionality as the Open dialog box shown later in Figure 3-10.

   The one difference is that when you click on a file, the Open button changes to Create New, as illustrated. This lets you know that you are opening a copy of the document.

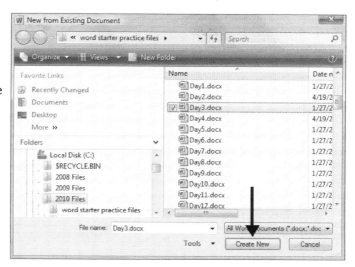

Figure 3-8 New From Existing Document dialog box

2. Navigate to the folder that has the file that you want to use as the basis for the new document that you are creating.

3. Double-click on the file name to open the document.

You should see the document that you selected in the workspace. Usually, when you open a non template document, the file name is at the top of the workspace. If you look at the top of your workspace you will not see the name of the file that you double-clicked on. Instead, you see "'Document and a number", as shown in Figure 3-9 . This means that the changes that you make will only be saved in this copy of the original document. When you save this document, use a different file name then the original one unless you are saving the document to a different folder.

Document3 - Microsoft Word Starter

Figure 3-9 Result of using the New from existing option

This process is the same as using the Open dialog box to select a file and then using the SAVE AS command. The benefit of using the New from existing option is that it is more difficult to overwrite the original file by mistake, thus helping to keep your blood pressure low <smile>.

How To Find Documents That You Create If you organize the documents that you create by saving them in folders, they will be easier to find, thus saving you time and reducing the stress that comes from not being able to find the file that you need, in a timely manner. The majority of documents that I create are project related, so I create a folder for each project and store all of the documents for that project in the same folder, regardless of the software that was used to create each document. This means that I store word processing documents, spreadsheets, PDF files and image files in the same folder, as long as they are for the same project.

You can use the same technique or a different technique that better meets your needs. The worse thing that you can do in my opinion, is to store all of the documents that you create in the same folder. Months from now, you may not remember what some documents contain.

Opening An Existing Document The Recent panel (File tab ⇒ Recent panel) provides several options to open documents. On the right side of the panel by default, you will see a list of at least the last four documents that you have opened. If you changed the **NUMBER OF RECENT DOCUMENTS** option to a larger number, you will see more files in the Recent Documents list on the left.

To open a document at the top of the panel, click on the file name. If the file that you want to open is not displayed, use the Open command.

Using The Open Dialog Box

In addition to being able to open documents created in Word, you will see that you can open files that were created in other word processing packages. The steps below show you how to open a file type that is supported in Word, but not necessarily created in Word.

1. File tab ⇒ Open.

   You will see the dialog box shown in Figure 3-10.

   The list in the lower right corner of the figure contains the file types that Word supports.

   If you are not sure of the file type for the file that you want to open, select the **ALL FILES** option.

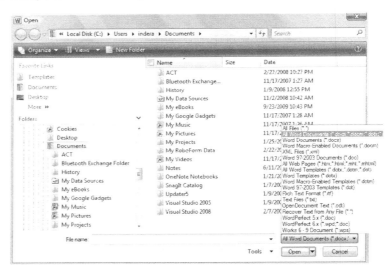

Figure 3-10 Open dialog box

2. Navigate to the folder that has the file that you want to open. Double-click on the file name to open the document.

Open Dialog Box Options

In addition to being able to open a variety of file types from the Open dialog box, the dialog box has other options, as explained below.

FILE NAME This field has the drop-down list shown in Figure 3-11. It displays files that you opened recently in Word, regardless of the file type.

In the figure, there are HTML and OpenOffice.org files that can be opened in Word.

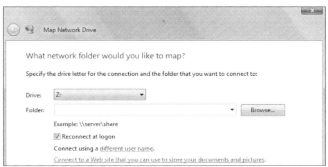

Figure 3-11 File name drop-down list

TOOLS BUTTON Opens a dialog box that is used to connect to a network drive, as shown in Figure 3-12.

You would select this option if you wanted to open a file that is on a network drive that the computer is not already connected to.

Figure 3-12 Map Network Drive dialog box

OPEN BUTTON The options shown in Figure 3-13 are used to select how you want to open the document. The options are explained in Table 3-4.

Figure 3-13 Open button options

Option	Description
Open	This is the default option. It opens the document so that it can be modified without restrictions.
Open Read-Only	Opens the document, but changes cannot be saved to the document.
Open as Copy	Creates a copy of the document and opens the copy and gives the document a different name by adding the word "Copy" and a number in front of the file name, as shown in Figure 3-14.
Open in Browser	The option is only available when an HTML document is selected to be opened because the document selected will be opened in a web browser.
Open with Transform	This option is only available when you open an XML file. This option is used to select the .XSL or .XSLT transform file.

Table 3-4 Open button options explained

Option	Description
Open in Protected View	Select this option if you are not sure if the file could have a security threat (virus, spyware, etc.). Selecting this option does not allow the file to be edited, unless you click the **ENABLE EDITING** button shown in Figure 3-15 or 3-16.
Open and Repair	Select this option when you need to recover text from a document that is damaged. If you select the Open button and see a message that there is something wrong with the file, select this option to repair the file so that it can be fixed and then opened.

Table 3-4 Open button options explained (Continued)

Copy (2)Day1.docx - Microsoft Word Starter

Figure 3-14 Open as Copy file name example

Opening More Than One Document At The Same Time
If you know that you need to work on more than one document, you can select more than one document to open if they are all in the same folder. Click on the first document that you want to open in the Open dialog box. Press and hold down the CTRL key, then click on each file that you want to open. Once you have selected all of the files that you open, click the Open button.

Using The Practice Files
Unless instructed otherwise, it is probably best to save the practice files with a different file name if you want to keep the changes that you make, so that when you go through the book, you will still have the original file. As you have read in this chapter, you have several options for not overwriting the original file, as listed below.
① Use the **NEW FROM EXISTING** option.
② Use the **OPEN AS COPY** option.
③ Use the **SAVE AS** option when you first open a file.

Figure 3-15 Protected view of the document

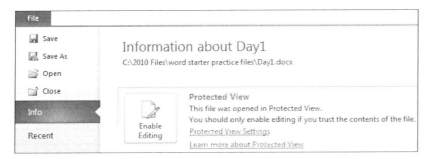

Figure 3-16 Protected view options

Recent Documents List

The Recent Documents list is shown in Figure 3-17. This list contains the documents that you have opened. If there are documents that you use all the time, you may want to add them permanently to the top of the list, as explained in the next section.

Figure 3-17 Recent Documents List

Pin A Document To The Recent Documents List

On the right side of Figure 3-17 above, you see the **PIN THIS ITEM TO THE LIST** option. Selecting this option will place the document in the top section of the Recent Documents list, as shown above, at the top of Figure 3-17. The document will stay there until you unpin it.

The icon will be different for files that are not pinned to the list. The Recent Documents list will display the last 20 documents that were opened. This includes the pinned documents. For example, if you pin seven documents, they will be displayed at the top of the Recent Documents list and the last 13 documents that were opened, are displayed below the pinned documents.

Keep the following in mind. If the **QUICKLY ACCESS THIS NUMBER OF RECENT DOCUMENTS** option is set to five for example and you have seven pinned documents, only five of the seven pinned documents will be displayed in the Recent Documents list on the left side of the panel.

If you right-click on a document in the Recent Documents section, you will see one of the two shortcut menus shown in Figure 3-18.

The shortcut menu on the left contains the options for a document that is not pinned. The shortcut menu on the right contains the options for a document that is pinned.

Figure 3-18 Shortcut menus

Selecting the **REMOVE FROM LIST** option will clear the file from both Recent Documents sections.

Recent Places List

The options in this section were shown earlier in Figure 3-17. They are a list of the folders that you have opened to get to the documents that you have opened. You can pin folders to the Recent Places list. If you use some folders on a regular basis, pinning them to this list will save you some time.

Not Saving Documents

If you close a document and do not save the changes, you will see the dialog box shown in Figure 3-19. If you click the **DON'T SAVE** button and have the **SAVE AUTORECOVER** option enabled, Word will save the document for you.

Figure 3-19 Save warning dialog box

Recover Documents

As you read in Chapter 2, Office Starter 2010 has the ability to recover documents. If you lose a document, try to recover it by clicking on the **RECOVER UNSAVED DOCUMENTS** option at the bottom of the Recent panel on the File tab. The files that can be recovered are in a folder called "Unsaved Files" and have the file type **.ASD**, as illustrated in Figure 3-20. When you need to recover a file, follow the steps below.

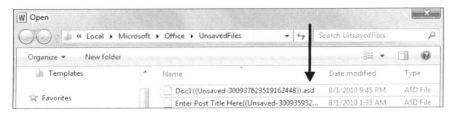

Figure 3-20 Files that can be recovered illustrated

1. If you do not have any files to recover, make a change to an existing document, close it without saving the change.

2. File tab ⇒ Recent panel ⇒ Recover Unsaved Documents link.

3. Double-click on the file in the Unsaved Files folder. You will see the options illustrated in Figure 3-21. Notice the following:

   ① In the title bar at the top of the workspace, you see (Unsaved File) [Read-Only]. This lets you know that you must give the file a different name then the one shown to fully recover the document.
   ② The **RECOVERED UNSAVED FILE** section shown in Figure 3-21 provides the tasks that you must complete in order to finalize the recovery of the document. Figure 3-22 shows the recover options for an auto saved document that can be restored.

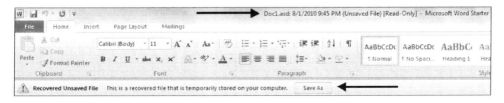

Figure 3-21 Recovered file

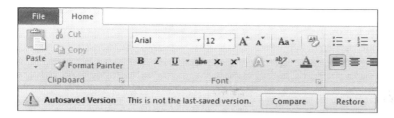

Figure 3-22 Autosaved recover options

4. Click the Save As button illustrated earlier in Figure 3-21.

5. Navigate to the folder that you want to save the document in, then type in the file name that you want.

Comparing Documents

The **COMPARE** button shown above in Figure 3-22 is used to display all copies of a document that was auto saved, as shown in Figure 3-23. The items in the left column show the changes by category, like Inserted or Header and Footer changes. If you scroll down the compared, original or revised document, the other documents will also scroll down.

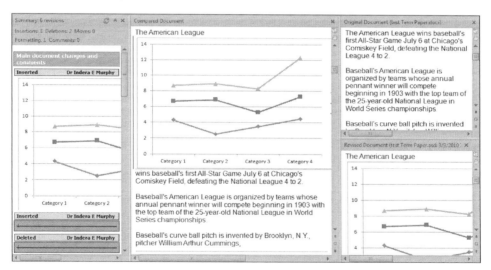

Figure 3-23 Compare documents window

The Difference Between Save And Save As

The **SAVE** command will save the file that is currently open, with the existing file name.

The **SAVE AS** command will save a file for the first time. You can also save an existing file with a new name, which means that you will have similar information in two documents, unless you delete one of the documents.

Using The Save As Dialog Box

In addition to being able to select the folder and file name for the document, the Save As dialog box shown in Figure 3-24 has other options, as explained below.

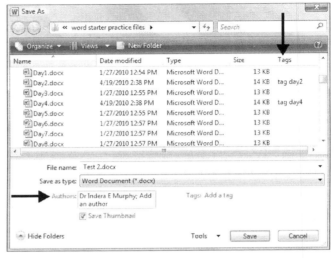

Figure 3-24 Save As dialog box

Save As Dialog Box Options

SAVE AS TYPE Is used to select the file format for the document. In addition to the file format options discussed earlier in Tables 3-1 and 3-2, you can also save documents in the following formats. Having the ability to save documents in these formats will allow you to share the documents with people that do not have Word 2007 or 2010. Some of the Word 2010 formatting and features may not be available when documents are saved in these formats.

① Word XML Document (.xml)
② Word 2003 XML Document (.xml)
③ Word 97-2003 & 6.0/95 - RTF (.doc)

AUTHORS Is used to change or add the documents authors. To change the author information, click in the field. You will see the option to add an author, as illustrated in Figure 3-24 above. Type in another authors name or change the current author information.

TAGS are used to enter keywords for the document. Often, the information entered in this field is used to search for documents. The tags can be seen in the Open and Save As dialog boxes in the Tags column, as illustrated in Figure 3-24 above.

SAVE THUMBNAIL If checked, this option is used to view a thumbnail size picture of the first page of the document in the Open or Save As dialog box in Word, as illustrated in Figure 3-25 or Windows Explorer, as illustrated in Figure 3-26. To see the thumbnail, the view must be set to Medium, Large or Extra Large icons.

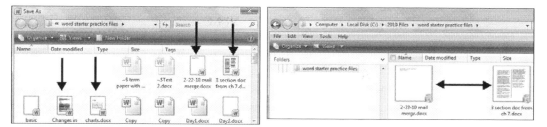

Figure 3-25 Thumbnail view in Word   **Figure 3-26** Thumbnail view in Windows Explorer

HIDE FOLDERS Clicking this button will hide the folders at the top of the Save As dialog box, as shown in Figures 3-27 and 3-28. Compare this version of the dialog box to the one shown earlier in Figure 3-24.

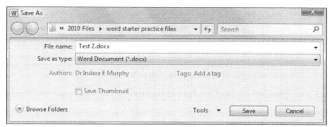

Figure 3-27 Folders hidden on the Save As dialog box

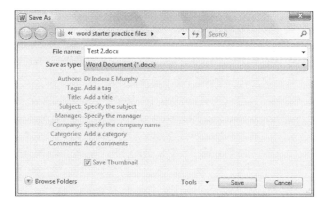

Figure 3-28 Another hidden view for folders

TOOLS The options shown in Figure 3-29 are used to select additional save options. They are explained below.

Figure 3-29 Tools button options on the Save As dialog box

Tools Button Options

MAP NETWORK DRIVE Select this option if you need to save the file to a network drive that the computer is not already connected to. [See Figure 3-12 earlier in this chapter]

SAVE OPTIONS Displays the save options on the Word Options dialog box.

WEB OPTIONS Opens the dialog box shown in Figure 3-30. The options are used to select the Internet options for the file that you are saving.

Figure 3-30 Web Options dialog box

COMPRESS PICTURES Opens the dialog box shown in Figure 3-31. The compress options are used to reduce the file size of images in the document. For the most part, you probably will not have to use this option, unless the image file size is very large or if the image needs to meet at least one of the options on the dialog box.

The Target output options are used to select the resolution of images in the document. Select the option that is closest to the type of document that you are creating.

Figure 3-31 Compress Pictures dialog box

Create Your Own Template

In Chapter 2 you read about the templates that are available in Word. Earlier in this chapter you read about the template file format extension and how to create a document using a template. In this section you will learn how to create your own template.

If you have created a document that has a lot of formatting and content that you would like to use for other document that you will create, you can save the document as a template. To do that, follow the steps below.

1. Open the document that has the content that you want to save as a template.

2. Remove any content or formatting that you do not want in the template.

3. File tab ⇒ Save As, then select the folder that you want to store the template in.

4. Type in a name for the template, then open the Save as type drop-down list and select Word Template. Click the Save button.

Using The Open And Save As Dialog Boxes For File Management

In addition to opening and saving documents with these dialog boxes, they also provide copy, delete and rename file management functionality, as shown in Figure 3-32.

This shortcut menu has other options that you may also find useful. These are the same options that Windows Explorer displays when you right-click on a file.

Depending on the software that you have installed, you may have different options on the shortcut menu then the ones half way down the menu.

Figure 3-32 Open and Save As dialog box shortcut menu

Renaming Files

You may find it easier to rename files in the Open or Save As dialog box, then renaming or deleting files in Windows Explorer. The steps below show you how to rename files in Word.

1. Open a new document or any word processing document.

2. File tab ⇒ Open, or File tab ⇒ Save As.

3. Right-click on the file that you want to rename in the dialog box, then select **RENAME**, as shown above in Figure 3-32.

4. Type in the new file name, then press Enter. The document will be renamed.

Deleting Files In The Open And Save As Dialog Boxes

Click on the file that you want to delete in the Open or Save As dialog box, then select one of the options below to delete the document.

① Press the **DELETE** key, then click Yes to send the document to the Recycle Bin.
② Select the Delete option on the shortcut menu shown above in Figure 3-32.

Converting Documents To The New File Type

What I noticed after installing Office Starter 2010 is that documents created in Word 2003 are automatically displayed with a different file type name, as shown in Figure 3-33. Documents that do not have Microsoft Word Document as file type name can be converted after they are opened in Word Starter.

To convert the document to the new file format, open the Save As dialog box, then open the Save as type drop-down list and select Word Document (*.docx).

Name	Date modified	Type
Crystal Reports 2008 For ACT! Front Matter.doc	1/6/2010 8:05 PM	Microsoft Office Word 97 - 2003 Document
Crystal Reports For ACT 2010 Table of contents.doc	1/7/2010 12:27 AM	Microsoft Office Word 97 - 2003 Document
Day1.docx	1/27/2010 11:54 AM	Microsoft Word Document
Day2.docx	1/27/2010 11:54 AM	Microsoft Word Document

Figure 3-33 Word file types

Compatibility Mode

When you open a document that is not in the new file format, it will be opened in **COMPATIBILITY MODE,** as illustrated at the top of Figure 3-34. This means that the document does not have access to the new features in Word Starter. For example, I opened a document that was saved in Word 2003 format and noticed that the Themes option on the Page Layout tab was not enabled. You can use the Document to convert practice file to convert a file to the new file format.

Figure 3-34 Compatibility mode illustrated

Using The Compatibility Checker

If you are creating or editing a document in Word 2010 and know that some people will need to open it in Word 2003, you should use the Compatibility Checker to see how the document will convert to Word 2003 or earlier. This process will identify the features that are not supported in earlier versions of Word. To see how this feature works, follow the steps below.

1. Open the C-Checker.docx document.

2. File tab ⇒ Info panel ⇒ Check for Issues ⇒ Check Compatibility. You will see the dialog box shown in Figure 3-35.

The options in the Summary section are the items that will be changed or removed if the document is saved in an older file format.

With the changes being made in the dialog box, the document may not look the same when it is saved in the older file format.

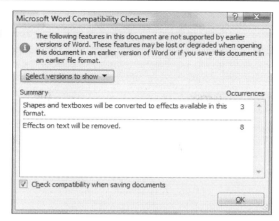

Figure 3-35 Microsoft Word Compatibility Checker dialog box

Insert And Over Type Modes

Insert and overtype are the options for adding text to a document. The majority of the time you use the Insert mode whether you know it or not. Insert mode is used to add more text to the document. Overtype mode deletes the character to the right of the insertion point, each time you type a character. If you have turned on the overtype mode and did not realize it, you know how frustrating it can be. Have no fear, there is a solution that will prevent you from turning on the overtype option without knowing it. Your keyboard has an Insert key, which is often right next to the Delete key. Often, you could hit the Insert key by mistake.

In Word, the Overtype mode is controlled by an option on the Word Options dialog box. I know what you are saying, "That's great, but what if I press the Insert key on the keyboard?" The answer is that when the option on the dialog box is enabled, pressing the Insert key on your keyboard does not override the setting. How cool is that?

Hiding White Space

If you have already created or edited documents with more than one page in Word Starter, you have seen the white space above and below the pages in the Print Layout view. I don't know why it's called "white space" when it is really gray <smile>. If it was white, we wouldn't see it. The benefit of hiding the white space is to be able to see more of the document on the screen. You can hide the white space between the pages by following the steps below.

1. Open the document that you want to hide the white space in, then switch to the Print Layout view if necessary.

2. Hold the mouse pointer in the "white" space at the top or bottom of a page, as shown in Figure 3-36.

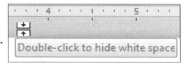

Figure 3-36 Mouse pointer in position to hide white space

3. When you see the option shown above in Figure 3-36, double-click as prompted and the white space between the pages in the document will disappear. Save the document.

Using Document Properties

Document properties are used to add information about the document to the document. This feature is more helpful if the document will be shared or edited by more than one person. To add or edit document properties, follow the steps below after you have opened the document.

1. File tab ⇒ Info panel ⇒ Properties section. On the right side of the panel, you will see the options shown in Figure 3-37.

The options below the Properties button display information about the document. To add a title, tag, comment or author, click in the field to the right of the option and type in the information.

The **TITLE** field can also be updated if a header building block that has the "Type the document title" field is added to the document. The information that you type in this field will update the Title field shown in Figure 3-37.

Except for the **LAST PRINTED** property, the properties that have gray text can be changed.

The **RELATED PEOPLE** options are used to add and edit authors of the document. If you hold the mouse pointer over the **ADD AN AUTHOR** field, you will see the options illustrated in Figure 3-37.

Figure 3-37 Properties section on the Info panel

Clicking the button at the end of the Author field will open the address book, which allows you to select an author from the address book.

The **OPEN FILE LOCATION** option displays the folder that the file is saved in.

2. Add or change the properties as needed, then save the changes to the document.

Properties Button Options

Clicking the **PROPERTIES** button at the top of the Properties section displays the options shown in Figure 3-38. The options are explained below.

The **SHOW DOCUMENT PANEL** option displays the Document Properties panel shown in Figure 3-39. The options on this panel are used to enter basic information about the document.

Figure 3-38 Properties button options

The **ADVANCED PROPERTIES** option displays the dialog box shown in Figure 3-40. This dialog box can also be opened by clicking on the Document Properties option on the Document Properties panel shown in Figure 3-39.

The **SHOW ALL PROPERTIES** option will display more options in this section of the panel, as shown in Figure 3-41. Compare this to the options shown earlier in Figure 3-37.

Figure 3-39 Document Properties panel

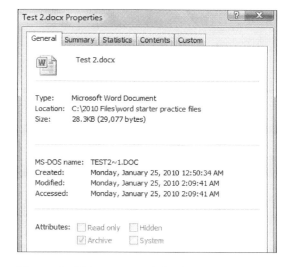

Figure 3-40 Properties dialog box

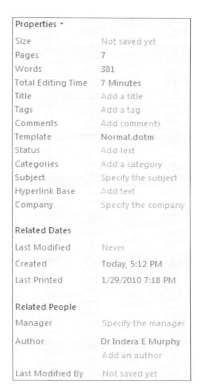

Figure 3-41 All (document) properties

Using Click And Type

This feature is used to place text, images and other objects in any blank space in the document, without selecting any options like alignment, tabs or pressing the Enter key. This option is only available in the Print Layout or Web Layout view. The steps below show you how to use this feature.

1.   Open a new or existing document, then switch to the Print Layout view.

2. Click any place in the document, then hold the mouse pointer in the location where you want to add text or an object.

The mouse pointer will change to one similar to the one shown in Figure 3-42.

Figure 3-42 Mouse pointer in click and type mode

3. Double-click, then add the text, image or object.

Selecting Text

After creating the initial draft of the document you will spend a lot of time, probably more time if the document is more than a few pages long, editing and formatting the text. Therefore, before you delve into Chapters 4 and 5, it is probably a good idea to learn about the options available for selecting text and objects in a document.

General Selecting Options

The general options to select text and objects are on the Home tab. These options are used to select all of the text or objects in the document at one time.

Using The Mouse To Select Text

I suspect that this is the way that most people select text. The tips and shortcuts discussed below will help you select text quicker when using a mouse, which is sometimes referred to as highlighting text.

① Double-click on a word to select it.

② Triple-click any place in a sentence to select the entire sentence.

③ Quadruple-click any place in a paragraph to select the entire paragraph.

Using The Keyboard To Select Text

With so many laptop and netbook users, using the keyboard to select text is growing. The tips and shortcuts discussed below will help you select text quicker when using the keyboard.

① CTRL+A selects the entire document.

② To select a group of words, place the insertion point in front of the first word that you want to select. Press the CTRL+Shift keys, then press the right arrow key. Every time that you press the right arrow key another word will be highlighted.

③ To select the last part of a line, place the insertion point at the beginning of the part of the line that you want to select, then press the Shift+End keys.

④ To select to the beginning of the line from where the insertion point is, press the Shift+Home keys.

⑤ To select more than one line of text, place the insertion point at the beginning of the text that you want to select. Press and hold down the Shift key, then press the arrow key that points in the direction of the text that you want to select. You can also use the Home, Page Up, Page Down and End keys with the Shift key to select text.

⑥ To select a paragraph, place the insertion point any place in the paragraph. Tap the touch pad four times.

Use The F8 Key To Select Text

The F8 key can be used in place of clicking with the mouse to select words, sentences or paragraphs, as explained below. In each example, you can place the insertion point in front of the word or in the word. After you have selected the text with the F8 key, press the ESC key.

   ① To select a word, press the F8 key twice.

   ② To select a sentence, press the F8 key three times.

   ③ To select a paragraph, press the F8 key four times.

   ④ To select the entire document, press the F8 key five times.

How To Select Text In Different Parts Of The Document

The steps below show you how to use the CTRL key to select text in different parts of the document, which will let you make the same change to all of the selected text at one time.

1. Press and hold down the **CTRL** key, then select the first block of text that you want to select.

2. Release the mouse button, but not the CTRL key.

3. Select the next block of text that you want to apply the change to.

4. Repeat steps 2 and 3 above until you have all of the text that you need selected, as shown in Figure 3-43.

> The "Black Sox" scandal threatens to undermi
> popularity of America's national pastime. Eight
> Chicago White Sox baseball team are indicted
> connection with last year's 5-to-3 World Series
>
> The "Louisville Slugger" bat is introduced by th

Figure 3-43 Different parts of the document selected

5. Make the changes that you need. When you are finished making the changes, click the mouse button.

Selecting Text
I suspect that most people always select text from left to right. I just wanted to let you know that you can also select text from right to left.

The Mini Toolbar

If you tried some of the select text options discussed earlier, you probably saw the toolbar shown in Figure 3-44. I am not sure why, but when the mini toolbar first displays, it is transparent.

Figure 3-44 Mini toolbar for text

When you place the mouse pointer over the mini toolbar, it will be visible. If you do not want to use this toolbar, you can disable it on the Word Options dialog box.

These are not the only options on the mini toolbar that you will see in Word. Depending on the task, the mini toolbar will display other options. Figure 3-45 shows the mini toolbar options that you will see when a chart is selected.

Figure 3-45 Chart mini toolbar

Outline View

In Chapter 1 you read about the four page view options. The Outline view is the only view that has its own tab, as shown in Figure 3-46. The buttons in the Outline Tools group are explained in Table 3-5. The other options in the group are explained below.

Outlining Tab

Figure 3-46 Outline Tools group buttons illustrated

Option	Description
1	**PROMOTE TO HEADING 1** Changes the selected heading to the highest level.
2	**PROMOTE** Changes the selected heading to the next heading level up.
3	**DEMOTE** Changes the selected heading to the next heading level down.
4	**DEMOTE TO BODY TEXT** Changes the selected heading to the lowest heading level.
5	**MOVE UP** Moves the item up in the outline.
6	**MOVE DOWN** Moves the item down in the outline.
7	**EXPAND** Displays the text under a heading.
8	**COLLAPSE** Hides the text under a heading.

Table 3-5 Outline Tools group buttons explained

SHOW LEVEL Is used to select the levels of the document to display.

SHOW TEXT FORMATTING If checked, the text will be shown with its formatting.

SHOW FIRST LINE ONLY If checked, only the first line of each section will be displayed. Figure 3-47 shows the document with this feature enabled. Figure 3-48 shows the document with this feature disabled.

Figure 3-47 Show first line only option enabled

Figure 3-48 Show first line only option disabled

Master Document Group

The options in this group are used to create and edit master documents. The options are explained below.

SHOW DOCUMENT Displays subdocuments and additional options in the group, as shown on the right of Figure 3-49.

These options are used to create and edit subdocuments. The options are explained in Table 3-6.

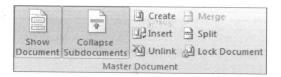

Figure 3-49 Additional Master Document group options

Additional Master Document Group Options

Option	Description
Create	Is used to create a new subdocument. (2)
Insert	Is used to add an existing document as a subdocument. (2)
Unlink	Removes the link to inserted subdocuments and copies the content from the subdocument into the Master document.
Merge	Combines two or more subdocuments into one subdocument.
Split	Separates a subdocument into two subdocuments. Place the insertion point where you want to split the subdocument.
Lock Document	Is used to lock links to subdocuments, so that any changes made to the external subdocuments are not brought into the copy of the subdocument that is in the master document.

Table 3-6 Additional Master Document group options explained

(2)   Subdocuments must be added after a heading, not in the body text. The **SHOW DOCUMENT** button must be clicked to create a new subdocument. You will see the options on the right of Figure 3-49 above.

COLLAPSE SUBDOCUMENTS Is only available in documents that have subdocuments. This option displays and hides subdocuments.

The **CLOSE OUTLINE VIEW** button in the Close group closes the Outline view and displays the document in the Print Layout view.

Master Documents

The Master Document feature is used to create one large document either by creating all of the content in the master document or by adding existing documents to the master document. Master documents can contain links to other documents, which are called subdocuments. Each chapter in this book would be a subdocument. Then a master document would be created to allow the Table of Contents and index to be created for the entire book. Like many other features in Word, there is more than one way to create a master document, as discussed below.

① Take an existing document and split it into subdocuments, usually by chapter.
② Use existing documents and combine them into one document. This involves creating a master document template that has all of the styles and other elements that are needed for the entire document.

③ Create a master document without any existing documents. You will create the entire document as needed from scratch.

Regardless of the way that you create master documents, they all have one thing in common, you need to have a plan of what has to be included in the master document. The better the plan, the less problems you will run into when working on a master document. If the concept of a master document has you a bit puzzled or you cannot visualize what it looks like, try thinking of a master document as a container that holds other documents.

What may not be obvious is that the Table of Contents and Index should be created in the Master document if the final product has more than one document. The problem is that Word Starter does not have Table of Contents and Index functionality, which means that you would have to create them manually. Ironically, creating a Table of Contents or Index is why most people create a master document.

What Is The PDF File Format?

PDF stands for Portable Document Format. When a file is saved in PDF format, the formatting of the document is saved in the PDF file. The PDF file will look like the file does on your computer, when it is opened on another computer, even if the other computer does not have the software that the document was originally created in or if it is opened on a computer without a different operating system, like Linux. When printed, PDF files print exactly as they appear on the computer screen. Unlike many of the other file formats, PDF files do not have a lot of functionality to modify the content in the document.

PDF files are a very popular file format for documents that need to be placed on the Internet. For example, many companies place their product user guides on their web site in PDF format. At some point you will probably have the need to create a PDF file.

If you are going to share a document that will be printed, you should save the document in PDF format and distribute the PDF file instead of distributing the file in another file format. One reason that you should do this is because each printer has a different configuration, which can cause lines of text in a document to be moved to the next page, thus messing up your well designed layout.

Viewing And Printing PDF Files

To view or print a PDF file, you need the full version of Adobe Acrobat or the free Adobe Acrobat Reader. Many computers sold today come with the free reader installed. If you want the free reader or want to update to the latest version of the reader, go to www.get.adobe.com and click on the "Get Adobe Reader" button. You do not have to download or install any of the other software on the download page for the reader to work.

Embedding Fonts

When you are creating PDF files, the fonts in the Word document need to be embedded in the PDF file that you create. Even if you are not going to create a PDF file, the fonts should be embedded in the document if you are going to share the file with someone else or if you are going to use the file on another computer. The reason is because the fonts that you used in the document may not be on another computer.

When that is the case, Windows will use a different font to replace fonts that it cannot find. While that is better then not displaying the parts of the document that have a font that Windows can't find, the replacement font will probably alter the layout of the document.

What Is The XPS File Format?

XPS stands for XML Paper Specification. The XPS format was created by Microsoft. The XPS format is similar to the PDF file format and provides the same functionality of saving the formatting, not allowing changes to the document and ensuring that the document will print as you intended.

Viewing And Printing XPS Files

To view and print XPS files, you need the XPS viewer. It is built into Windows Vista and Windows 7. If the XPS file will be viewed on a computer with an older version of Windows or a non Windows computer, you can download the viewer from www.microsoft.com/whdc/xps/viewxps.mspx.

How To Create PDF And XPS Files

Selecting the option illustrated on the left side of the Share panel on the File tab shown in Figure 3-50 displays the Create A PDF/XPS button on the right. Clicking this button opens the dialog box shown in Figure 3-51.

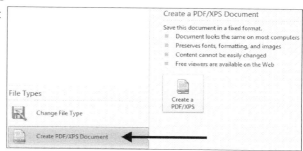

Figure 3-50 Create PDF/XPS Document options

The options at the bottom of the dialog box are used to create the PDF and XPS files.

Notice that the file type has been changed to PDF. If you want to create an XPS file, open the **SAVE AS TYPE** drop-down list and select XPS Document.

The customization options on the dialog box are explained below.

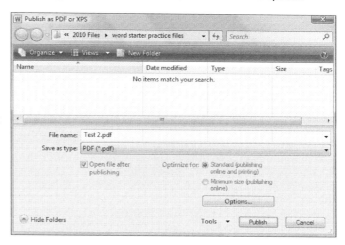

Figure 3-51 Publish as PDF or XPS dialog box

Publish As PDF Or XPS Dialog Box Customization Options

OPEN FILE AFTER PUBLISHING If checked, this option causes the PDF or XPS file to be opened after you create it.

OPTIMIZE FOR Select the **MINIMUM SIZE** option if the PDF file will only be used online, otherwise, select the Standard option.

TOOLS Is used to save the PDF or XPS file to a network drive.

OPTIONS Opens the dialog box shown in Figure 3-52 when creating a PDF file or the dialog box shown in Figure 3-53 when creating an XPS file. The options are explained below.

PUBLISH Creates the PDF or XPS file.

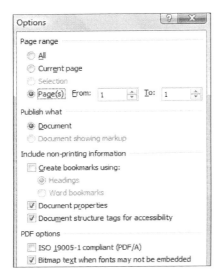

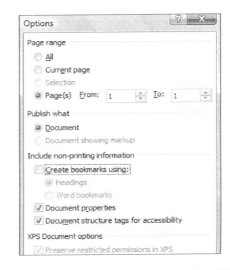

Figure 3-53 Options dialog box for XPS files

Figure 3-52 Options dialog box for PDF files

Options Dialog Box Options Explained

PAGE RANGE The options in this section are used to select the pages in the document that you want to be converted to PDF or XPS format.

PUBLISH WHAT Select the Document option unless the document that you are converting to PDF or XPS format has markups that you want included.

MARKUPS Select this option if the document has handwritten objects that you want included in the PDF or XPS file. [See Chapter 6, Ink Group]

INCLUDE NON-PRINTING INFORMATION The options in this section are used to create bookmarks from the heading styles or from bookmarks that are in the document. If the document does not use any of the built-in heading styles or does not have any bookmarks, these options are not enabled. The Document Properties option will add the properties section of the Info panel (on the File tab) to the PDF or XPS file.

PDF OPTIONS (Only for PDF files)
The **ISO 19005-1 COMPLAINT (PDF/A)** option is used to make the PDF file PDF/A compliant, which leaves out PDF features that are not suited for long term archiving.

If checked, the **BITMAP TEXT WHEN FONTS MAY NOT BE EMBEDDED OPTION** allows Word to embed unknown fonts into the file as a .bmp file. I think that it is best to use fonts that Word recognizes.

XPS DOCUMENT OPTIONS (Only for XPS files) Preserves restricted permissions in XPS.

. . . .

THE HOME TAB (EDITING OPTIONS)

As you will see, Word has a lot of options that you can use to help make editing documents easier. You will learn the following editing techniques:

☑ Using the Clipboard
☑ Using Cut, Copy and Paste
☑ Using the Format Painter
☑ Using the Undo and Repeat commands
☑ Drop and Drag
☑ Find and Replace
☑ Spell checking a document

CHAPTER 4

Editing Overview

Editing documents is often a task that many people do not like because it is time consuming. Often, it can take longer to edit a document then it did to type it the first time. One way to reduce the amount of time it takes to edit a document besides not making as many mistakes to begin with <smile>, is to have above average editing skills. That is the goal of this chapter, to teach editing tips and shortcuts. Many of the tasks that you will learn in this chapter have more than one way to be completed. You can also access many options more than one way.

It is worth the time in the long run to experiment and try different ways to complete the same task. I think that this is good because it will enable you to be able to quickly select the most appropriate method for the editing task at hand. You may find that you prefer one method over another.

Document Shortcut Menu

Many of the editing and formatting options that you will use the most are on what I refer to as the Document shortcut menu. This menu is available any time that you have a document open. When you right-click in the document you will see the shortcut menu shown in Figure 4-1.

The options on the menu provide quick access to options on the Ribbon. The options are explained in Table 4-1. The first section of the menu has options from the Clipboard group that you will learn about later in this chapter. Depending on the text or object that is selected before you open this shortcut menu, additional options will appear on the shortcut menu, as illustrated in Figure 4-2.

Figure 4-1 Document shortcut menu

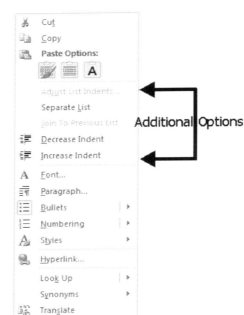

Figure 4-2 Document shortcut menu with text selected

Document Shortcut Menu Options

Option	Description
Font	Opens the Font dialog box. The options are used to customize the fonts used in the document. The majority of options on the Font tab are in the Font group on the Home tab.
Paragraph	Opens the Paragraph dialog box. The options on the Paragraph dialog box are used to select the alignment, indentation and spacing options for the selected paragraphs.
Bullets	The options are used to add bullets to a part of the document or modify bullets that are already in the document.
Numbering	The options are used to add numbers to a part of the document or modify numbers that are already in the document.
Styles	The options are used to add styles to a part of the document, clear or modify styles that are already in the document.
Hyperlink	Opens the Insert Hyperlink dialog box, which is used to create a link in the document or edit an existing link.
Look Up	[See Look Up Options at the end of this chapter]
Synonyms	[See Synonyms at the end of this chapter]
Translate	[See Table 4-10 later in this chapter]

Table 4-1 Document shortcut menu options explained

The Windows Clipboard

The clipboard is a temporary holding area for any type of data including graphics, text and media files. The clipboard is a tool that is part of the Windows operating system. Once the data is in the clipboard you can paste it into a document in any application that recognizes data in the clipboard. For example, you could copy information from an Excel spreadsheet and paste it in a Word document.

Clipboard Group

The Clipboard group shown in Figure 4-3 contains some of the options that you will use the most when editing documents. The options in this group are used to copy, paste and delete part of a document. The options are explained in Table 4-2.

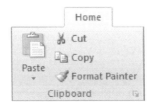

Figure 4-3 Clipboard group options

Clipboard Group Options

Option	Description
Paste	Displays the options or a subset of the options shown in Figure 4-4. The Paste button options are explained in Table 4-3. The keyboard shortcut is CTRL+V.
Cut	Deletes the selected text or object from the document and places it in the clipboard. The keyboard shortcut is CTRL+X.
Copy	Makes a copy of the selected text or object and places it in the clipboard. The keyboard shortcut is CTRL+C.
Format Painter	Applies existing formatting in the document to another part of the document. [See Using The Format Painter later in this chapter]
Dialog Box Launcher	Opens the Clipboard task pane, which is covered later in this chapter.

Table 4-2 Clipboard group options explained

Paste Button Options

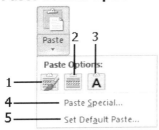

Figure 4-4 Paste button options

Option	Description
1	**KEEP SOURCE FORMATTING** Pastes the cut or copied text with the same formatting as the original text.
2	**MERGE FORMATTING** Pastes the cut or copied text with the same formatting as the original text, plus the formatting around where the text will be pasted.
3	**KEEP TEXT ONLY** Pastes the cut or copied text without the formatting from the original text.
4	**PASTE SPECIAL** Opens the Paste Special dialog box, which is covered below.
5	**SET DEFAULT PASTE** Displays the Advanced panel of the Word Options dialog box so that you can customize the paste options.

Table 4-3 Paste button options explained

Paste Special Dialog Box

The dialog box shown in Figure 4-5 is used to link or embed other documents into the current document. The options are explained below.

Select the **PASTE** option if you are going to embed the document.

Select the **PASTE LINK** option if you want to link to another document.

If checked, the **DISPLAY AS ICON** option will display an icon in the document instead of the pasted text. The icon is a link to the document. Click on the icon in the document to display the linked document.

The **CHANGE ICON** button opens the dialog box shown in Figure 4-6.

The **RESULT** section explains what the option that is selected means.

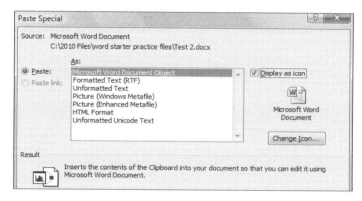

Figure 4-5 Paste Special dialog box

Change Icon Dialog Box

The options on this dialog box are used to select the icon that will be displayed in the document.

The **ICON** option is used to select a different Word icon that will be displayed in the document.

The **BROWSE** button is used to select an image file that is not a Word icon.

The **CAPTION** option is used to type in the text that you want to appear next to the icon in the document. The caption should be as descriptive as possible, so that other users of the document know that they are about to open another document.

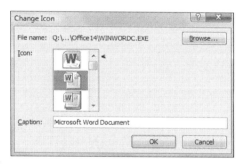

Figure 4-6 Change Icon dialog box

Clipboard Task Pane

If you do a lot of cutting and pasting, the Clipboard task pane shown in Figure 4-7 may be helpful because it displays the items in the Windows clipboard. The task pane displays up to the last 24 items that were cut or copied in the document.

I wish that there was an option to save the contents of the clipboard with the document because I do not always finish editing the entire document at one time. So for now, I paste everything in the task pane into a new document and save it.

The options at the bottom of the task pane are explained in Table 4-4.

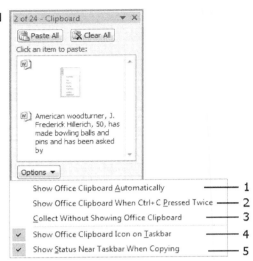

Figure 4-7 Clipboard task pane

Clipboard Task Pane Options

Option	Description
1	**SHOW OFFICE CLIPBOARD AUTOMATICALLY** If checked, the Clipboard task pane will automatically open when the Cut or Copy command is used.
2	**SHOW OFFICE CLIPBOARD WHEN CTRL+C PRESSED TWICE** If checked, you can use the keyboard to copy and open the Clipboard task pane by selecting what you want to copy, then pressing and holding down the CTRL key and pressing the C key twice.
3	**COLLECT WITHOUT SHOWING OFFICE CLIPBOARD** If checked, items are added to the Clipboard task pane, but the task pane is not displayed. This options overrides the two options above.
4	**SHOW OFFICE CLIPBOARD ICON ON TASKBAR** If checked, an icon for the Clipboard task pane is placed in the lower right corner of the Windows taskbar, as illustrated in Figure 4-8. Double-clicking on the icon will display the Clipboard task pane.
5	**SHOW STATUS NEAR TASKBAR WHEN COPYING** If checked, a tool tip will display temporarily in the Windows taskbar area when content is cut or copied to the clipboard, as illustrated in Figure 4-9.

Table 4-4 Clipboard task pane options explained

Figure 4-8 Clipboard icon in Windows taskbar

Figure 4-9 Tool tip in Windows taskbar

Use The Clipboard Task Pane With More Than One Document
The items placed in the Clipboard task pane can be used in other documents. To see this in action, open a document, then open the Clipboard Task Pane. Copy two items in the document and delete a paragraph. You should see three items in the task pane. Open a different document. You will see the same three items in the task pane. At this point, you can paste any or all of these items into the second document. If you delete an item from the task pane, it is no longer available to either document.

Creating Practice Text
In Chapter 1 you read about the practice files that you can download and use to work through the exercises. You also have the option of generating random text and using that instead. The steps below show you how to generate text.

1. Open a new document.
2. Type =rand(10,15), then press Enter. This code will generate 10 paragraphs that each have 15 sentences. You can enter any number of paragraphs and sentences that you want. This code also works in an existing document.

Using Cut, Copy And Paste

These three options are used to re-arrange and delete parts of a document. You can use the New Classes Letter file to practice.

1. Highlight the first paragraph in the document. Right-click on the highlighted text. You should see the shortcut menu shown earlier in Figure 4-2. Select COPY on the shortcut menu.

2. Right-click on the line under the word "Sincerely" and select PASTE. You should see a copy of the first paragraph at the bottom of the letter.

3. Highlight the paragraph at the end of the document. Right-click on it, then select CUT. The paragraph should be deleted.

Using The Format Painter

This is a pretty cool feature. It is used to copy the formatting from text in one part of the document to another part of the same document or to a different document that is open, with a mouse click. There are two types of formatting that can be copied: CHARACTER FORMATTING, which includes the font, font size and font color. PARAGRAPH FORMATTING copies character and paragraph formatting if the paragraph mark is selected. Borders can also be copied using the Format Painter. The steps below show you how to use the Format Painter.

Double-clicking on the Format Painter button allows you to apply the formatting more than once in the document.

1. Open the Multi Page file, then display the Louisville Slugger section of the document. As you can see, the header is bold and italic.

2. Select the header, then double-click on the Format Painter button.

3. When you hold the mouse pointer over text in the document, it will change to a **PAINT BRUSH**, as illustrated in Figure 4-10.

Figure 4-10 Mouse pointer in position to apply formatting

4. Click on two or three parts of the paragraph. The formatting will change to the same as the heading.

Using The Undo And Repeat Commands

1. Click on the arrow next to the Undo button on the Quick Access toolbar.

The **UNDO** list should look similar to the one shown in Figure 4-11. This list shows the actions (changes) that you made to the document. This feature can be useful if you need to remove an action that you have added to the document.

If you want to undo several changes, click the arrow shown at the top of Figure 4-11. Other then the first option in the list, you cannot select a specific item in the list to undo. If you click on the third option from the top of the list, the first three actions will be undone.

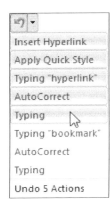

Figure 4-11 Undo list

 Undo And Repeat Shortcuts
① **CTRL+Z**, will undo the last action.
② **CTRL+Y**, will repeat the last action.

How To Move (Drop And Drag) Text

Drop and drag is a term that you may have heard before, but were not quite sure what it meant. It means to move content from one section of a document to another section of the same document. It works the same way that cut and paste works. You can use either method to accomplish the same task. Drop and drag is easier to use if you are moving text to another part of the document that is visible on the screen because there are no commands, options or buttons to select. The steps below show you how to drop and drag text.

1. Highlight the second paragraph in the New Classes Letter document.

2. Click on the highlighted text with the left mouse button and drag the mouse pointer down until it is at the end of the first sentence in the third paragraph, as illustrated in Figure 4-12.

Our higly skilled training team is looking forward to s
We will soon be offering the following classes on the

So come on in and see what we have to offer. Be on
we will be mailing soon that can be applied to any of

Figure 4-12 Drop and drag technique illustrated

You should see a dotted square below the insertion point while you are dragging the text.

3. Release the mouse button. The second paragraph should now be in the middle of the third paragraph.

    You will see the options shown in Figure 4-13. The **SET DEFAULT PASTE** option displays the Advanced panel on the Word Options dialog box.

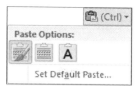

Figure 4-13 Paste options

4. Click the Undo button to put the second paragraph back to where it was.

 Drop And Drag Tip
As you just read, using the left mouse button to drop and drag will move the text from one location in the document to another location. If you want to place a **COPY** of the text in another location, before dragging it to another location, hold down the **CTRL** key while using the left mouse button to drop and drag the text. The mouse pointer will have a plus sign instead of the dotted square.

 Drop And Drag Between Documents
Usually when you need to copy content from one document to another, copy and paste is used. Just like you can drop and drag in the same document, you can drop and drag between documents, even if the second document is not a Word document. To do that, follow the steps below.

1. Open the document that has the text that you want to move or copy, then make the window half the size of the computer screen.
2. Open the document that you want to place the copied or moved text to, then make the window half the size of the computer screen so that you can see both documents.
3. In the first document, select the text that you want to drag, then drag it to where you want it in the second document.

Editing Group

The options in this group are used to find, replace and select text.

Using The Find And Replace Commands

These commands are used when you need to change (or delete) the same text in several places in the document. These commands will search the entire document, or just the part of the document that you select.

The **FIND** command is used to search for text or formatting in a document. If you prefer to use the Find option from Word 2003, select the Replace command, then click on the Find tab. The **REPLACE** command is used to search for text or formatting in a document and replace or delete it. Every occurrence that matches your search criteria will be replaced with what you specify.

Additional Find And Replace Options

If you click the **MORE** button on the Find and Replace dialog box, you will see the options shown in Figure 4-14.

These search options provide more control over the search.

Table 4-5 explains the search options.

Figure 4-14 Additional search options

Search Options

Option	Description
Search	Is used to select the direction of the search. **ALL** will search the entire document, regardless of where the insertion point is in the document. **DOWN** will start the search where the insertion point is in the document and only search to the end of the document. **UP** will start the search where the insertion point is in the document and only search up to the beginning of the document.
Match Case	If checked, this option will only retrieve words that are in the same case (upper, lower or a combination of both) that you enter in the **FIND WHAT** field. If you type "brooklyn" in the Find what field and check the Match Case option, the word "Brooklyn" would not be retrieved, because it is in a different case then what you typed in.
Find whole words only	If checked, this option will only find words that have all of the characters that you type in the Find what field. If the word has more characters than you enter, it will not be found. If you type the word "brook" in the Find what field and check the Find whole words only option, the word Brooklyn will not be retrieved.
Use wildcards	When this option is selected, wildcard characters can be used to search for text. For example, the **QUESTION MARK** is used to find one character. The **ASTERISK** is used to find more than one character. This wildcard character is more flexible, but often returns a lot of results that are not relevant.
Sounds like	Finds words that sound like the word that you are searching for. This is helpful if you cannot spell the word that you want to search for.
Find all word forms	Finds words that are similar. This option works similar to a thesaurus.
Match prefix	Finds words that have the same characters at the beginning of the word like the word that you are searching for.
Match suffix	Finds words that have the same characters at the end of the word like the word that you are searching for.
Ignore punctuation characters	If checked, punctuation in a word will be ignored when searching for a match.

Table 4-5 Search options explained

Option	Description
Ignore white-space characters	If checked, non-printing characters like tabs, spaces and paragraph marks are ignored during the search.

Table 4-5 Search options explained (Continued)

Reading Highlight Button

The **HIGHLIGHT ALL** option shown in Figure 4-15 is used to highlight each occurrence in the document of what you searched for.

The steps below show you how to use this option.

Figure 4-15 Reading Highlight button options

1. In the Find what field, type in what you want to search for.

2. Click the **READING HIGHLIGHT** button, then select Highlight All.

Any text that matched your search criteria will be highlighted in the document. You will also see how many times the search criteria was found in the document, as illustrated in Figure 4-16. You can clear the highlighting or leave it in the document. If the document is printed, the highlighting is not printed.

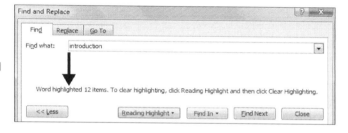

Figure 4-16 Result of search

Find In Button

The options in the drop-down list shown in Figure 4-17 are used to select the part of the document that you want to search in. The default is the **MAIN DOCUMENT** option.

Figure 4-17 Find In button options

Using The Find Command

As you just read, you can look for a specific word or phrase in a document. This feature is useful, especially in long documents. If a document has 50 pages and you need to find the word Brooklyn, it could take a while to visually go through all 50 pages of the document. Instead, you could follow the steps below to have Word find each occurrence of the word or phrase for you. You can use the Term Paper document for practice.

1. Home tab $\Rightarrow$ Editing group $\Rightarrow$ Replace $\Rightarrow$ Find tab.

2. Type brook in the **FIND WHAT** field.

3. Click the More button. Check one of the options (either Match case or Find whole words only), then click the **FIND NEXT** button. Did you get the results that you expected? You can play with these options to get a feel for how they can help you find what you are looking for.

4. Close the Term Paper document. If prompted, discard the changes.

Using The Replace Command

The letterhead of the New Classes Letter has the company name as Capri Book Company. You will see the company name as Capri Company, twice in the first paragraph. Instead of looking through the entire document to find out where the company name needs to be changed and typing the word **BOOK** in each place, you can use the Replace command. The steps below show you how to replace text in a document.

1. Home tab ⇒ Editing group ⇒ Replace. You will see the Find and Replace dialog box.

2. Type Capri Company in the **FIND WHAT** field.

If you are thinking that you could just type Capri or Company and not both words in the Find what field, you could get unexpected results. If you only used one of the words, the search would find the word in the letterhead and add the replacement text there also. This is not what you want.

3. Press the Tab key, then type Capri Book Company in the **REPLACE WITH** field.

You should have the fields filled in, as shown in Figure 4-18.

Figure 4-18 Search criteria

 The **REPLACE** option is used to view each occurrence before it is changed, which will allow you to skip an occurrence if necessary. The **REPLACE ALL** option makes all of the changes at one time.

4. Click the **REPLACE ALL** button.

You should see the message shown in Figure 4-19.

The message tells you how many times the text was replaced.

Figure 4-19 Replacement message

5. Click OK, then close the Find and Replace dialog box. Save the changes.

Using Special Characters As Search Criteria

The options on the Special button are used to search for non printing characters like paragraph marks, tab characters and manual page breaks.

Go To Command

This command is used to display different parts of the document.

The options on this tab are shown in Figure 4-20 and are explained in Table 4-6.

Figure 4-20 Go To tab options

Option	What It Displays . . .
Page	A page in the document. Select this option and type in the page number that you want to display on the right, as shown above in Figure 4-20, then click the GO TO button.
Section	A section of the document. (1) (2)
Line	The line number in the document. (1) (2)
Bookmark	The content closest to the bookmark name that you enter.
Comment	The comments created by the reviewers name that you enter.
Footnote	A footnote in the document. Footnotes are located at the bottom of the page.
Endnote	An endnote in the document. All endnotes are usually located at the end of the document, which is why I'm not sure why this option is necessary. (2)
Field	A field in the document. (2)
Table	A table in the document. (2)
Graphic	A graphic in the document. (2)
Equation	A formula in the document. (2)
Object	An object in the document. (2)
Heading	A heading in the document. (2)

Table 4-6 Go To tab options explained

(1) This option is helpful if you have the same option enabled on the status bar.

(2) The item displayed is based on where the insertion point is and the number that you enter in the field. For example, if you enter a 3 in the field, the third item from where the insertion point is in the document will be displayed, not necessarily the third item from the beginning of the document.

Navigation Task Pane

This task pane replaces the **DOCUMENT MAP** feature in previous versions of Word and is used to search for text or other objects in the document. You may find this task pane useful in long documents. Type in the text that you want to search for, then press Enter.

As illustrated in Figure 4-21, there are three ways to display the search results in the Navigation task pane.

Home tab ⇒ Editing group ⇒ Find button, displays this task pane. The options are explained in Table 4-7.

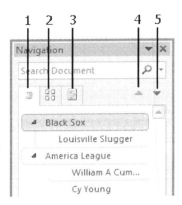

Figure 4-21 Navigation task pane

Navigation Task Pane Options

Option	Description
1	**BROWSE THE HEADINGS IN YOUR DOCUMENT** As shown in Figure 4-21 above, text that has a heading style is displayed.
2	**BROWSE THE PAGES IN YOUR DOCUMENT** Displays a thumbnail of each page in the document, as shown in Figure 4-22. In the task pane, click on the page that you want to view and it will be displayed.
3	**BROWSE THE RESULTS FROM YOUR CURRENT SEARCH** Displays the portions of the document that has the text or object that you searched for, as shown in Figure 4-23.
4	**PREVIOUS SEARCH RESULT** Displays the previous item that met the search criteria.
5	**NEXT SEARCH RESULT** Displays the next item that meets the search criteria.

Table 4-7 Navigation task pane options explained

How To Search For Non Text Content

Click on the magnifying glass button illustrated in Figure 4-24 to display the search options. These options are used to search for objects like tables, images or equations. The options are explained in Table 4-8.

Navigation Task Pane Search Options

Option	Description
Options	Opens the Find Options dialog box shown in Figure 4-25. Almost all of the options are the same as the search options explained earlier in Table 4-5.
Advanced Find	Displays the Find tab on the Find and Replace dialog box. (3)
Replace	Displays the Replace tab on the Find and Replace dialog box. (3)
Go To	Displays the Go To tab on the Find and Replace dialog box. (3)

Table 4-8 Navigation task pane search options explained

Option	Description
Graphics	If selected, the first image file in the document is displayed. Click the down arrow search button to display the next image file in the document.
Tables	Finds the tables in the document.
Equations	Finds the formulas in the document.
Footnotes/ Endnotes	Finds the footnotes and endnotes in the document. (4)
Comments	Is used to select the reviewers whose comments you want to view. (4)

Table 4-8 Navigation task pane search options explained (Continued)

(3)   This option was discussed earlier in this chapter.
(4)   This option can only be used if you open a document that already has footnotes, endnotes or comments because you cannot add them to a document in Word Starter.

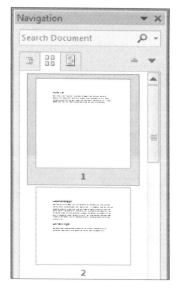

Figure 4-22 Thumbnail view of search results

Figure 4-23 Content view of search results

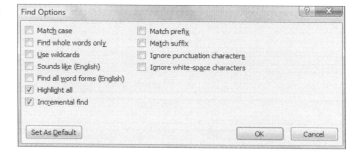

Figure 4-24 Navigation task pane search options

The **INCREMENTAL FIND** option is used to enable the type ahead searching. As you type an entry in the Search field in the task pane, results start to be displayed.

Figure 4-25 Find Options dialog box

Select Button

The Select button is in the Editing group on the Home tab.

The options shown in Figure 4-26 are used to select objects in the document that are stacked on top of each other.

The options are explained in Table 4-9.

Figure 4-26 Select button options

Option	Description
Select All	Selects all of the content in the body of the document except headers, footers and footnotes. It is primarily used when you need to make the same change to the entire document, like changing the line spacing from single to double.
Select Objects	Selects all non text objects in the body of the document.
Select Text with Similar Formatting	To enable this option in Word Starter, the Mark grammar errors as you type option on the Proofing panel on the Word Options dialog box must be enabled. This option is used to select all text that has the same format or style as the text that you selected.
Selection Pane	Displays the **SELECTION AND VISIBILITY** task pane shown in Figure 4-27.

Table 4-9 Select button options explained

Selection And Visibility Task Pane

The task pane shown in Figure 4-27 is used to keep track of images, shapes and other items that are stacked on top of each other in the document. Each item is in its own layer.

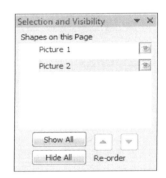

Figure 4-27 Selection and Visibility task pane

Proofing Group

The options in this group are used to check the document for spelling and grammar errors, use the Thesaurus and more, as shown in Figure 4-28. The options are explained in Table 4-10.

Figure 4-28 Proofing group options

Option	Description
Spelling & Grammar	Opens the Spelling and Grammar dialog box, which has options for fixing spelling errors.
Research	Opens the Research task pane. The options are used to search reference books and research related web sites for more information about the selected word or phrase in the document.
Thesaurus	Finds words that are similar in meaning to the word that you selected in the document.
Translate	The options shown in Figure 4-29 are used to translate the selected text or document into a different language.
Set Proofing Language	Opens the dialog box shown in Figure 4-30. The options are used to select the language that the proofing tools, like the spell checker and grammar checker will use. Unless you need to spell check the document in a different language, there is probably no reason to change the options on this dialog box.
Word Count	[See Chapter 1, Word Count Options]

Table 4-10 Proofing group options explained

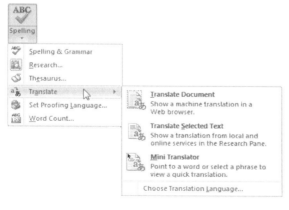

Figure 4-29 Translate options

Figure 4-30 Language dialog box

Using The Spell Checker

Once you have finished working on the document it is a good idea to check the spelling. By default, the **AUTO SPELLCHECKER** option is enabled. You will see a red squiggly line under words that are not spelled correctly, based on the spelling options that you have selected. To activate the spell checker you can use one of the following three options.

   ① Press the F7 key.
   ② Right-click on the misspelled word in the document to display the shortcut menu.
   ③ Home tab ⇒ Proofing group ⇒ Spelling ⇒ Spelling & Grammar.

> The Spell Check dialog box can only be accessed when the document has a spelling error. If you have a need to open the Spell Check dialog box in a document that does not have any misspelled words, type a word incorrectly in the document to open the Spell Check dialog box.

1.   Open the New Classes Letter document.

> I usually put the insertion point at the beginning of the document before spell checking it. I do this because the spell checker only has to go through the document once and I am not prompted to start checking from the beginning of the document. Doing this is optional.

2.   Start the spell checker.

     You should see the dialog box shown in Figure 4-31.

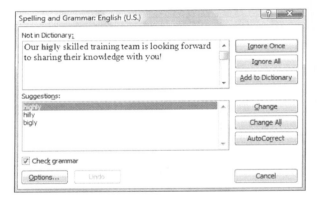

Figure 4-31 Spelling and Grammar dialog box

You will see that the misspelled word is in bold (red) in the **NOT IN DICTIONARY** section of the dialog box. It is helpful to see the words around the misspelled word if no words are suggested because you may not know what the word should be without being able to see the sentence that it is in.

3.   Click the **CHANGE ALL** button to change every occurrence of the word in the document to the word that is highlighted in the **SUGGESTIONS** section of the dialog box.

The reason that you may want to use the **CHANGE ALL** button instead of the **CHANGE** button is because you may have misspelled the same word, the same way, more than once. Change All will change the word every place that it is misspelled the same way in the document. This is very useful, especially in long documents.

4.   Change the word "git" to `gift`. Save the changes.

When you proof read a document, you may see a word that the spell checker did not catch. This will happen if the word is already in the dictionary. What I found out is that all word processors do not use the same dictionary. For example, in OpenOffice.org, the word "git" is in the default dictionary. I am bringing this to your attention because I suspect that you may not be aware of the fact that different word processing software uses different dictionaries. Even though you rely on the spell checker dictionary, it is still a good idea to proof read the document.

 If you only want to spell check part of the document, highlight the part that you want to spell check before starting the spell checker.

Spell Check Buttons

The buttons on the Spelling dialog box shown above in Figure 4-31 are explained below.

IGNORE ONCE If a word that you typed in is not in the dictionary, but you want to use it, click this button and the current occurrence of the word will be skipped.

IGNORE ALL Is used to skip the same word every time that it is in the document.

ADD TO DICTIONARY If a word is not in the dictionary but you know that it is correct, you should add it to a dictionary. Adding a word to the dictionary means that from that point on, the word will not be marked as being incorrect. A good use of this option is to add peoples names and street names that you use often to the dictionary.

CHANGE Is used to change the word that has been marked as not being spelled correctly.

CHANGE ALL Is used to change the same word every time that it is found in the document.

AUTO CORRECT Is used to add the incorrect word and the word that is replacing it, to the list on the AutoCorrect tab on the Auto Correct dialog box.

OPTIONS BUTTON Is used to open the Proofing panel on the Word Options dialog box.

Using The Spell Check Options On The Shortcut Menu

I think that most people use the Spelling dialog box that you used in the previous section. There is another way to find suggestions and correct misspelled words. This method does not have all of the features that the Spell check dialog box has, but you may find it convenient sometimes. Follow the steps below to use the spell check options on the shortcut menu.

1. Open a new document and type the word `higly` (Yes, I know it is spelled wrong.), then press the Enter key.

2. Right-click on the word that you just typed. You will see the shortcut menu shown in Figure 4-32.

   At the top of the shortcut menu are suggestions for the misspelled word. Notice that they are the same suggestions as the ones shown above in Figure 4-31. If you see the word that you want, you can select it from the shortcut menu.

   If you need spelling features that are not on the shortcut menu, select the **SPELLING** option on the shortcut menu and the Spell check dialog box will open.

Figure 4-32 Spell check shortcut menu

Custom Dictionaries

Custom dictionaries are used to store words that you know are correct, but are not in the Microsoft Office standard dictionary. When you click the **ADD TO DICTIONARY** button on the Spelling and Grammar dialog box shown earlier in Figure 4-31 or on the shortcut menu shown above in Figure 4-32, you are adding the word to the default custom dictionary (file name custom.dic) not to the standard dictionary.

Custom Dictionary Dialog Box

The custom.dic dictionary is the default custom dictionary that comes with Office products. This dictionary, as well as, the standard dictionary are shared by all Microsoft products that have spell check functionality. The default custom dictionary will probably handle all of your needs, but if it doesn't, you can create more custom dictionaries. The steps below show you how to view, edit and create custom dictionaries.

1. File tab ⇒ Options ⇒ Proofing panel ⇒ Custom Dictionaries button. You will see the dialog box shown in Figure 4-33. The buttons and options are explained in Table 4-11.

Figure 4-33 Custom Dictionaries dialog box

Option	Description
Edit Word List	Displays the words that are in the dictionary that is selected, as shown in Figure 4-34.
Change Default	This button is enabled when there are two or more custom dictionaries. This option is used to select which custom dictionary Word should check first. If you have more than one custom dictionary, select the one that has the words that you use most.
New	Is used to create a new dictionary.
Add	Is used to add an existing dictionary to the list.
Remove	If you want to remove (not delete) a custom dictionary from the list, select the dictionary, then click the Remove button.
File Path	Displays the location of the selected dictionary.
Browse	Is used to select a different location for the dictionary that is selected. Use this option if the location of a custom dictionary has been moved to another folder or network drive.
Dictionary Language	Is used to select the language of the words in the dictionary. Unless you have a good reason to select a specific language, accept the default **ALL LANGUAGES** option.

Table 4-11 Custom Dictionaries dialog box options explained

To add a word to the dictionary, type it in the Word(s) field, then click the Add button.

To delete a word in the dictionary, select it in the Dictionary list, then click the Delete button.

To delete all of the words in the dictionary, click the Delete All button.

If you want to add several words, open the Custom.dic file in Notepad.

Figure 4-34 Custom.dic dialog box

How To Create A New Dictionary

1. Click the New button shown earlier in Figure 4-33.

    You will see the dialog box shown in Figure 4-35.

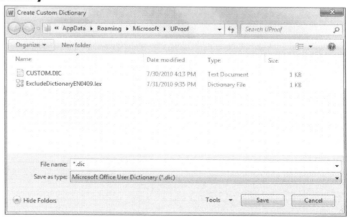

Figure 4-35 Create Custom Dictionary dialog box

2. Type in the file name for your new dictionary, then press Enter or click the Save button.

3. Add the words to the dictionary.

> **Custom Dictionary Tips**
> ① If you add words to the custom.dic dictionary or a dictionary that you create, you may want to back up these files. By default, the dictionaries are in this location (in Windows Vista). C:\Users\Account Name\AppData\Roaming\Microsoft\Proof.
> Replace "Account Name" with your Windows login account name. If you cannot find the file in this location, search your hard drive for the file.
>
> ② If you buy a new computer and have added words to this dictionary, copy the file from your old computer to the new computer and place the file in the path shown above. When prompted to overwrite the existing file, click Yes.
>
> ③ From time to time, it is a good idea to view the words in your custom dictionary to make sure that you have not added words that are not correct.

Using The Research Task Pane

The options shown in Figure 4-36 are used to find more information online about the word, phrase or topic that you enter in the Search for field. Clicking the **RESEARCH OPTIONS** link at the bottom of the task pane opens the dialog box shown in Figure 4-37. These options are links to online reference tools that you can use.

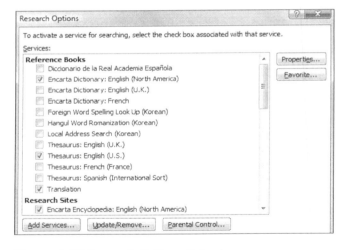

Figure 4-37 Research Options dialog box

Figure 4-36 Research task pane

Research Options Dialog Box

This dialog box is used to select additional sources to automatically include in your search. The buttons are explained below.

The **PROPERTIES** button opens the Service Properties dialog box, which displays information about the service that you selected.

The **FAVORITE** button is used to change your favorite service to the one that is currently selected.

The **ADD SERVICES** button is used to add more web sites to search.

The **UPDATE/REMOVE** button is used to update or remove services that are already installed.

The **PARENTAL CONTROL** button opens the dialog box shown in Figure 4-38. This dialog box is used to password protect the options selected on the Research task pane.

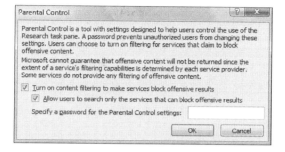

Figure 4-38 Parental Control dialog box

Using The Thesaurus

The Thesaurus is used to find another word that has a similar meaning for the word or phrase that you select. The steps below show you how to use the Thesaurus.

1. Select the word in the document that you want to find another word for.

   Home tab ⇒ Proofing group ⇒ Spelling ⇒ Thesaurus.

   You will see the Research task pane with the Thesaurus option selected, as shown in Figure 4-39.

   The word that you selected in the document should be in the **SEARCH FOR** field.

Figure 4-39 Thesaurus options on the Research task pane

2. Select one of the options in the list in the middle of the task pane. The words in this list are used to select the meaning of the word that you selected. In this example, I selected "advancing" as the meaning, as shown above in Figure 4-39.

3. When you find the word that you want to use, click on it to open the drop-down list shown above in Figure 4-39, then select **INSERT**. The word that you selected will replace the word in the document.

Look Up Options

This option is on the Document shortcut menu shown earlier in Figure 4-1.

The services shown on the right of Figure 4-40 are a subset of the services on the Research task pane. You can select one of the options to search.

Figure 4-40 Look Up shortcut menu options

If the service that you want to search is not on the sub menu, select the **RESEARCH OPTIONS** option. You will see the Research Options dialog box shown earlier in Figure 4-38. The services that you select on this dialog box will appear on the Look Up sub menu.

Synonyms

This option is on the document shortcut menu. It is used to find words that have a similar meaning as the word selected in the document. Figure 4-41 shows the submenu options.

You can select one of the words in the list or select the Thesaurus option to display the Research task pane.

Figure 4-41 Synonyms menu options

THE HOME TAB (FORMATTING OPTIONS)

 In this chapter you will learn about the following formatting options on the Home tab.

- ☑ Using fonts
- ☑ Using bold, italic and underline
- ☑ Text effects
- ☑ Creating a bulleted list
- ☑ Paragraph alignment
- ☑ Line spacing
- ☑ Tab stops
- ☑ Adding borders
- ☑ Applying styles

CHAPTER 5

Formatting Overview

The three types of formatting that can be applied to documents are explained below.

① **CHARACTER FORMATTING** Is usually applied to characters or words in a paragraph. Fonts are an example of character formatting. The Font dialog box has character formatting options.

② **PARAGRAPH FORMATTING** This formatting is applied to the entire paragraph. Examples of paragraph formatting are line spacing and alignment. The Paragraph dialog box has the paragraph formatting options.

③ **SECTION FORMATTING** This formatting is applied to part of the document (called a section) or the entire document. Examples of section formatting include the margins and page size. The Page Setup dialog box has the section formatting options.

Formatting Advice

The best formatting advice that I can give you is to not set up formatting as if you are using a typewriter. Doing things like pressing the space bar to indent text can cause problems if you have to change the page margins. The reason that software has all of the options that it has is to make creating and modifying documents easier. Using styles will help alleviate many of the document formatting issues that you may have.

As a computer programmer, I fully understand that software has bugs, but I hope that you do not let that stop you from exploring options that will allow you to create better looking documents, in less time.

As an online college professor, students submit their papers to me electronically. At one point I was shocked by the formatting that many students used, which includes the following:

① Putting the page number on the last line in the body of the document instead of in the header or footer section.

② Inconsistent line spacing between paragraphs or sections.

③ Creating numbered lists manually and forgetting to renumber the remaining items in the list when they inserted a new item or deleted an item from the list.

④ Using inappropriate font formatting.

If you have used any of the options just mentioned, hopefully this chapter will show you a better way to format documents.

Font Group

The options shown in Figure 5-1 are used to format the fonts used in the document. They are explained in Table 5-1.

The majority of options in this group require text to be selected before the option can be used.

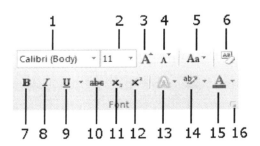

Figure 5-1 Font group options

Option	Description
1	**FONT** Is used to select a font from the list shown later in Figure 5-6.
2	**FONT SIZE** Is used to select the size of the font.
3	**GROW FONT** Increases the font size by one font size.
4	**SHRINK FONT** Reduces the font size by one font size.
5	**CHANGE CASE** The options shown in Figure 5-2 are used to change the case (upper or lower).
6	**CLEAR FORMATTING** Is used to remove all of the formatting.
7	**BOLD** Makes the selected text bold.
8	**ITALIC** Makes the selected text italic.
9	**UNDERLINE** Adds a line below the text. Figure 5-5 shows the options.
10	**STRIKETHROUGH** Draws a line through the text, as shown in Figure 5-4. This is usually done for editing purposes.
11	**SUBSCRIPT** Reduces the font size and places the text below the rest of the text around it.
12	**SUPERSCRIPT** Reduces the font size and places the text above the rest of the text around it.
13	**TEXT EFFECTS** [See Using Text Effects later in this chapter]
14	**TEXT HIGHLIGHT COLOR** Changes the background color of the selected text.
15	**FONT COLOR** Changes the color of the selected text.
16	**DIALOG BOX LAUNCHER** Opens the Font dialog box shown in Figure 5-7.

Table 5-1 Font group options explained

Change Case Options

The options are explained in Table 5-2.

Figure 5-2 Change Case options

Option	Description
Sentence case	Capitalizes the first word of the sentence.
Lower case	Changes the selected text to all capital letters.
Upper case	Changes the selected text to all lower case letters.
Capitalize Each Word	Capitalizes the first letter of each word in the sentence.
Toggle case	Is used to switch between two case views. For example, the text on the left in Figure 5-3 is changed to the text on the right, after this option is applied.

Table 5-2 Change Case options explained

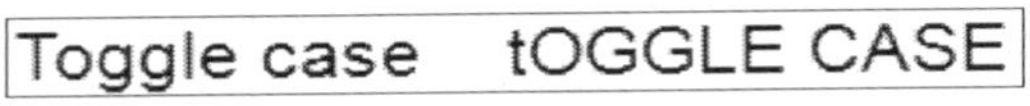

Toggle case tOGGLE CASE

Figure 5-3 Toggle case option applied

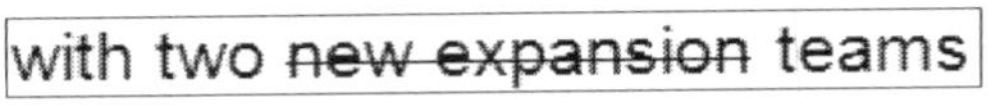

with two ~~new expansion~~ teams

Figure 5-4 Strikethrough option applied

Underline Options

The **MORE UNDERLINES** option opens the Font tab, shown later in Figure 5-7.

The **UNDERLINE COLOR** option displays the color palette so that you can select a color for the underline.

Figure 5-5 Underline options

Font List Sections

The font drop-down list has several sections, as illustrated in Figure 5-7.

The **THEME FONTS** section lists the fonts from a theme that are being used in the document.

The **RECENTLY USED FONTS** section displays up to the last 10 fonts that were applied to the document, even if they have since been removed from the document.

The **ALL FONTS** section lists all of the fonts that can be used in the document. If you know that there is a font on your computer that does not appear in this section, the font may not be installed correctly.

Figure 5-6 Font list sections illustrated

Font Dialog Box

The options on the Font tab shown in Figure 5-7 are used to select the font. Many of the options on this tab are in the font group shown earlier in Figure 5-1.

The options on the Advanced tab shown in Figure 5-8 are used to change character spacing. The Text Effects button opens the dialog box shown later in Figure 5-13.

Figure 5-7 Font dialog box

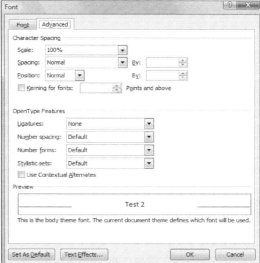

Figure 5-8 Advanced tab on the Font dialog box

Change The Font And Font Size

The steps below show you how to change the font and font size. You can use the New Classes Letter file to practice.

1. In the letter, click in front of the word **DEAR**.

   Hold down the left mouse button and drag the mouse down until the entire letter is selected, as shown in Figure 5-9.

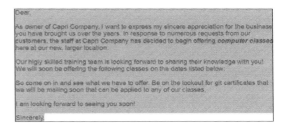

Figure 5-9 Text selected

2. Open the Font drop-down list and select the Arial font.

3. With the text still selected, open the Font Size drop-down list and select 12. Click on a blank space in the document to deselect the text.

Font Size Tip
If the font size that you need to use is not in the drop-down list, highlight whatever size is showing at the top of the list, then type in the size that you want. You can also type in half sizes like 9.5, as shown in Figure 5-10.

Figure 5-10 Font size changed to a half size

Using The Bold, Italic And Underline Options

These three options are used to emphasize parts of a document. The steps below show you how to use the bold, italic and underline options.

1. In the last sentence of the first paragraph in the New Classes Letter document, select the words **COMPUTER CLASSES.**

2. Click the Bold button, then click the Italic button. Click on a blank space in the document. The first paragraph should look like the one shown in Figure 5-11.

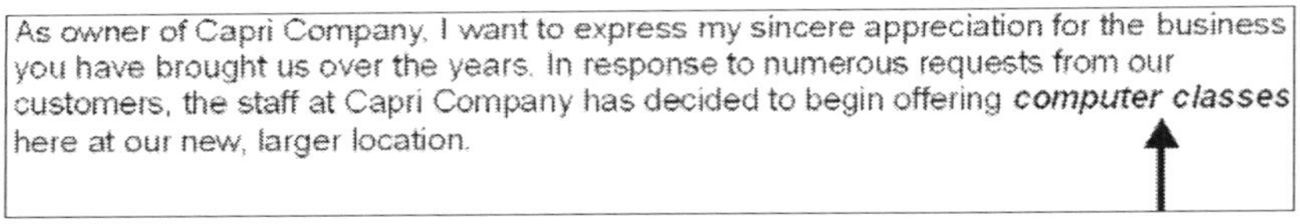

As owner of Capri Company, I want to express my sincere appreciation for the business you have brought us over the years. In response to numerous requests from our customers, the staff at Capri Company has decided to begin offering *computer classes* here at our new, larger location.

Figure 5-11 Words bolded and italicized

3. Place the mouse pointer on the blank line above the word **SINCERELY**, then press Enter. Press the Tab key once and type, Don't wait until the last minute to get the training that you need.

4. Press Enter. Select the sentence that you just typed, then click the Underline button. The document should look like the one shown in Figure 5-12.

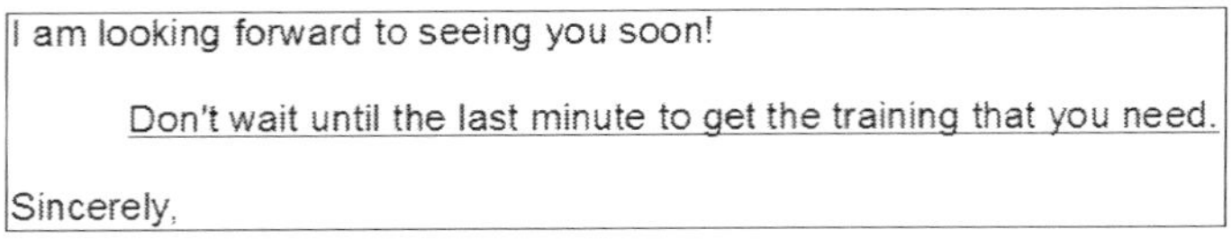

I am looking forward to seeing you soon!

    Don't wait until the last minute to get the training that you need.

Sincerely,

Figure 5-12 Underlined text illustrated

Format Text Effects Dialog Box

The **TEXT EFFECTS** options are used to change the outline or fill of text.

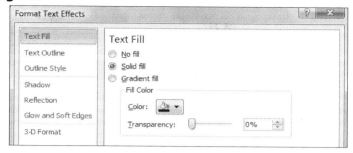

Figure 5-13 Format Text Effects dialog box

Using Text Effects

The options shown in Figure 5-14 are used to apply an effect to text, as shown in Figure 5-15.

You can select a text effect from the top of the gallery to apply to the text. The options at the bottom of the gallery are explained below.

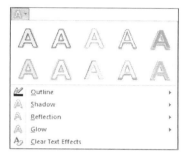

Figure 5-14 Text Effects gallery

Figure 5-15 Text effect added to a document

Text Effect Options

Selecting the Outline, Shadow, Reflection and Glow effects options shown above in Figure 5-14 will display additional options that are used to customize the text effect.

The **OUTLINE** text effect options are used to add or change the border of the text effect.

The **SHADOW** text effect options shown in Figure 5-16 are used to add a shadow to the outside or inside of the text. Clicking the Shadow Options button opens the Format Text Effects dialog box shown earlier in Figure 5-13.

The **REFLECTION** text effect options are used to add a reflection below the text.

The **GLOW** text effect options are used to add a glow effect and color to text.

The **CLEAR TEXT EFFECTS** option is used to remove the text effect from the selected text. If applying a text effect was the last change made to the document, you can click the Undo button on the Quick Access toolbar to remove the text effect.

Figure 5-16 Shadow Text Effect options

Paragraph Group

The options shown in Figure 5-17 are used to change the paragraph formatting, add bullets, line numbers, indents, line spacing, borders, display paragraph marks and alignment. The options are explained in Table 5-3.

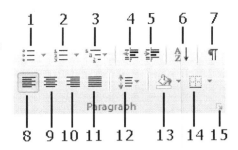

Figure 5-17 Paragraph group options

Option	Description
1	**BULLETS** Creates a bulleted list.
2	**NUMBERING** Creates a numbered list.
3	**MULTILEVEL LIST** Creates a multilevel list, as shown in Figure 5-18.
4	**DECREASE INDENT** Decreases the amount of space that the selected text is indented.
5	**INCREASE INDENT** Increases the amount of space that the selected text is indented.
6	**SORT** Sorts the text or data in rows or columns. Clicking this button opens the dialog box shown in Figure 5-19.
7	**PARAGRAPH MARKS** Are used to display or hide symbols and paragraph marks, as shown in Figure 5-21. These symbols are not printed.
8	**ALIGN TEXT LEFT** Is how the paragraph that you are reading is aligned. All of the characters in this paragraph on the left margin are aligned vertically. This is the default alignment of Word and every other word processing package that I have used.
9	**CENTER** Positions the text on each line in the paragraph between the left and right margins.
10	**ALIGN TEXT RIGHT** Is the opposite of Align Text Left. All of the characters on the right margin are aligned vertically.
11	**JUSTIFY** Is a combination of the Left and Right alignment options. All of the lines in the paragraph are aligned on the right and the left. This is accomplished by adding space between words. This means that all lines in the paragraph are the same width. Novels often have this type of alignment.
12	**LINE AND PARAGRAPH SPACING** Changes the line spacing for part of the document or the entire document.
13	**SHADING** The options shown in Figure 5-22 are used to add a background color to the selected text, as illustrated in Figure 5-23.
14	**BORDERS** Adds a border around text or an object.
15	**DIALOG BOX LAUNCHER** Opens the Paragraph dialog box shown later in Figure 5-36.

Table 5-3 Paragraph group options explained

Multi Level List Gallery

Clicking the **ALL** option in the upper left corner of the gallery shown in Figure 5-18 displays the menu in the upper right corner of the gallery.

The All option is the default and will display all of the sections of the gallery. The other options on the menu will hide the other sections of the gallery.

The options at the bottom of the gallery are explained below.

CHANGE LIST LEVEL Is used to select a different list level for the selected items in the list.

DEFINE NEW MULTILEVEL LIST Is used to create a new multilevel list.

DEFINE NEW LIST STYLE Is used to create a new list style.

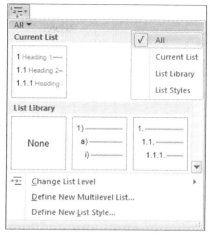

Figure 5-18 Multi level list gallery

Sort Options

The options on the dialog box shown in Figure 5-19 are used to select how the data will be sorted.

Clicking the **OPTIONS** button on the Sort dialog box opens the dialog box shown in Figure 5-20. These options are used to customize the sort.

If text is selected before the Sort dialog box is opened, the name of the dialog box is **SORT TEXT**.

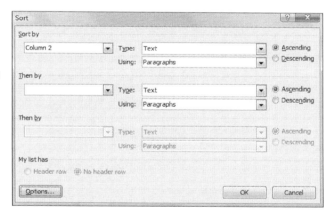

Figure 5-19 Sort dialog box

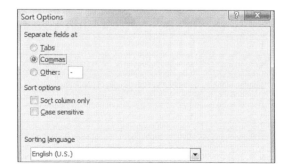

Figure 5-20 Sort Options dialog box

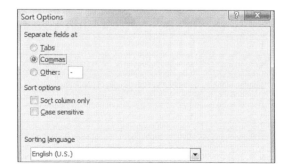

Figure 5-21 Paragraph marks

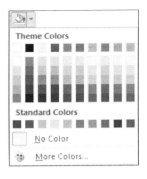

Shaded Text

Figure 5-23 Shading applied to text

Figure 5-22 Shading options

Bulleted Lists

The options on the gallery shown in Figure 5-24 are used to create and edit bulleted lists. The options shown are some of the bullet styles that can be applied to the list. The options at the bottom of the gallery are explained below.

The **CHANGE LIST LEVEL** option displays a list of bullet options that are used to select a different list level for the selected items in the bulleted list.

The **DEFINE NEW BULLET** option opens the dialog box shown in Figure 5-25. The options are used to create a custom bullet style. You can use your own image file for the bullet, by clicking the Picture button and then click the Import button.

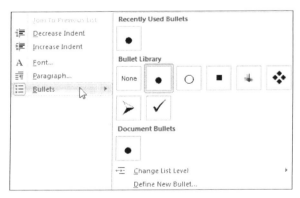

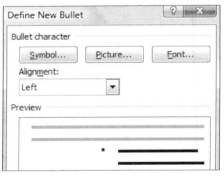

Figure 5-25 Define New Bullet dialog box

Figure 5-24 Bullets gallery

Using Bullets

Bullets are often used to make lines of text stand out in a document. They are also used to create lists, format and organize content, as are numbered lists. There are two ways to create a bulleted list, as discussed below.

① Position the mouse pointer where you want the first bullet, then select a bullet style from the gallery. Start typing the items for the bulleted list. Press the Enter key after each item. Each time you press the Enter key, another bullet will appear.

② Type the list of items. Select all of the items, then select a bullet style from the gallery.

Create A Bulleted List

1. Open the New Classes Letter document.

2. Select the body of the letter, then change the font size to 11.

3. Move the mouse pointer to the line below the second paragraph, then press Enter.

4. Type `Introduction To Multimedia`. Press the Tab key three times. The mouse pointer should be at the 3 inch mark on the ruler.

5. Type `January 9th`, then press Enter.

6. Type `Introduction To Web Page Design`. Press the Tab key twice. Type `January 10th`, then press Enter.

7. Type `Introduction To Networking`. Press the Tab key three times. Type `January 11th`, then press Enter.

8. Highlight the three lines that you just typed. Home tab ⇒ Paragraph group ⇒ Click the Bullets button.

The list should look like the one shown in Figure 5-26.

Save the changes.

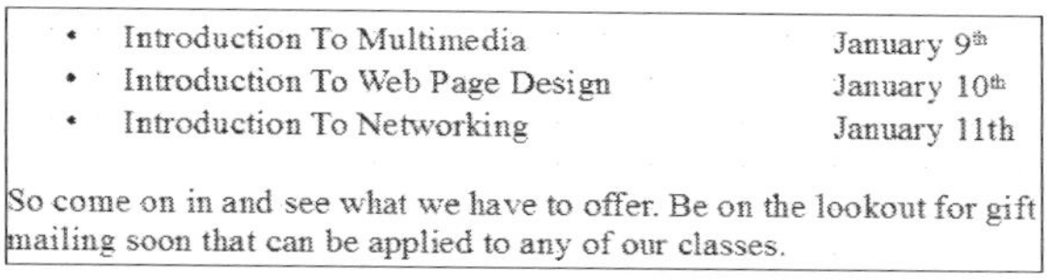

• Introduction To Multimedia	January 9th
• Introduction To Web Page Design	January 10th
• Introduction To Networking	January 11th

So come on in and see what we have to offer. Be on the lookout for gift mailing soon that can be applied to any of our classes.

Figure 5-26 Bulleted list in the document

How To Change The Bullet Style

There are several bullet styles that you can select from. The bulleted list that you just created used the default bullet style. The steps below show you how to change the bullet style.

1. Right-click in the bulleted list and hold the mouse pointer over the Bullets option on the shortcut menu. You should see the bullets gallery shown earlier in Figure 5-24.

2. Select the first bullet style option in the second row.

Your letter should look like the one shown in Figure 5-27.

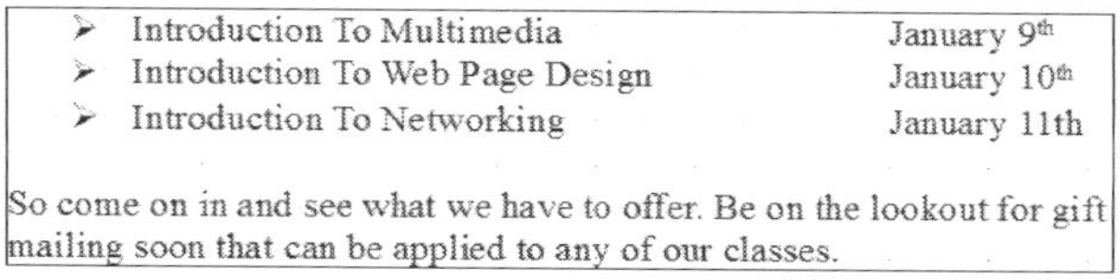

➢ Introduction To Multimedia	January 9th
➢ Introduction To Web Page Design	January 10th
➢ Introduction To Networking	January 11th

So come on in and see what we have to offer. Be on the lookout for gift mailing soon that can be applied to any of our classes.

Figure 5-27 Bullet style changed

How To Remove Bullets

If you have created a bulleted list and later decide that you do not want the bullets, follow the steps below to remove the bullets. You can just read this section now.

1. Highlight the bulleted list in the document.

2. In the Bullets gallery, select the option **NONE**, as shown earlier in Figure 5-24. The bullets will be removed.

Creating Multi Level Lists

The bulleted list shown in Figure 5-28 is known as a **MULTI LEVEL** or **INDENTED** list because there is a list within a list. The easiest way to create this style of bulleted or numbered list is to create the entire list at the same level. Once the entire list is created, highlight the items that need to be indented to create the sublevel, then press the Tab key. If you need to move an item up one level, select it, then press the **SHIFT+TAB** keys.

The **INCREASE INDENT** and **DECREASE INDENT** options in the Paragraph group should not be used to create the sublevels in the bulleted list. Instead, use the **CHANGE LIST LEVEL** option in the bullets gallery or the **ADJUST LIST INDENTS** option on the shortcut menu, shown in Figure 5-29. This option opens the dialog box shown in Figure 5-30. The options on the Adjust List Indents dialog box are used to customize the indent of the bulleted list. The last two options on the shortcut menu are explained below.

The **SEPARATE LIST** option will split the bulleted list into two lists.

The **JOIN TO PREVIOUS LIST** option will move the selected items (usually items in a different level) up to the previous level and change the bullet style to match the style of the level that the items are moved to.

You can also use the markers on the ruler to position the sublevel items by selecting all of the items that need to be indented, then drag the corresponding marker on the ruler to the location that the items need to be indented to.

To change the bullet style for the second level shown in Figure 5-28, highlight the second level items select a different bullet style in the bullet gallery.

 You can follow the same process to create a numbered list with multiple levels.

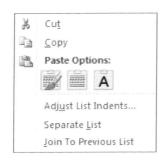

Figure 5-28 Multi level bulleted list

Figure 5-29 Document shortcut menu

Figure 5-30 Adjust List Indents dialog box

Numbered Lists

Numbered lists are very similar to bulleted lists. They are created the same way. The difference is that bulleted lists use images and numbered lists use a numerical sequence. Figure 5-31 shows the numbering list options.

SET NUMBERING VALUE (On the Numbering gallery) Is used to select a different starting number for the level on the dialog box shown in Figure 5-32.

CONTINUE FROM PREVIOUS LIST (On the Set Numbering Value dialog box) If checked, the numbers will be increased by one, as each level is created, as shown in Figure 5-33.

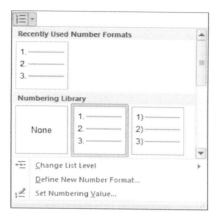

Figure 5-33 Consecutive numbering

Figure 5-32 Set Numbering Value dialog box

Figure 5-31 Numbering gallery

Create A Numbered List

The steps below show you how to create a numbered list.

1. Open a new document.

2. Type `Introduction To Multimedia`, then press Enter.
   Type `Introduction To Web Page Design`, then press Enter.
   Type `Introduction To Networking`, then press Enter.

3. Highlight the list, then click the **NUMBERING** button in the Paragraph group on the Home tab. The list should look like the one shown in Figure 5-34.

   | 1. Introduction To Multimedia |
   | 2. Introduction To Web Page Design |
   | 3. Introduction To Networking |

Figure 5-34 Numbered list

 How To Change The Numbered List Style
If you want to change the style of the numbered list, highlight the list, right-click on the list and select Numbering. Select a different numbering style on the Numbering gallery shown earlier in Figure 5-31.

Setting Paragraph Alignment

You can set the paragraph alignment in one of four ways. Figure 5-35 shows each of the paragraph alignment options. They were explained earlier in Table 5-3.

Figure 5-35 Paragraph alignment options

Paragraph Dialog Box

The dialog box shown in Figure 5-36 is used to format paragraphs in a document.

Indents And Spacing Tab

The options on the Indents and Spacing tab are used to select the alignment, indentation and spacing options. Most of these options are in the Paragraph group on the Home or Page Layout tab.

The **TABS** button opens the Tabs dialog box, which you will learn about later in this chapter.

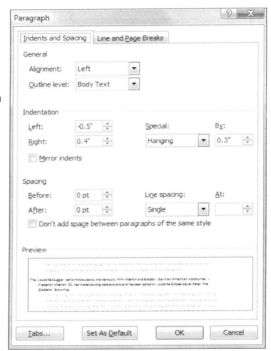

Figure 5-36 Indents and Spacing tab

 You can right-click in the paragraph and select Paragraph on the shortcut menu to open the Paragraph dialog box.

Indentation Options

The Indentation options shown in Figure 5-37 are similar to the Paragraph alignment options that you may already be familiar with. There are also two buttons in the Paragraph group for indenting text. Indent options are applied to change the placement of text in the paragraph.

Figure 5-37 illustrates the three basic types of indentation.

Figure 5-37 Indentation options illustrated

Unlike paragraph alignment, you can use more than one indentation option in the same paragraph. Figure 5-38 shows what is known as a **HANGING INDENT**. To create this type of indentation, enter a negative number in the **LEFT** Indentation field. Open the Special drop-down list and select **HANGING**, then change the **BY** option to a positive number, as shown earlier in Figure 5-36.

> The American League wins baseball's first All-Star Game July 6 at Chicago's Comiskey Field, defeating the National League 4 to 2. The American League wins baseball's first All-Star Game July 6 at Chicago's Comiskey Field, defeating the National League 4 to 2.

Figure 5-38 Hanging indent

 Left And Right Indent Options
These are the two most popular indent options. They have their own options in the Paragraph group on the Page Layout tab, as shown in Figure 5-39. If you use these options often, it may be easier to access them on the Page Layout tab then it is to open the Paragraph dialog box.

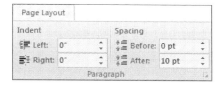

Figure 5-39 Paragraph group options on the Page Layout tab

Use The Ruler To Set Paragraph Indents

In addition to being able to set paragraph indents with options on the tabs and the Paragraph dialog box, they can also be set on the horizontal ruler. Figure 5-40 illustrates the options on the ruler that are used to set up paragraph indents.

Click in the paragraph that you want to indent. If you want to indent more than one paragraph, select them. Drag the buttons to the location on the ruler to create the indent size that you need. The options are explained in Table 5-4.

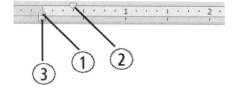

Figure 5-40 Paragraph indent options

Option	Description
1	Is used to set the left indent for a hanging indent.
2	Is used to set the indent for the first line of the paragraph.
3	Is used to move both indents at the same time.

Table 5-4 Paragraph indent options explained

Nonprinting Characters

Displaying characters that do not print may help you figure out why part of a document is not being displayed or printed as you thought that it would. Figure 5-41 shows a paragraph that needs to be fixed.

The "Black Sox" scandal threatens to undermine the prestige and popularity of America's   national pastime. Eigh last year's Chicago White Sox baseball team are indicted in September for fraud in connection   with last year's 5-to-3

Figure 5-41 Paragraph that needs to be fixed

Figure 5-42 shows the same paragraph with the nonprinting characters option enabled.

Table 5-5 explains the nonprinting characters.

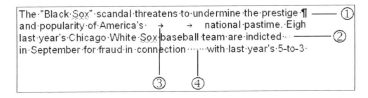

Figure 5-42 Paragraphs with nonprinting characters option enabled

Option	Description
1	The Enter key was pressed.
2	The Enter and Shift keys were pressed.
3	The Tab key was pressed.
4	The space bar was pressed more than once.

Table 5-5 Nonprinting character options explained

Spacing Options

There are three types of paragraph spacing. The one that you are probably most familiar with is **LINE** spacing. Keep in mind that a "paragraph" in word processing software does not only apply to a section of the document with multiple lines of text. A paragraph is also a section header. The other two paragraph spacing options are used to add space before and after the paragraph that they are applied to.

Before And After Paragraph Spacing Options

These options are on the Indents and Spacing tab on the Paragraph dialog box shown earlier in Figure 5-36 and work exactly as their names imply. The **BEFORE** paragraph option will add space before (above) the paragraph that is selected. The **AFTER** paragraph option will add space after (below) the paragraph that is selected.

These options are most often used with section headings in a document. All of the section headings in this book use both of these spacing options. Figure 5-43 illustrates the **BEFORE** and **AFTER** paragraph spacing options.

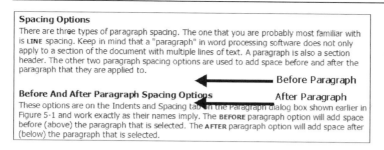

Figure 5-43 Before and After paragraph spacing options illustrated

Using these spacing options helps make the section headings stand out in the document. They also allow more consistent and precision spacing then the line spacing options provide. The Before and After paragraph spacing options are also in the Paragraph group on the Page Layout tab, as shown earlier in Figure 5-39.

Line Spacing Options

The line spacing options on the Paragraph dialog box shown in Figure 5-44 are useful if you need to use the last three options in the drop-down list because the **AT** field next to it provides additional functionality. Line spacing options can also be accessed from the Paragraph group on the Home tab, as shown in Figure 5-45. Notice that the options are different. The **LINE SPACING OPTIONS** option shown in Figure 5-45 opens the Paragraph dialog box shown earlier in Figure 5-36.

AT LEAST Is used to set the minimum line spacing needed. Select this option if the line will have a font size larger than the other font size on the line.

EXACTLY Is used to set a fixed line spacing.

MULTIPLE Is used to change single line spacing by increasing or decreasing it.

Figure 5-44 Line spacing options

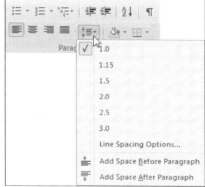

Figure 5-45 Line spacing options

The line spacing option is used to select the amount of space between the lines of text in a paragraph. The default option is Single. As shown above in Figures 5-44 and 5-45, there are other line spacing options. The steps below show you how to change the line spacing. You can use the Term Paper document for practice.

1. Click in the second paragraph. Home tab ⇒ Paragraph group ⇒ Dialog box launcher.

2. On the **INDENTS AND SPACING** tab, open the **LINE SPACING** drop-down list, then select Double.

   Click OK.

   The second paragraph should now be double spaced, as shown in Figure 5-46.

> The "Louisville Slugger" bat is introduced by the Kentucky firm Hillerich and Bradsby. German-American woodturner, J. Frederick Hillerich, 50, has made bowling balls and pins and has been asked by Louisville Eclipse player Peter "the Gladiator" Browning, 26, to make an ashwood bat that will replace one that Browning has broken. Browning has made his own bats of seasoned timber aged in his attic, but although he had averaged three hits per game with his homemade bats, he does even better with Hillerich's bat.
>
> The American League wins baseball's first All-Star Game July 6 at Chicago's Comiskey Field, defeating the National League 4 to 2.

Figure 5-46 Double spaced paragraph

Line And Page Breaks Tab

The options shown in Figure 5-47 are used to configure how paragraphs that do not fit on a page are handled.

Pagination Options

The options in this section are used to select options for paragraphs that do not fit at the bottom of a page.

If checked, the **WIDOW/ORPHAN CONTROL** option does not allow a paragraph to be split onto two pages. A widow line appears at the top of the page. An orphan line appears at the bottom of the page.

The **ORPHAN** portion of the option does not allow the first line of a paragraph to be the only line of the paragraph that prints at the bottom of the page.

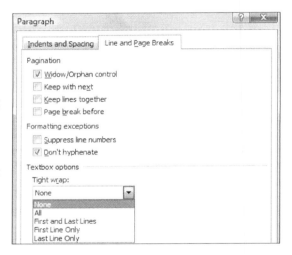

Figure 5-47 Line and Page Breaks tab

The **WIDOW** portion of the option does not allow the last line of the paragraph to be the only line of the paragraph to print at the top of a page.

To keep a paragraph heading from printing on the last line of a page and the paragraph that goes with the heading printing at the top of the next page, select the **KEEP WITH NEXT** option for the heading styles that the document uses.

The **KEEP LINES TOGETHER** option prevents a paragraph from being split onto two pages. The paragraph is automatically forced to the next page if it doesn't fit on the current page. Even if checked, this option is ignored if the Widow/Control option is selected.

The **PAGE BREAK BEFORE** option inserts a manual page break where the insertion point is in the document. This gives you control over where the page breaks are in the document.

Formatting Exceptions Options

The options in this section will be applied to the part of the document that is selected before the Paragraph dialog box is opened.

The **SUPPRESS LINE NUMBERS** option is used to hide line numbers in the paragraphs that are selected.

The **DON'T HYPHENATE** option is used to suppress hyphenation for the selected text.

Textbox Options

The **TIGHT WRAP** option is only available when a text box object is selected in the document. The options in the drop-down list shown above in Figure 5-47 are used to select how the text is wrapped in the text box.

Tab Stops

The options shown in Figure 5-48 are used to create, edit and delete tab stops. The options are explained below.

TAB STOP POSITION This option is used to select the location of the tab stops. The numbers entered in this field will appear as markers on the ruler.

ALIGNMENT The options in this section are used to select the alignment of the text at the tab stop.

The **DECIMAL** alignment option is used to line up numbers that have a decimal point.

The **BAR** alignment option inserts a vertical bar at the tab stop position.

LEADER The options in this section are used to select the character that appears to the left of the tab stop.

Figure 5-48 Tabs dialog box

Setting Tab Stops

Word has default tab stops preset at every half inch. The default tab stops are displayed on the ruler. To see where the preset tabs are located, press the Tab key a few times. Each stop represents a default tab stop. If these tab stops are not what you need for a particular document or section of a document, follow the steps below to change the tab stops. The steps below show you how to set tab stops at every inch.

> Tab stops that you create override some or all of the default tab stops in the current document. For example, if you create tab stops in the range 0.75" to 2.75", any default tab stop in that range are removed. The default tab stops outside of that range remain unchanged.

1. Double-click in the margins on the ruler to open the Tabs dialog box.

2. Click the Clear All button. This will delete the tab stop that you created when you double-clicked on the ruler to open the Tabs dialog box.

3. In the Tab stop position field type a 1, then click the Set button.
    In the Tab stop position field type a 2, then click the Set button.
    In the Tab stop position field type a 3, then click the Set button.
    The dialog box should have the options shown above in Figure 5-48.

4. Click OK. You should see tab stop markers at the 1, 2 and 3 inch marks on the ruler, as shown in Figure 5-49. Press the Tab key a few times. The mouse pointer will stop at the 1 inch mark, instead of the ½ inch mark.

Figure 5-49 New tab stops on the ruler

5. Leave the document open.

Changing The Default Tab Stops

The default tab stops cannot be deleted, but their spacing can be changed. As you saw in the **DEFAULT TAB STOPS** field show earlier in Figure 5-48, the default tab stops are at every half an inch. The steps below show you how to change the default tab stops to be at every inch.

1. Open the Tabs dialog box.

2. Clear all of the tab stops.

3. Change the Default tab stops option to 1 inch, then click OK.

4. When you press the Tab key, the insertion point stops at every inch instead of every half an inch.

How To Delete A Tab Stop

The steps below show you how to delete a tab stop.

1. Open the Tabs dialog box.

2. In the Tab stop position list, click on the tab stop that you want to delete.

3. Click the **CLEAR** button, then click OK. The tab stop that you selected should not be on the ruler.

Use The Ruler To Create Tab Stops

In addition to being able to click on the ruler to create a tab stop, the Tab Selector button to the far left of the ruler is used to select a specific type of tab stop alignment.

Figure 5-50 shows the Tab Selector button and some tab markers on the ruler.

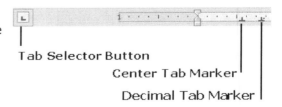

Figure 5-50 Tab Selector button and markers

If you hold the mouse pointer over the Tab Selector button, you will see a description of the tab stop type. Click on this button until you see the tab stop type that you want to create. The options on this button are Left tab, Center tab, Right tab, Decimal tab, Box tab, First Line Indent and Hanging Indent.

The icon on this button changes. When you see the tab stop that you want to create, click on the ruler where you want to place the tab stop. On the ruler you will see a marker with the same image as the option that you selected on the Tab Selector button. You can move the tab stop marker on the ruler as needed. To remove a tab stop on the ruler, click on it, then drag it off the ruler.

Borders

Borders are often used to make certain parts of a document stand out. An example of borders and shading added to text are the tip boxes in this book. In Word, the borders can be single, double, bold or a colored line.

You can also place borders on the left, right, top or bottom of a paragraph. An example of a partial border is the single line at the top of this page, right below the page header information.

The options shown in Figure 5-51 are used to add borders to text, tables or other objects. The image next to each option shows where the border will be added (or removed from).

The **DIAGONAL DOWN BORDER** and **DIAGONAL UP BORDER** options are used in table cells, as shown in Figure 5-52.

The non border options (the last four in Figure 5-51) are explained below.

The **HORIZONTAL LINE** option is used to add a horizontal line where the insertion point is, as shown in Figure 5-53.

The **DRAW TABLE** option is used to manually add a table to the document. This option displays the Table Tools Design and Layout tabs.

The **VIEW GRIDLINES** option is used to display the gridlines of a table when it or any of its cells do not have a border applied, as shown in Figure 5-54.

Figure 5-51 Border options

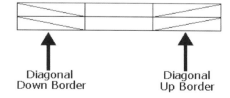

Figure 5-52 Diagonal border options illustrated

that we will be mailing soon that can be applied

I am looking forward to seeing you soon!

Figure 5-53 Horizontal line option

Figure 5-54 View gridlines option

Borders And Shading Dialog Box

The **BORDERS AND SHADING** option shown earlier in Figure 5-51 opens the dialog box shown in Figure 5-55. The options on this dialog box are used to add borders and shading to text, tables and pages in the document.

The **HORIZONTAL LINE** button opens the dialog box shown in Figure 5-56. The options on this dialog box are used to add a decorative horizontal line to the document.

The **OPTIONS BUTTON** on the Borders tab opens the dialog box shown in Figure 5-57. The **OPTIONS BUTTON** on the Page Border tab opens the dialog box shown in Figure 5-58. The options on these dialog boxes are used to select the distance between the border and the text.

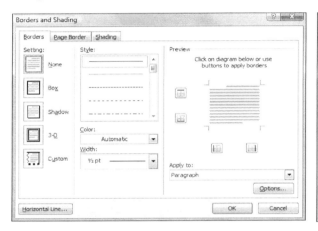

Figure 5-55 Borders and Shading dialog box

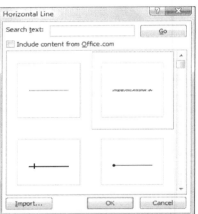

Figure 5-56 Horizontal Line dialog box

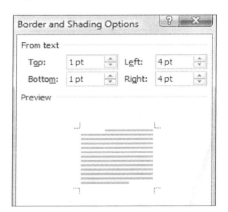

Figure 5-57 Border and Shading Options dialog box (from the Borders tab)

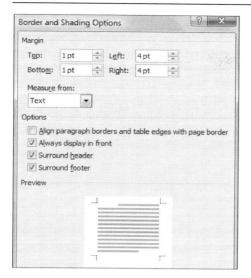

Figure 5-58 Border and Shading Options dialog box (from the Page Border tab)

How To Add A Border

The instructions below show you how to add a border around text or an object.

1. Select the text, table or object that you want to add a border to.

2. Home tab ⇒ Paragraph group ⇒ Borders drop-down list.

3. Select the border option that you want to use or select the Borders and Shading option to open the Borders and Shading dialog box to create a custom border.

Page Borders can be added to the entire document or individual pages in the document. For example, you may only want a page border on the cover page of the document. To accomplish this, on the Page Border tab, open the **APPLY TO** drop-down list and select **THIS SECTION** if the cover page is the only page in the section or select the **THIS SECTION - FIRST PAGE ONLY** option if there are other pages in the section that the cover page is in.

How To Add A Page Border

The previous section showed you how to add a border to text or an object in the document. The steps below show you how to add a border to the page. Adding a border to a page is very similar to adding a border to text.

1. Open the document that you want to add the page border to.

2. Home tab ⇒ Paragraph group ⇒ Borders drop-down list ⇒ Borders and Shading ⇒ Page Border tab.

3. Select the page border options that you want. They are similar to the options on the Borders tab.

 The page border is only visible in the Print Layout view.

How To Add Shading

The steps below show you how to add shading to text or to the entire page.

1. Select the text, table or object that you want to add shading to.

2. Home tab $\Rightarrow$ Paragraph group $\Rightarrow$ Borders drop-down list $\Rightarrow$ Borders and Shading $\Rightarrow$ Shading tab.

3. Select the Fill color and Pattern from the options shown in Figure 5-59 that you want to use as shading.

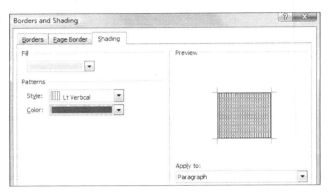

Figure 5-59 Shading tab

4. Select Paragraph in the Apply to drop-down list to apply the shading to the selected text.

To apply shading to the entire document, press CTRL+A, then open the Borders and Shading dialog box. Click on the Shading tab, then select the shading color that you want.

If you added a border and shading to a header in the document, it would look similar to the one shown in Figure 5-60. If you added a border to an image, it would look similar to Figure 5-61.

Figure 5-60 Borders and shading added to the title of the document

Figure 5-61 Borders added to the images

What Are Styles?

Styles are predefined formats that can be applied to text, images and entire documents. Word comes with several built-in styles. If you cannot find a built-in style that meets your needs, you can create your own style. You can also modify the styles that come with Word. The most used style is the **NORMAL** page style. By default, this is the style that all new documents are created from.

Benefits Of Using Styles

The best reason to use styles instead of manually formatting parts of the document is to keep the formatting consistent throughout the document. If you decided that the formatting for text that has the same style needs to be changed from bold to italic for example, you do not need to look for every word that is bold and manually change it to italic. You change the style to italic and all of the text that has that style applied to it, is automatically updated to the new style. The longer the document, the more you need to use styles.

Styles Group

The options shown in Figure 5-62 are used to apply styles, save styles that you create and remove the formatting from the selected text.

The three options at the bottom of the gallery are explained below.

The **SAVE SELECTION AS A NEW QUICK STYLE** option is used to save a style that you created, including modifying a style that comes with Word.

The **CLEAR FORMATTING** option removes the style from the selected text. If the mouse pointer is in a paragraph, the styles will be removed from the paragraph.

The **APPLY STYLES** option opens the task pane shown in Figure 5-64. The options are used to apply styles that are not in the style gallery, as shown in Figure 5-65.

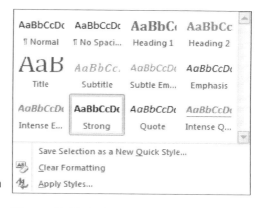

Figure 5-62 Styles gallery

To see more than one row of styles at a time in the gallery, click on the **MORE** arrow button illustrated in Figure 5-63.

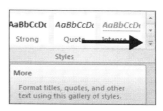

Figure 5-63 More arrow button illustrated

The **REAPPLY** button applies the style in the Style Name field to the selected text.

The **MODIFY** button opens the dialog box shown in Figure 5-66.

Clicking the **STYLES** button displays the task pane shown in Figure 5-67.

Figure 5-64 Apply Styles task pane

Figure 5-65 Additional styles

The options on this dialog box are used to modify styles. If you want the changes that you make to the style to be available for all documents, select the **NEW DOCUMENTS BASED ON THIS TEMPLATE** option.

The **STYLE TYPE** field is how you link a style, as illustrated in Figure 5-66.

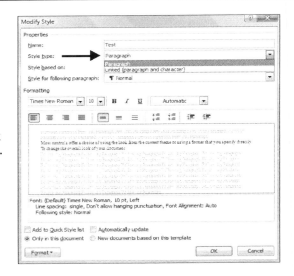

Figure 5-66 Modify Style dialog box

Styles Task Pane

Word supports the styles that are explained in Table 5-6. Not all styles have a symbol. The second column in the table has the symbol that is displayed next to the style on the Styles task pane, as shown on the right of Figure 5-67.

The options on the Styles task pane are used to apply, create and manage styles. This is another way to apply a style. The style options are displayed how they will look when applied to text. The options on the task pane are explained in Table 5-7.

Holding the mouse pointer over a style in the list, as shown in Figure 5-68, displays the attributes for the style.

Clicking at the end of a style displays the options shown in Figure 5-69. The options are used to modify the style. You will see different options on this list depending on the features that the style has enabled.

Figure 5-67 Styles task pane

Figure 5-68 Style attributes

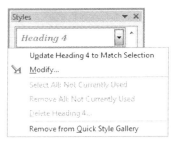

Figure 5-69 Style drop-down list

Style	Symbol	This Style Is Used For . . .
Character	**a**	Individual parts of a paragraph, like fonts, bold and italic formats.
Paragraph	¶	Borders, line spacing, tabs and text alignment.
Linked	¶a	Styles that work with both paragraph and character style types.
List		Bullet and numbered lists.
Table		Text formatting, row and column colors and gridlines in tables.

Table 5-6 Style types explained

Styles Task Pane Options

Option	Description
Show Preview	If checked, the styles are displayed with their formatting. Figure 5-70 shows the styles without this option enabled.
Disable Linked Styles	If checked, styles that are linked to another style are not displayed.
New Style button	Opens the dialog box shown in Figure 5-71. The options are used to create a new style based on the current style. The options on the Format button shown in Figure 5-72 are used to further customize the new style.
Style Inspector button	Opens the task pane shown in Figure 5-73. The information on this task pane lets you know if the formatting was applied manually or by using a style. Formats in the gray boxes (illustrated) were applied manually. The options are used to view the layers of the formatting of the style.
Manage Styles button	Opens the dialog box shown in Figure 5-74.
Options link	Clicking this link opens the dialog box shown later in Figure 5-76.

Table 5-7 Styles task pane options explained

Figure 5-70 Show Preview option disabled

Figure 5-71 Create New Style From Formatting dialog box

Figure 5-72 Format button options   **Figure 5-73** Style Inspector task pane

The options on this dialog give you access to all of the styles, which allows you to set default options, edit style options, create new styles and delete styles, all in one place.

The styles that are marked **HIDE UNTIL USED** are not automatically displayed on the Styles gallery or the Styles task pane. Once you apply one of these styles, it will be displayed in the Styles gallery and task pane.

The **IMPORT/EXPORT** button opens the dialog box shown in Figure 5-75.

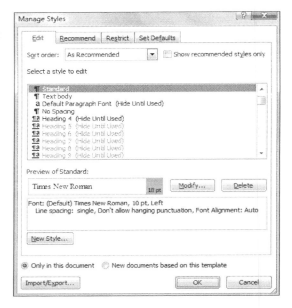

Figure 5-74 Manage Styles dialog box

The options on the Styles tab are used to copy styles between the document and the **GLOBAL TEMPLATE**, Normal.dotm.

Figure 5-75 Organizer dialog box

The options on the dialog box shown in Figure 5-76 are used to customize how styles are displayed on the Styles task pane.

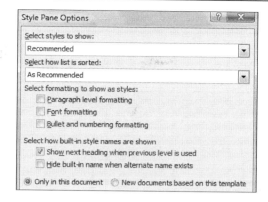

Figure 5-76 Style Pane Options dialog box

Change Styles Options

The options shown in Figure 5-77 are used to manage style sets, which are shown on the right of the figure.

A **STYLE SET** is a collection of styles. Each of the style sets shown on the right of the figure have heading styles, a normal style, a caption style, as well as, a style for many of the options shown earlier in Figure 5-70.

The options on the submenus for the Colors, Fonts and Paragraph Spacing are used to modify the selected style set.

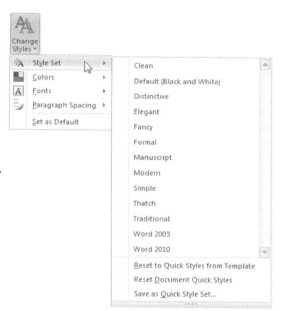

Figure 5-77 Change Styles and Style Set options

View The Style Sets

To see the differences between the style sets, follow the steps below.

1. Open the Multi Page document.

2. Home tab ⇒ Styles group ⇒ Change Styles ⇒ Style Set.

3. Hold the mouse pointer over each style set and view the differences in the document.

Paragraph Spacing (Style Options)

The options shown in Figure 5-78 are used to change the spacing. If you hold the mouse pointer over an option, you will see the Before, After and Line spacing that the paragraph style has. You will also see it applied to the text in the document.

The **CUSTOM PARAGRAPH SPACING** option opens the Set Defaults tab on the Manage Styles dialog box, shown earlier in Figure 5-74. The options are used to change the paragraph spacing.

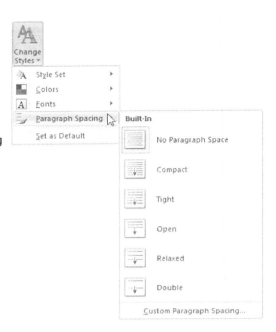

Figure 5-78 Paragraph Spacing style options

THE INSERT TAB

Overview The options on the Insert tab are used to enhance documents. You will learn about the following.

- ☑ How to apply templates
- ☑ How to add image and clip art files to a document
- ☑ How to create hyperlinks
- ☑ How to add text to the header and footer sections
- ☑ How to use WordArt and Drop Caps

CHAPTER 6

Overview

The options on the Insert tab are used to add objects and functionality to documents that make them look more professional. The options on this tab are how you can customize documents. Figure 6-1 shows the Insert tab. The options are explained below.

Figure 6-1 Insert tab

Pages Group

The options in this group are used to add pages to a document and split existing pages in a document. The options are explained in Table 6-1.

Option	Description
Cover Page	The options shown in Figure 6-2 are cover page templates. Like the templates that you read about in Chapter 2, the cover page templates have place holders for you to enter information. These templates automatically insert a new page at the beginning of the document and places the cover page there.
Blank Page	Inserts a new page where the insertion point is in the document.
Page Break	Adds a page break in the document where the insertion point is in the document. If the insertion point is in a paragraph, the text after the insertion point will be moved to the top of the next page. The **BREAKS** option on the Page Layout tab has additional page break options.

Table 6-1 Pages group options explained

Cover Page Templates

The cover page templates are called **BUILDING BLOCKS**.

The header and footer options on this tab, as well as, the watermark option on the Page Layout tab also have building blocks.

The **MORE COVER PAGES FROM OFFICE.COM** option displays additional cover page templates.

The **REMOVE CURRENT COVER PAGE** option deletes the cover page from the document.

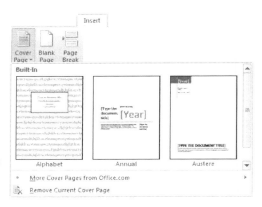

Figure 6-2 Cover page templates

Some of the fields in the cover page templates have drop-down lists and some fields cause additional tabs to be displayed.

For example, some templates have a date field, as shown in Figure 6-3. You can type in the date or click on the down arrow and select the date from the calendar.

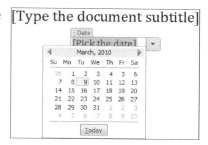

Figure 6-3 Date field in a template

Using The Cover Page Templates

The steps below show you how to add a cover page template to a document.

1. Open the document that you want to add a cover page to.

2. Insert tab ⇒ Pages group ⇒ Cover Page, then select the template that you want to use.

3. Modify the template as needed.

Tables Group

The options in this group are covered in Chapter 9.

Illustrations Group

The options in this group are used to add images to a document, which includes photos, clip art and shapes. Image or graphic files, as they are also called, add visual elements to point something out, demonstrate some of the content in the document or capture the readers attention. The options are explained in Table 6-2.

Option	Description
Picture	Adds image files. Clicking this button opens the dialog box shown in Figure 6-4.
ClipArt	Adds image files that are on your computers hard drive or on office.com.
Shapes	Adds shapes like arrows and callouts to a document.
Chart	Adds a chart to the document. Charts are covered in Chapter 10.

Table 6-2 Illustrations group options explained

Difference Between Picture Files And Clip Art

In the Illustrations group you see both of these options. While they both are used to add image files to a document, the ClipArt option also has the ability to add audio and video files to a document.

Insert Picture Dialog Box

This dialog box works like the Open dialog box, meaning that the left side of the dialog box is used to navigate to the folder that has the image file that you want to add to the document and then select the image file on the right side of the dialog box.

Above the **ALL PICTURES** button in the lower right corner of the dialog box, you will see a list of the file types that Word recognizes as image files.

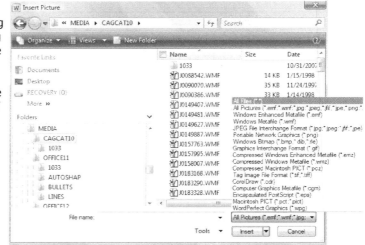

Figure 6-4 Insert Picture dialog box

Insert Options

Figure 6-5 shows the insert options that you can select on the Insert Picture dialog box for how you want the image to be added to the document.

After you select the image, select one of the options explained in Table 6-3.

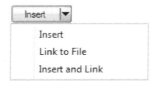

Figure 6-5 Picture Insert options

Option	Description
Insert	This is the default option. Select this option when you want to embed the image in the document. This option causes the document file size to increase.
Link to File	Is used to create a link to the image file. This means that the image is not actually saved in the document. It also means that if the image file is changed, you will see the changes in your document.
Insert and Link	Links to the image and embeds the image in the document.

Table 6-3 Picture Insert options explained

Adding Pictures To A Document

The steps below show you how to add a picture to a document.

1. Click in the document where you want to add the picture. The location does not have to be exact because you can move the picture file.

2. Insert tab ⇒ Illustrations group ⇒ Picture.

3. Navigate to the folder where the image file is that you want to add. If you do not know where any image files are on your hard drive, navigate to the folder with the practice files for this book.

4. Double-click on the image file and it will be added to the document. If you are using the practice files, double-click on the image6.jpg file.

Resizing Image Files

Many times, the image is not the size that you need it to be. To resize the image, click on one of the size handles surrounding the image, as illustrated in Figure 6-6 and drag it in the direction that you want to resize the image to.

As you are resizing the image, you will see a translucent copy of the image, as shown in Figure 6-6. Why, I have no idea.

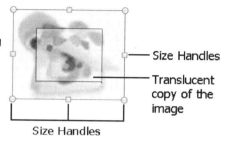

Size Handles

Translucent copy of the image

Size Handles

Figure 6-6 Size handles and translucent image

Resize Tips
The tips below will help you resize an image.
① Holding down the Shift key when resizing an image will keep the image in proportion.
② Holding down the CTRL key when resizing an image will keep the center of the image anchored. This means that the image will not move when it is resized.

Rotating Image Files

If you need to rotate an image, follow the steps below. Like resizing the image, rotating it causes a translucent copy of the image to appear.

1. Click on the handle at the top of the image, as illustrated in Figure 6-7.

Rotating Handle

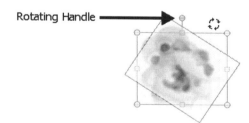

Figure 6-7 Rotating handle illustrated

2. Move the handle in the direction that you want the image rotated, then release the mouse button.

Picture Mini Toolbar And Shortcut Menu

Figure 6-8 shows the Mini toolbar for pictures.

Figure 6-9 shows shortcut menu for pictures.

Figure 6-8 Picture mini toolbar

The **EDIT PICTURE** option is used to change clip art files.

The **SAVE AS PICTURE** option is used to save the image file in the format of your choice.

The **CHANGE PICTURE** option is used to select a different picture.

Figure 6-9 Picture shortcut menu

Picture Tools Format Contextual Tab

When an image in the document is selected, the Picture Tools Format tab will appear. This tab contains options for customizing the picture. Figure 6-10 shows the Picture Tools Format tab. The options are used to adjust and crop the image, as well as, add borders and effects. The options are explained below.

Figure 6-10 Picture Tools Format tab

Adjust Group

The options in this group are used to modify a specific aspect of the image. The options are explained in Table 6-4.

Option	Description
Remove Background	Is used to remove the background from the image. Clicking on this option displays the tab shown in Figure 6-11. The options on this tab are used to select the part of the image to remove.
Corrections	The options shown in Figure 6-12 are used to change the sharpness, brightness and contrast of the image. The **PICTURE CORRECTIONS OPTIONS** option opens the dialog box shown in Figure 6-13. This dialog box contains additional options for modifying image files.
Color	This gallery displays options to change the color, tone and saturation of the image.
Artistic Effects	The options shown in Figure 6-14 are used to make the image look more like a painting or sketch.
Compress Pictures	[See Chapter 3, Figure 3-31]
Change Picture	Opens the Insert Picture dialog box shown earlier in Figure 6-4. This option will replace the selected image in the document with the new one that you select.
Reset Picture	Selecting this option will remove all of the changes that you made to the image.

Table 6-4 Adjust group options explained

Figure 6-11 Background Removal tab

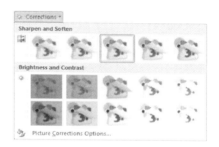

Figure 6-12 Corrections gallery

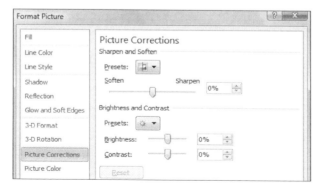

Figure 6-14 Artist Effects gallery

Figure 6-13 Format Picture dialog box

Picture Styles Group

The options in this group add effects to the border of an image. The options are explained in Table 6-5.

Option	Description
Picture Styles	The options are used to apply a background or frame around the image. The **MORE** button displays the styles in the gallery.
Picture Border	The options are used to select the color, weight and line style for the border around the image. The Picture Border options are similar to the paragraph border options that were covered in Chapter 5.
Picture Effects	The options shown in Figure 6-15 are used to add effects to the image. Many of the options are the same as the text effects that were covered in Chapter 5.
Dialog Box Launcher	Opens the Insert Picture dialog box shown earlier in Figure 6-4.

Table 6-5 Picture Styles group options explained

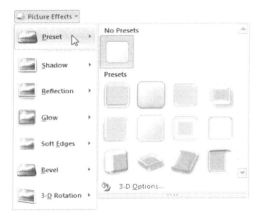

Figure 6-15 Picture Effects options

Arrange Group

The options in this group are used to change the location of the image. The options are explained in Table 6-6. The Wrap Text and Rotate options are the ones that you will probably use the most.

Option	Description
Position	The options shown in Figure 6-16 are used to select where the image will appear on the page. If the image is positioned near text, the text is wrapped around the image automatically. The **MORE LAYOUT OPTIONS** option opens the dialog box shown in Figure 6-17. The options on this dialog box are used to set up the **ABSOLUTE** and **RELATIVE** positioning and anchor the image to text.

Table 6-6 Arrange group options explained

Option	Description
Wrap Text	The options shown in Figure 6-18 are used to select how text will be displayed around the image. The image next to each option shows how the text will be wrapped. The **MORE LAYOUT OPTIONS** option opens the dialog box shown in Figure 6-19.
Bring Forward	The options are used to move the image up in the layers of the document.
Send Backward	The options are used to move the image down in the layers of the document.
Selection Pane	[See Chapter 4, Selection And Visibility Task Pane]
Align	The options are used to position (line up) the image with the page or align the image in a paragraph of text. For example, Figure 6-23 shows the image with the Align Left option selected. Selecting the Align Center option moves the image to the center of the paragraph, as shown in Figure 6-24.
Group	The options are used to put the selected objects (like images and shapes) into a group so that they can be moved as a single object.
Rotate	The options shown in Figure 6-25 are used to rotate and flip objects. The **MORE ROTATION OPTIONS** option opens the dialog box shown in Figure 6-26. These options are used to customize the rotation.

Table 6-6 Arrange group options explained (Continued)

Figure 6-16 Position options

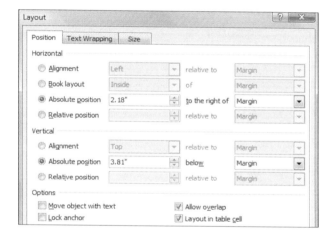

Figure 6-17 Position tab on the Layout dialog box

Wrap Text Options

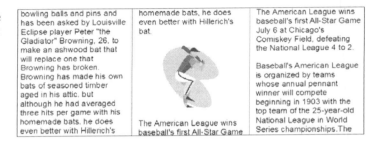

Figure 6-18 Wrap Text options

Figure 6-19 Text Wrapping tab on the Layout dialog box

Figure 6-20 shows an image with the **THROUGH** wrap text option applied.

bowling balls and pins and has been asked by Louisville Eclipse player Peter "the Gladiator" Browning, 26, to make an ashwood bat that will replace one that Browning has broken. Browning has made his own bats of seasoned timber aged in his attic, but although he had averaged three hits per game with his homemade bats, he does even better with Hillerich's

homemade bats, he does even better with Hillerich's bat.

The American League wins baseball's first All-Star Game

The American League wins baseball's first All-Star Game July 6 at Chicago's Comiskey Field, defeating the National League 4 to 2.

Baseball's American League is organized by teams whose annual pennant winner will compete beginning in 1903 with the top team of the 25-year-old National League in World Series championships.The

Figure 6-20 Through wrap text option applied

Wrapping Style Options The options in this section of the dialog box shown earlier in Figure 6-19 are used to select how the text will be wrapped around the object. The **IN LINE WITH TEXT** option puts the object into the line of text, meaning that the object is treated like a character on the line. The **SQUARE** option wraps the text around the frame of the object.

Wrap Text Options The options in this section of the dialog box shown earlier in Figure 6-19 are only available with the **SQUARE, TIGHT** and **THROUGH WRAPPING** style options. These options are used to select which side of the image the text will be wrapped on.

Using The Wrapping Style Options

1. Open the Term Paper document.

2. Place the mouse pointer before the word **GLADIATOR** on the fourth line in the second paragraph, then add an image to the document. You can use the baseball2.tif file. Make the image larger.

3. Picture Tools Format tab ⇒ Arrange group ⇒ Wrap Text ⇒ Square. Your document should look like the one shown in Figure 6-21.

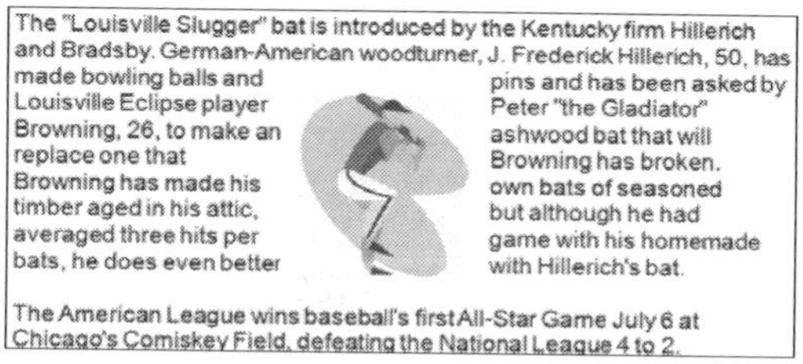

The "Louisville Slugger" bat is introduced by the Kentucky firm Hillerich and Bradsby. German-American woodturner, J. Frederick Hillerich, 50, has made bowling balls and Louisville Eclipse player Browning, 26, to make an replace one that Browning has made his timber aged in his attic, averaged three hits per bats, he does even better pins and has been asked by Peter "the Gladiator" ashwood bat that will Browning has broken. own bats of seasoned but although he had game with his homemade with Hillerich's bat.

The American League wins baseball's first All-Star Game July 6 at Chicago's Comiskey Field, defeating the National League 4 to 2.

Figure 6-21 Text wrapped around the image using the square style

Using The Wrap Text Options

1. Right-click on the image ⇒ Wrap Text ⇒ More Layout Options ⇒ Tight option.

2. Select the **LEFT ONLY** wrap text option shown earlier in Figure 6-19, then click OK.

   Your document should look like the one shown in Figure 6-22.

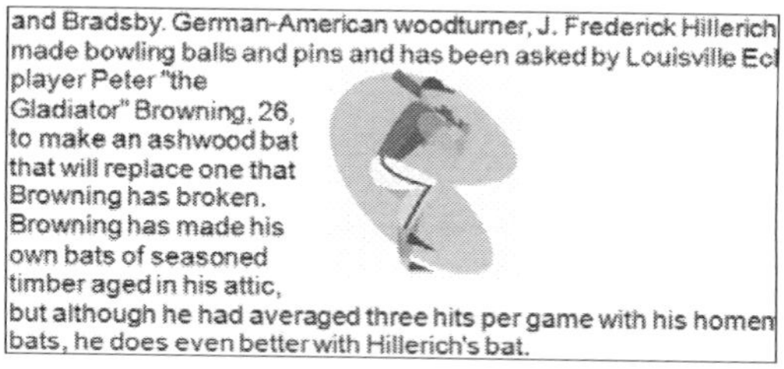

and Bradsby. German-American woodturner, J. Frederick Hillerich made bowling balls and pins and has been asked by Louisville Ecl player Peter "the Gladiator" Browning, 26, to make an ashwood bat that will replace one that Browning has broken. Browning has made his own bats of seasoned timber aged in his attic, but although he had averaged three hits per game with his homem bats, he does even better with Hillerich's bat.

Figure 6-22 Tight text wrapping style and wrap text options applied to the image

If you wanted less white space on the left side of the image, you could use the **DISTANCE FROM TEXT** options shown earlier in Figure 6-19. If that does not help, you would have to edit the image and remove some of the white space that is around the image.

3. Save the document with a new file name.

Alignment Examples

The first World Series baseball champion Boston team against the National League 5 games to 3.

Figure 6-23 Align Left (image) option

The first World Series baseball League's Boston team against the Boston wins 5 games to 3. championship pits the American National League's Pittsburgh team.

Figure 6-24 Center (image) option

Figure 6-25 Rotate options

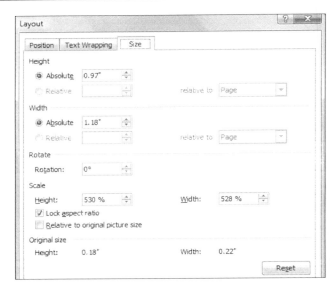

Figure 6-26 Size tab on the Layout dialog box

Size Group

The options in this group are used to resize an image or an object. They are explained in Table 6-7.

Option	Description
Crop	The options are used to remove part of the image. The **CROP TO SHAPE** option shown in Figure 6-27 will change the shape of the image to the shape that you select in the gallery.
Shape Height	Is used to change the height of the shape.
Shape Width	Is used to change the width of the shape.
Dialog Box Launcher	Opens the Layout dialog box shown above in Figure 6-26.

Table 6-7 Size group options explained

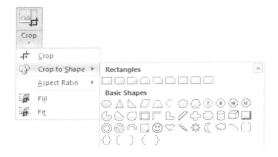

Figure 6-27 Crop options

Using Clip Art

In addition to being able to add clip art, this option is also used to add video files to a document.

Selecting the ClipArt button on the Insert tab displays the task pane shown in Figure 6-28. The options are explained in Table 6-8.

When clip art is added to the document the Picture Tools Format tab is available, just like it is for pictures. [See Picture Tools Format Contextual Tab, earlier in this chapter]

Figure 6-28 Clip Art task pane

Option	Description
Search For	Is used to type in the category of media files that you want to search for.
Results should be	The options shown in Figure 6-29 are used to select the types of media files that you want included in the search.
Include Office.com content	If checked, this option will search the web site for the category of media files that you select.
Find more at Office.com	This link opens the image section of the web site so that you can search for images.

Table 6-8 Clip Art task pane options explained

The **VIDEOS** option retrieves animated image files, not videos like the kind that you create with a camcorder.

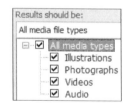

Figure 6-29 Media file types

How To Add Clip Art To A Document

1. Open the document that you want to add clip art to, then click near the location where you want to add the clip art.

2. Insert tab ⇒ Illustrations group ⇒ ClipArt.

3. Type in the category that you want in the Search for field. For the exercise, type books.

4. Open the Results drop-down list and clear the Videos and Audio options, then click the Go button.

5. After the files have been retrieved, scroll down the list of clip art to find what you want. When you find the file, double-click on it to add it to your document.

Creating Your Own Clip Art Collection

As you saw in the exercise above, a lot of the clip art is online and not on your computers hard drive. If you find clip art that you want to use again, you can copy the file to your computers hard drive. To do that, follow the steps below.

1. Open the ClipArt task pane.

2. Search for the clip art that you want to copy to the hard drive.

3. Click on the arrow on the right side of the image in the Task pane.

    You will see the menu shown in Figure 6-30.

    Select the **MAKE AVAILABLE OFFLINE** option.

Figure 6-30 Clip art menu option

4. You will see the Copy to Collection dialog box. Click on one of the folders to save the file in or create your own folder. Click OK after you have selected the folder.

Using Shapes

The options in this gallery are used to add shapes to the document. The shapes can be used alone for decorative or illustration purposes or they can be placed behind text to emphasize the text. The shapes that you recently used are displayed at the top of the list in the Recently Used Shapes section. The options in this gallery are the same options that the **CROP TO SHAPE** option has. [See Figure 6-27, earlier in this chapter]

The **NEW DRAWING CANVAS** option at the bottom of the shapes gallery is used to combine shapes and text that you want to use as one image. It works like the group option that you read about earlier in this chapter. The difference is that this option is used to select the shapes that you want to group together. Selecting this option adds a square to the document that you can resize and add shapes to, as shown in Figure 6-31.

Once the canvas is added to the document, the Drawing Tools Format tab will be displayed. At this point, text and shapes can be added to the canvas, which allows them to be treated as one object, as shown in Figure 6-32.

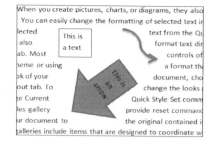

Figure 6-31 Drawing canvas with shapes and text

Figure 6-32 Text wrapped around objects in the canvas

Drawing Canvas Shortcut Menu

The shortcut menu shown in Figure 6-33 has three options that are used to change the size of the canvas. Right-click on the frame of the drawing canvas to display the shortcut menu.

Select **FIT** to reduce the Drawing Canvas to the size of the objects in the canvas.

Select **EXPAND** to make the drawing canvas larger.

Select **SCALE DRAWING** when you need to manually resize the drawing canvas and the objects in the canvas.

Figure 6-33 Drawing canvas shortcut menu

Adding Shapes To A Document

The steps below show you how to add shapes to a document.

1. Insert tab ⇒ Illustrations group ⇒ Shapes.

2. Click on the shape that you want to add to the document. The mouse pointer will change to a cross hair.

3. Draw a box in the location in the document, the size that you want the shape to be. You can resize the shape as needed.

Shapes Mini Toolbar And Shortcut Menu

Figure 6-34 shows the mini toolbar.

Figure 6-35 shows the shortcut menu.

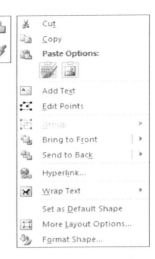

Figure 6-34 Shapes mini toolbar

The **ADD TEXT** option on the shortcut menu is used to add text to the shape.

Figure 6-35 Shapes shortcut menu

Drawing Tools Format Contextual Tab

When a shape in the document is selected, the Drawing Tools Format tab will appear. This tab contains options for customizing the shape. Figure 6-36 shows the Drawing Tools Format tab. The options are used to add other shapes, apply styles to shapes and add text to shapes. The options are explained below in Tables 6-9 to 6-12.

Figure 6-36 Drawing Tools Format tab

Insert Shapes Group

The options in this group are used to add shapes to the document and are explained in Table 6-9.

Option	Description
Shapes	[See Figure 6-27 earlier in this chapter]
Edit Shapes	Is used to change the selected shape to a different one. This option is also used to change the points of the shape. The points are the size handles. This lets you change the dimensions of the shape. On the left of Figure 6-37 is the original shape. On the right is the shape after the **EDIT POINTS** option on the Edit Shapes drop-down list was used to change the shape.
Draw Text Box	Is used to add a text object to the document.

Table 6-9 Insert Shapes group options explained

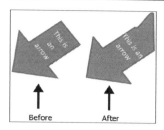

Figure 6-37 Edit Points option applied to a shape

Shape Styles Group

The options in this group are used to add or modify a shapes style. The options are explained in Table 6-10.

Option	Description
Shapes	This gallery contains the styles that can be applied to the shape.
Shape Fill	The options are used to change the interior color of the shape. Gradients and textures can also be applied to the interior of the shape.
Shape Outline	The options are used to change the border color and border color weight (size) of the shape.
Shape Effects	The options are used to add effects to the shape. Many of the options are the same as the Text Effects that you read about in Chapter 5.
Dialog Box Launcher	Opens the dialog box shown in Figure 6-38.

Table 6-10 Shape Styles group options explained

Figure 6-38 shows the Format Shape dialog box. This dialog box has options for customizing shapes.

Some of the options on the Drawing Tools Format tab have an option that opens this dialog box.

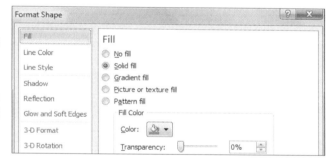

Figure 6-38 Format Shape dialog box

WordArt Styles Group

The options in this group are used to apply styles to text that is part of a shape or text in a Draw Text box object. The options are explained in Table 6-11.

Option	Description
Styles	The options shown in Figure 6-39 are used to apply WordArt to text or remove Word Art.
Text Fill	The options are used to change the color of the text or apply a gradient color to the text.
Text Outline	The options are used to change the border color and border color weight (size) of the text.
Text Effects	The options are used to add effects to the WordArt. Many of the options are the same as the Text Effects that you read about in Chapter 5.
Dialog Box Launcher	Opens the dialog box shown in Figure 6-40.

Table 6-11 WordArt Styles group options explained

Figure 6-39 WordArt Styles gallery

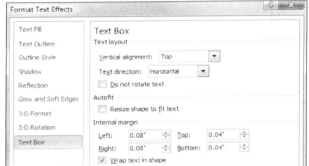

Figure 6-40 Format Text Effects dialog box

Text Group

The options in this group are used to modify text in a text box, like WordArt. The options are explained in Table 6-12.

Option	Description
Text Direction	The options shown in Figure 6-41 are used to rotate text. The **TEXT DIRECTION OPTIONS** option opens the dialog box shown in Figure 6-42. The options are also used for rotating text.
Align Text	The options shown in Figure 6-43 are used to select how the text is aligned in the text box.
Create Link	Is used to create a link between text boxes.

Table 6-12 Text group options explained

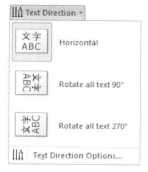

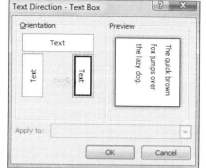

Figure 6-41 Text Direction options

Figure 6-42 Text Direction - Text Box dialog box

Figure 6-43 Align Text options

Creating A Link To A Text Box

If you are thinking why in the world would you need to create a link from one text box to another, you are not alone. It took me a while to figure out a use for this feature. The reason that I came up with is if the text box is at or near the bottom of the page and there is not enough space on the page for all of the text in the box to fit on the page. You would create a text box on the next page, which would allow the overflow of text in the first box to flow into the second text box. The steps below show you how to link two text boxes together.

1. Add a text box at the bottom of a page.

2. Add a lot of text to the text box. Make the text box smaller.

3. Add an empty text box some place on the next page of the document. It does not have to be at the top of the page.

4. Click on the first text box, then Drawing Tools Format tab ⇒ Text group ⇒ Create Link button.

   The mouse pointer will change to the one shown in Figure 6-44.

Figure 6-44 Symbol for linking text boxes

5. Scroll down, then click in the second text box. If you added enough text to the first text box, you will see some of the text in the second text box.

Arrange Group

The options in this group are the same as the ones on the Picture Tools Format tab. [See Table 6-6 earlier in this chapter]

Size Group

The options in this group are the same as the ones on the Picture Tools Format tab. [See Table 6-7 earlier in this chapter]

Links Group

If you have used the Internet you have used **HYPERLINKS**, which are often called "Links". Word has hyperlink functionality on the Insert tab that you can add to documents. Hyperlinks are used to move from one part of a document to another or to go to external locations like a web site. Hyperlinks can be created with text and objects like images. Hyperlinks can also be used to open a new email window. There are four types of hyperlinks that you can create in a document as discussed below.

     ①   To an existing file or web site.

     ②   To a location in the current document, as shown in Figure 6-45.

     ③   To a new document.

     ④   To an email address.

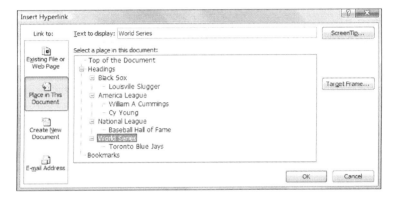

Figure 6-45 Insert Hyperlink dialog box

Depending on the type of hyperlink, you have to provide different types of information. Generally, you have to provide the following. You have to provide what you want to link to, the location of what you want to link to and the text that you want to use for the link in the document.

The **TEXT TO DISPLAY** field shown above in Figure 6-45 is used to store the text for the link. If you select the text in the document before opening the Insert Hyperlink dialog box, the text will be displayed in this field. If you do not want to use text that is in the document, you can type in the text that you want to use in this field. The link will be placed where the insertion point is in the document.

How To Create A Hyperlink To A Web Page

Out of all of the hyperlink options, this is probably the most popular. The steps below show you how to create a link to a web page.

1. Open the Multi Page document.

2. In the second paragraph, select the words Louisville Slugger.

3. Right-click on the highlighted text and select Hyperlink. In the Text to display field at the top of the dialog box, you should see the words that you selected.

4. In the **ADDRESS** field type `www.slugger.com`, then click OK.

If your computer is connected to the Internet and you click on the link that you just created, the web site will be displayed.

How To Create A Hyperlink To A Location In The Document

Often, when creating hyperlinks, you have the ability to link to a bookmark in the document. The steps below show you how to create a hyperlink to a location in the document without using a bookmark. You can use the Multi Page practice file.

1. In the first paragraph, select the words "World Series".

2. Insert tab ⇒ Links group ⇒ Hyperlink. Click the **PLACE IN THIS DOCUMENT** button.

3. Click on the World Series header, as shown above in Figure 6-45, then click OK. If you click on the link that you just created, the World Series section of the document will be displayed.

Header & Footer Group

Headers and footers are most often used to print information that you want to appear at the top or bottom of pages in the document. Headers print at the top of the page and footers print at the bottom of the page. Items commonly placed in headers and footers include page numbers, the date, copyright information or the document name.

You can put almost everything in the header and footer sections of a document that you can put in the body of a document, including clip art. The header and footer sections of a document have a dotted line, as shown at the top of Figure 6-46. The options in the group are explained in Table 6-13.

Figure 6-46 Header section

Option	Description
Header	The templates shown in Figure 6-47 are used to select a style for the header section of the document. (1)
Footer	The templates are used to select a style for the footer section of the document. They are the same as the header options. (1)
Page Number	The options shown in Figure 6-48 are used to select the placement and format of the page number.

Table 6-13 Header & Footer group options explained

(1)   Some of the options in this gallery have a page number.

Header Gallery

The gallery shown in Figure 6-47 contains templates that you can use to format the header section.

If you scroll down the list of templates you will see that some templates just have text and other templates have text and page numbers. This makes it easy to set up the header and footer sections because you can select the template that is closest to your needs and delete the items that you do not need.

The majority of these templates have a corresponding footer template.

The **MORE HEADERS FROM OFFICE.COM** option displays additional header styles that you can use.

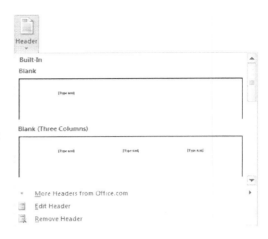

Figure 6-47 Header gallery

The **EDIT HEADER** option displays the header section of the document, so that you can make changes.

The **REMOVE HEADER** option deletes the header section of the document.

Page Number Options

The options shown in Figure 6-48 are explained in Table 6-14.

Figure 6-48 Page Number options

Option	Description
Top of Page	The options are used to select the style and location of the page number in the header section.
Bottom of Page	The options are used to select the style and location of the page number in the footer section.
Page Margins	The options are used to select the left or right margin as the location for the page number.
Current Position	The options are used to place the page number where the insertion point is, in the header or footer section.

Table 6-14 Page Number options explained

Option	Description
Format Page Numbers	Opens the dialog box shown in Figure 6-49. The options are used to change the format of the page number in the header or footer section.
Remove Page Numbers	Removes the page number from the header or footer section depending on which section the insertion point is in. This option only works for the page number options discussed in this table. If you added a page number another way, this option will not remove it.

Table 6-14 Page Number options explained (Continued)

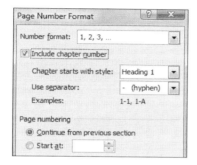

Figure 6-49 Page Number Format dialog box

Header & Footer Tools Design Contextual Tab

When a header or footer section is added to a document, the Header & Footer Tools Design contextual tab shown in Figure 6-50 is available. The options on the Design tab are explained below.

Figure 6-50 Header & Footer Tools Design tab

Header & Footer Group

[See Table 6-13, earlier in this chapter]

Insert Group

The options in this group are explained in other sections of this chapter, as listed in Table 6-15.

Option	Description
Date & Time	[See Text Group, later in this chapter]
Picture	[See Illustrations Group, earlier in this chapter]
ClipArt	[See Illustrations Group, earlier in this chapter]

Table 6-15 Insert group options explained

Navigation Group

The options in this group are used to display header and footer sections, as explained in Table 6-16.

Option	Description
Go to Header	Displays the header section on the current page.
Go to Footer	Displays the footer section on the current page.
Previous	Displays the prior header or footer section. (2)
Next	Displays the next header or footer section. (2)
Link to Previous	Is only available in documents that have two or more header or footer sections. This option will link the current header or footer section to the previous header or footer section so that the current header or footer section has the same style and content as the previous section. This option will also break the connection between the current header or footer section and the previous one.

Table 6-16 Navigation group options explained

(2) This is based on where the insertion point is in the document.

Options Group

The options in this group are used to customize the header and footer sections. They are explained in Table 6-17.

Option	Description
Different First Page	Selecting this option allows the first page (of the document or section of the document) to have different header or footer information then the other pages in the document or section of the document.
Different Odd & Even Pages	Selecting this option allows the odd and even pages to have a different style and content, like the header section in this book.
Show Document Text	Displays or hides the body of the document so that only the header and footer sections appear on the computer screen.

Table 6-17 Options group options explained

Position Group

The options in this group are used to set the spacing and alignment for the header and footer sections. They are explained in Table 6-18.

Option	Description
Header from Top	Is used to select how much space the header section should have.
Footer from Bottom	Is used to select how much space the footer section should have.
Insert Alignment Tab	Is used to add a tab stop in the header or footer section. Selecting this option opens the dialog box shown in Figure 6-51. These options are similar to the tab stop options. [See Chapter 5, Tab Stops]

Table 6-18 Position group options explained

Figure 6-51 Alignment Tab dialog box

Close Group

The **CLOSE HEADER AND FOOTER** option will close the Header and Footer Tools Design tab. You can also double-click in the body of the document to close the Design tab.

How To Add A Text Only Header

The steps below show you how to add a header style that only has text.

1. Open the Term Paper document.

2. Insert tab ⟹ Header & Footer group ⟹ Header ⟹ Alphabet style.

3. Right-click on the sample header text and select **REMOVE CONTENT CONTROL**, then type in the text that you want to appear in the header section.

4. Save the document as Text only header.

Add Page Numbers To The Document

1. Open the Text only header document that you created in the previous exercise.

2. Insert tab ⟹ Header & Footer group ⟹ Page Number ⟹ Bottom of Page ⟹ Plain Number 1 style.

How To Change The Font Size Of Text In The Header Or Footer

You may find that the font size of the information in the header or footer section is not the right size. Follow the steps below to change the font size of the text.

1. Highlight the text that you want to change the font size of in the header or footer section. In this case, select the page number in the footer section.

2. Open the Font Size drop-down list on the mini toolbar, then select 8.

Creating Different Odd And Even Page Header Or Footer Section Information

All of the header and footer section exercises that you have completed so far had the same information in these sections on every page. As you saw in the header gallery, there are built-in styles that will create odd/even page styles for you. If you look at the header and footer section information on this page and the next page of this book, you will see that the information in the header and footer section is different. The steps below show you how to create different odd and even page header/footer information from scratch.

1. Open the Multi Page document.

2. Insert tab $\Rightarrow$ Header & Footer group $\Rightarrow$ Header $\Rightarrow$ Puzzle (Odd Page) style.

3. Check the Different Odd & Even Pages option in the Options group on the Header & Footer Tools Design tab.

4. Click in the header section on page 2, then Insert tab $\Rightarrow$ Header & Footer group $\Rightarrow$ Header $\Rightarrow$ Puzzle (Even Page) style.

If you put the insertion point in the header style you will see the Table Tools contextual tabs. That is because this particular header style is created in a table. To change the background color of the page number, you need to use the shading option on the Table Tools Design tab.

5. If you preview pages 2 and 3, the header sections will like the ones shown in Figure 6-52.

Figure 6-52 Different odd and even page header information

Text Group

The options in this group are used to add text elements to the document. The options are explained in Table 6-19.

Option	Description
Text Box	The options shown in Figure 6-53 are different styles of text boxes. The Drawing Tools that were covered earlier in this chapter can be used with the options in this gallery.
WordArt	This gallery displays the WordArt styles that can be applied to text.
Drop Cap	The options shown later in Figure 6-58 are used to position the text that the drop cap will be applied to.
Date & Time	Opens the dialog box shown later in Figure 6-61. The options are used to select the format of the date or time that is added to the document.

Table 6-19 Text group options explained

Text Box Gallery

As shown in the gallery, text boxes can be added any place in the document. The other content can be wrapped around the text box. You can type in the text box or you can paste text into the text box. The text is formatted based on the style of the text box.

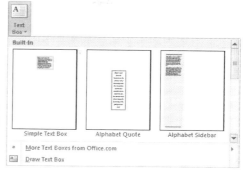

The **MORE TEXT BOXES FROM OFFICE.COM** option shown in Figure 6-53 displays additional text box styles that you can add to the document.

The **DRAW TEXT BOX** option is used to manually draw a text box in the document.

Figure 6-53 Text Box gallery

Using Text Boxes

The steps below show you how to add a side bar text box to a document.

1. Open the Term Paper document.

2. Insert tab ⇒ Text group ⇒ Text Box ⇒ **ANNUAL SIDEBAR** style.

3. Make the text box smaller and shorter, as shown on the right side of Figure 6-54.

Figure 6-54 Sidebar textbox style added to a document

4. To add your text, right-click in the text box and select **REMOVE CONTENT CONTROL**, then type or paste in your content. If needed, use the options on the Drawing Tools Format tab to modify the text box to meet your needs.

Adding WordArt To A Document

If you are creating a newsletter or brochure, you may want to add a title across the columns at the top of the document. This can be accomplished by using the WordArt tool.

1. Open the Multi Columns document.

2. At the beginning of the first column type `Baseball Term Paper`, then select the text.

3. Insert tab ⇒ Text group ⇒ WordArt ⇒ Select a style from the WordArt gallery.

4. Resize the frame around the text so that it is as wide as the three columns.

5. Center the WordArt in the frame, as shown in Figure 6-55, then save the changes.

Figure 6-55 WordArt added to a document

How To Change The Text Direction

The steps below show you how to change the direction of the WordArt text that you created in the previous exercise.

1. Click on the WordArt text in the Multi Columns document.

2. Drawing Tools Format tab ⇒ Text group ⇒ Text Direction ⇒ Select the **ROTATE ALL TEXT 270°** option.

3. Rotate the text box, then move the text box to the left of the text, as shown in Figure 6-56.

Figure 6-56 Text direction of WordArt changed

Using Drop Caps

The Drop Cap option is used to create a large capital letter, usually at the beginning of a sentence or paragraph. The steps below show you how to add a drop cap to a document.

The **DROP CAP OPTIONS** option shown in Figure 6-57 opens the dialog box shown in Figure 6-58.

The options on this dialog box are used to customize the drop cap.

Figure 6-57 Drop Cap options

Figure 6-58 Drop Cap dialog box

1. Open the Term Paper document. The mouse pointer should be at the beginning of the document.
2. Insert tab ⇒ Text group ⇒ Drop Cap ⇒ Select the **DROPPED** option.
3. Insert tab ⇒ Text group ⇒ Drop Cap ⇒ Select the Drop Cap Options option.
4. Change the **LINES TO DROP** option to 4. Click OK. The document should look like the one shown in Figure 6-59.

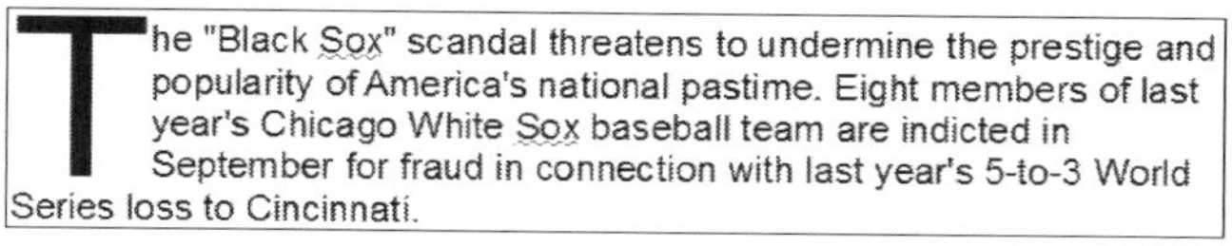

The "Black Sox" scandal threatens to undermine the prestige and popularity of America's national pastime. Eight members of last year's Chicago White Sox baseball team are indicted in September for fraud in connection with last year's 5-to-3 World Series loss to Cincinnati.

Figure 6-59 Drop cap added to the document

Because the drop cap is in a frame, you can resize and move it as needed. Resizing a drop cap is the same as resizing an image. The shortcut menu shown in Figure 6-60 displays the options for drop caps.

Cut
Copy
Paste Options:
A
Borders and Shading...
Drop Cap...

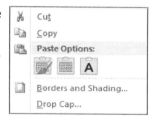

Figure 6-60 Drop cap shortcut menu options

Adding A Date To A Document

I think most people type the date in the document. The main reason that you would use the options on the Date and Time dialog box shown in Figure 6-61 is if you wanted to have the date or time updated each time the document is opened.

If checked, the **UPDATE AUTOMATICALLY** option will refresh the date or time in the document and display current information based on the computer that the document is opened on.

Date and Time
Available formats:
2/20/2010
Saturday, February 20, 2010
February 20, 2010
2/20/10
2010-02-20
20-Feb-10
2.20.2010
Feb. 20, 10
20 February 2010
February 10
Feb-10
2/20/2010 12:00 PM
2/20/2010 12:00:02 PM
12:00 PM
12:00:02 PM
12:00
12:00:02
Language:
English (U.S.)
Update automatically
Set As Default
OK
Cancel

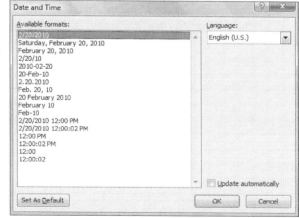

Figure 6-61 Date and Time dialog box

Symbols Group

The **SYMBOL** drop-down list shown in Figure 6-62 displays some of the symbols that you can add. Some of the special characters that you can add to a document are shown in Figure 6-63.

Figure 6-62 Some of the symbols that you can add to a document

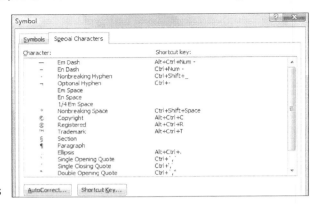

Figure 6-63 Special Characters

If you select a different font like Wingdings, you will see other symbols that you can use, as shown in Figure 6-64.

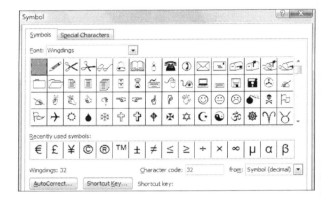

Figure 6-64 Wingdings symbols

Adding Symbols And Special Characters To A Document

Follow the steps below to learn how to add symbols or special characters to a document.

1. Place the insertion point in the document where you want to add the symbol or special character, then Insert tab ⇒ Symbols group ⇒ Symbol ⇒ More Symbols.

2. On the Symbol dialog box, double-click on the symbol or special character that you want to use.

 If you want the symbol or special character to be displayed smaller or larger, select it in the document, then change the font size.

Using The AutoCorrect Dialog Box

This feature will automatically correct some typing errors right after you make them. If you see a change right after it is made that you do not want, you can press CTRL+Z to remove the change.

By default, AutoCorrect is enabled.

Word comes with several auto correct entries, some of which you may have already used and not known. If you find that you are constantly making the same spelling error, you could create an auto correct entry for it. Figure 6-65 shows the AutoCorrect dialog box.

One of the most common misspelled words is **AND**. As you scroll down the list, look for this word in the second column.

There is more than one way to open the AutoCorrect dialog box, as discussed below.

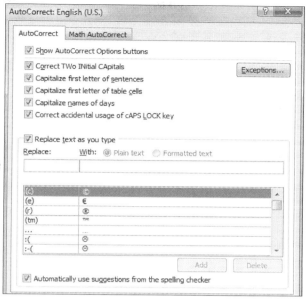

Figure 6-65 AutoCorrect dialog box

① Right-click on any word in the document that is not spelled correctly (a word with a red squiggly line under it), then select AutoCorrect ⇒ AutoCorrect Options. You will see the dialog box shown in Figure 6-66. Notice that it has more tabs than the version shown above in Figure 6-65. [See More AutoCorrect Tabs later in this chapter]

② Insert tab ⇒ Symbols group ⇒ Symbol ⇒ More Symbols ⇒ AutoCorrect button.

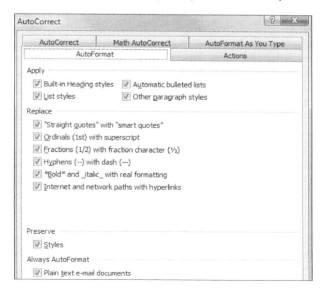

Figure 6-66 Another version of the AutoCorrect dialog box (with more tabs)

AutoCorrect Tab Options

There are many uses for the Auto Correct feature. The options on the AutoCorrect tab can be useful if you like using shortcuts. Suppose you do not want to type out the days of the week. You could create an auto correct entry that would allow you to type "mon" and have it automatically replaced with "Monday". If you use a symbol on a regular basis that is not already in the list, you can create an auto correct entry that will add the symbol to the document.

The options on the AutoCorrect dialog box ignore text in the document that is in quotes.

How To Create An Auto Correct Entry

The steps below show you how to create an AutoCorrect entry.

1. Open the AutoCorrect dialog box.

2. Type `tue` in the **REPLACE** field, then press the Tab key and type `Tuesday` in the **WITH** field.

   Your dialog box should have the options shown in Figure 6-67.

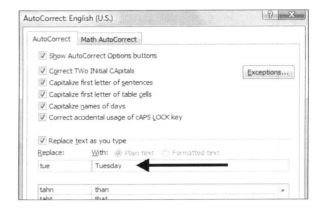

Figure 6-67 New Auto Correct entry

When creating an auto correct entry, what you type in the Replace field cannot already exist in the list. If it does, you will overwrite the existing Auto Correct entry when you save the new entry.

3. Click the **ADD** button, then click OK. Type `tue` in the document, then press the space bar. You should see the word Tuesday.

How To Create An Auto Correct Entry For A Symbol

Creating an auto correct entry for a symbol will save time if you use a symbol frequently. I use the ⇒ symbol frequently in this book. Having an Auto Correct entry for it saves me a lot of time. Follow the steps below to create this type of Auto Correct entry.

1. Insert tab ⇒ Symbols group ⇒ Symbol ⇒ More Symbols.

2. Open the Font drop-down list and select **SYMBOL**.

3. Scroll down and click on the symbol illustrated in Figure 6-68, then click the AutoCorrect button.

   You should see the arrow symbol in the With field.

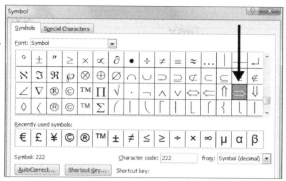

Figure 6-68 Symbol illustrated

4. Type >chk in the Replace field.

   Do not put a space between the > and the letter C.

   Your dialog box should have the options shown in Figure 6-69.

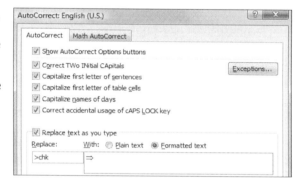

Figure 6-69 Auto Correct entry for the arrow symbol

5. Click the Add button. Click OK, then click Close on the Symbol dialog box.

6. Move to a new line in the document. Type >chk, then press the space bar. You should see the arrow.

How To Delete An Entry On The AutoCorrect Dialog Box

If there is an entry on the Auto Correct Dialog Box that you do not want to use, click on the entry in the list, then click the **DELETE** button.

Unexplained Changes If you find that what you type is not what is in the document, it is very possible that options that are selected on some of the tabs on the AutoCorrect dialog box are the reason why. I believe that the creators of this dialog box meant well, but some of the options drive many people crazy, including yours truly. I think that it is worth the time to learn more about the options on the AutoCorrect dialog box and clear the options that you really will not use. Doing this may save you some time, stress and aggravation.

How To Turn Off AutoCorrect Options
If you do not want to use the AutoCorrect feature, File tab ⇒ Options ⇒ Proofing panel ⇒ AutoCorrect Options button. Remove the check mark for the options at the top of the tab shown above in Figure 6-69, that you do not want to use. This will turn the option off.

AutoCorrect Exceptions Dialog Box

The options on the First Letter tab, shown in Figure 6-70 are used to override capitalization after a period is typed in the document.

The reason that I clear the **AUTOMATICALLY ADD WORDS TO LIST** option on all three tabs is because I found that typing technical abbreviations interfered with the first letter being capitalized in the next sentence.

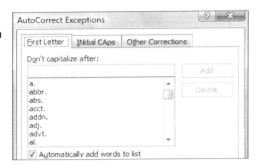

Figure 6-70 AutoCorrect Exceptions dialog box

Spell Check AutoCorrect Options

Figure 6-71 shows the AutoCorrect options for misspelled words. The options are explained below.

UNDO AUTOMATIC CAPITALIZATION Removes the capitalization that was added to the word. This option is for the first word of the paragraph.

Figure 6-71 Spell check AutoCorrect options

STOP AUTO-CAPITALIZING FIRST LETTER OF SENTENCES If selected, this option disables the **CAPITALIZE FIRST LETTER OF SENTENCES** option on the AutoCorrect tab on the AutoCorrect dialog box.

CONTROL AUTOCORRECT OPTIONS Opens the AutoCorrect dialog box.

Math AutoCorrect Tab Options

The options shown in Figure 6-72 are used to provide access to math symbols.

The options work the same as the text AutoCorrect options, by allowing you to create shortcuts for math related symbols.

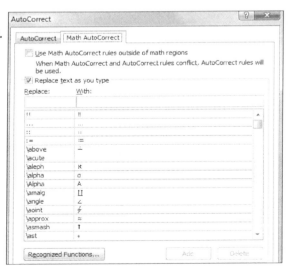

Figure 6-72 Math AutoCorrect tab

More AutoCorrect Tabs

As shown in Figure 6-73, depending on how the Auto Correct dialog box is opened, there are additional tabs, as explained below.

AUTO FORMAT TAB The options selected on this tab, shown earlier in Figure 6-66, will automatically be applied and replaced.

AUTO FORMAT AS YOU TYPE TAB The options shown in Figure 6-73 are used to set up formatting that will be applied when you type.

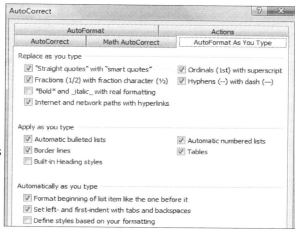

Figure 6-73 AutoFormat As You Type tab

ACTIONS TAB The options shown in Figure 6-74 are used to add options to the document shortcut menu.

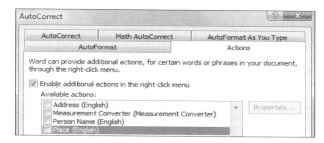

Figure 6-74 Actions tab

Ink Group

The **START INKING** option is used to add handwritten text, which is also known as **MARKUPS**, to the document. Clicking on this option displays the Ink Tools Pens tab shown in Figure 6-75.

Ink Tools Pens Contextual Tab

The options on this tab are used to customize the pen or highlighter.

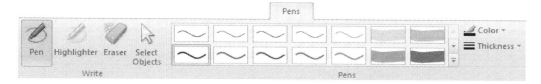

Figure 6-75 Ink Tools Pens tab

Write Group

The options in this group are used to select the writing tool. The options are explained in Table 6-20.

Option	Description
Pen	Select this option to use the stylus pen that came with your tablet computer to write on the document, as shown on the left of Figure 6-76.
Highlighter	Select this option to use the styles as a highlighter pen, as shown in Figure 6-77.
Eraser	Is used to remove ink (pen and highlighter) objects from the document.
Select Objects	Is used to select ink objects in the document.

Table 6-20 Write group options explained

Figure 6-77 Text highlighted with the highlighter tool

Figure 6-76 Handwritten text

Pens Group

The options in this group are used to select the pen or highlighter styles. The options are explained in Table 6-21.

Option	Description
Styles	The options shown in Figure 6-78 are used to select a pen or highlighter style and add styles to your Favorite Pens list.
Color	The options are used to select a pen or highlighter color.
Thickness	The options are used to select the thickness (size) of the pen or highlighter stroke.

Table 6-21 Pens group options explained

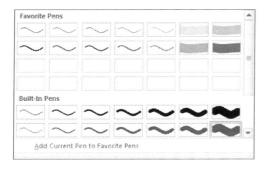

Figure 6-78 Pens (styles) gallery

Overview

This chapter covers the options on the Page Layout tab. You will learn about the following.

- ☑ How to apply themes
- ☑ How to set margins
- ☑ How to create columns
- ☑ How to add a watermark

CHAPTER 7

Overview

The options shown in Figure 7-1 are used to format the entire document. Many of the options are the same as those that are applied to individual paragraphs in the document. I consider the options on this tab to be the options that put the finishing touches on documents.

Figure 7-1 Page Layout tab

Themes Group

The options in this group are used to apply a color scheme, bulleted lists, fonts and effects to a document. In Chapter 5 you read how to format different parts of a document. You also read that style sets are a collection of individual styles. These take style sets to the next level. Word comes with 40 built-in themes.

In addition to the text in the body of the document, themes are used to change the color scheme of the following parts of a document: Headings, charts, WordArt, image border color and tables. If your document does not contain these parts of a document, when you select a theme, you will not notice a lot of changes. You may be use to the default font being Times New Roman. The default theme uses Calibri as the font for the body text in the document and Cambria as the font for headings. The options are explained in Table 7-1.

Option	Description
Themes	The gallery shown at the top of Figure 7-2 are some of the themes that can be applied to the document. If you hold the mouse pointer over a theme you can see it applied to the document.
Colors	The options are used to change the colors of the theme that is applied to the document and to create new theme colors as shown in Figure 7-3.
Fonts	The options are used to change the fonts for the selected theme. Selecting the **CREATE NEW THEME FONTS** option is used to create a new font theme on the dialog box shown in Figure 7-5. Like the Colors gallery, the Font gallery will display the font themes that you create at the top of the gallery.
Effects	The options are used to change the effects of the theme that is applied to the document. You cannot create your own theme effects.

Table 7-1 Themes group options explained

Theme Components

There are three components used to create a theme as discussed below.

① **Colors** Each part of a document (header, table or chart for example) has a pre-selected color in each theme. There are over 10 colors used in each theme.

② **Fonts** Each theme has up to two fonts, one for the headings and another for the body of the document, which is known as the **BODY TEXT**.

③ **Effects** Each theme has a text effect like outline or glow applied.

Shared Themes
Word, Excel and PowerPoint share the same themes. This is helpful for documents that require parts created from one or more of these software packages.

Themes Gallery

The **RESET TO THEME FROM TEMPLATE** option removes the last theme that was applied to the document.

The **BROWSE FOR THEMES** option is used to select a theme that is not in the gallery.

The **SAVE CURRENT THEME** option is used to save the theme that is applied to the document. This is helpful if you modified part of a built-in theme and want to be able to apply the modified theme to other documents.

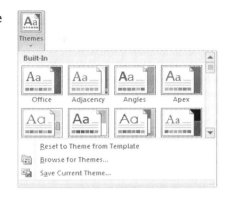

Figure 7-2 Themes gallery

For themes to appear in this gallery they must be stored in this folder.
C:\Users\Your User Name]\AppData\Roaming\Microsoft\Templates\Document Themes.

If you download themes, store them in this folder. Themes that you create should also have the extension **.THMX**.

Colors Gallery Options

The **CREATE NEW THEME COLORS** option at the bottom of the Colors gallery opens the dialog box shown in Figure 7-3. The initial color theme that is displayed on this dialog box is the one that is applied to the document.

The options on this dialog box are used to modify any of the colors in the theme. When you modify a color, you can save your changes as a new theme, which you can apply to other documents.

To save your changes, type in a name for the theme in the Name field at the bottom of the dialog box, then click the Save button. Your theme will be added to the Custom section of the theme colors gallery, as shown at the top of Figure 7-4.

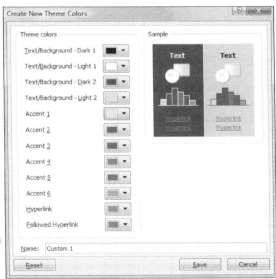

Figure 7-3 Create New Theme Colors dialog box

Custom colors that you create in Word are also available in Excel.

Figure 7-4 Custom theme color

Creating Theme Fonts

The options shown in Figure 7-5 are used to select the fonts for the current theme.

Figure 7-5 Create New Theme Fonts dialog box

How To Apply A Theme To A Document

The steps below show you how to apply a theme to a document.

1. Open the document that you want to apply a theme to.

2. Page Layout tab ⇒ Themes group ⇒ Themes ⇒ Select the theme that you want from the Themes gallery.

Saving Documents With Themes
If a Word 2010 document that is saved with a theme is opened in Word 2003 or earlier, the theme is converted to styles and can't be undone, even if you reopen the document in Word 2010.

Page Setup Group

The options in this group are applied to the entire document. They are explained in Table 7-2.

Option	Description
Margins	The options are used to select the amount of space that can contain the content. If you like the default margins in Office 2003 and earlier, there is an option in the gallery for those margins.
Orientation	The options are used to select **PORTRAIT** (the page is taller than it is wide, which is the default orientation for new documents) or **LANDSCAPE** (the page is wider than it is tall).

Table 7-2 Page Setup group options explained

Option	Description
Size	The options are used to select the paper, envelope or post-card size. If the size that you need is not visible in the gallery, select the **MORE PAPER SIZES** option. It will display the Paper tab on the Page Setup dialog box. Change the Width and Height options to the paper size that you need.
Columns	The options are used to select the number of columns for the entire document or the part of the document that is selected.
Breaks	Is used to set page, section and column breaks.
Line Numbers	The options shown in Figure 7-6 are used to add line numbers to the document in the left margin, as shown in Figure 7-7. Line numbers can only be seen in the Print Layout view. The line numbers start where the insertion point is in the document.
Hyphenation	The options shown in Figure 7-8 are used to select how you want the document hyphenated. Selecting the last option on the list opens the dialog box shown in Figure 7-9. These options are used to customize the hyphenation to meet the needs of the document.
Dialog Box Launcher	Opens the dialog box shown in Figure 7-10.

Table 7-2 Page Setup group options explained (Continued)

Line Numbers

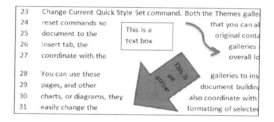

Figure 7-6 Line numbers options   **Figure 7-7** Line numbers added to a document

The dialog box shown in Figure 7-8 contain many of the options shown above in Figure 7-6. The difference is that the dialog box has options to customize the line numbers.

The **COUNT BY** option is used to select the frequency that line numbers should be printed. Selecting two in this field means that line numbers will print on every other line in the document.

To open this dialog box, select the Line Numbering Options option shown above in Figure 7-6, then click the Line Numbers button.

Figure 7-8 Line Numbers dialog box

Hyphenation

Hyphenation is used to split a word that will not fit at the end of a line and put part of the word on the next line. I personally do not like hyphenation in documents that are not using the Justify paragraph alignment. When using the Justify alignment option, often there are large spaces between words on the line which takes away from the formatting. The options are explained below.

NONE turns hyphenation off.

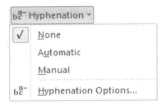

AUTOMATIC This is the default option. Select this option to allow Word to create the hyphenation based on the options that you select on the Hyphenation dialog box.

MANUAL Select this option if you want to be prompted for each word that Word wants to hyphenate. This gives you complete control over which words are hyphenated and which ones aren't.

Figure 7-9 Hyphenation options

The **HYPHENATION OPTIONS** option opens the dialog box shown in Figure 7-10.

The **HYPHENATION ZONE** option is used to select the maximum space between the last word and the right margin. Any word that is in this zone is likely to be hyphenated. .25" is the default.

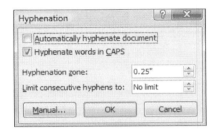

LIMIT CONSECUTIVE HYPHENS TO The number selected in this field is the maximum number of consecutive rows that can be hyphenated. The standard is two lines, which is what you would enter in this field.

Figure 7-10 Hyphenation dialog box

The Page Setup dialog box can also be opened on the Print Layout or Draft view by double-clicking on the ruler outside of the margins.

Figure 7-11 Page Setup dialog box

Manual Hyphenation
You can manually hyphenate a document. The downside to manually hyphenating a document is if you make changes to the document after the manual hyphenation, it is very possible that the line wrapping will change. This could cause some of the manually hyphenated words to no longer be at the end of the line, which will make the document look strange.

Margins

Making sure that you select the appropriate margins for the type of document that you are creating is important. For example, the margins for a movie script are wide, meaning that there is more white space on the page then there is content. The margins for most books is narrow, which allows a lot of content to be placed on a page. A book would look very strange if the interior pages had a wide margin.

Changing The Page Margins

The default margins will probably be sufficient for many of the documents that you create. If you need to change the margins follow the steps below. The steps below show you how to change the margins to 1.25 inches.

1. Open the Multi Page document.

2. Page Layout tab ⇒ Page Setup group ⇒ Margins ⇒ Custom Margins.

3. On the Margins tab, change all four margins (Top, Left, Bottom and Right) to 1.25", as shown in Figure 7-12, by selecting the number in the field and typing in the new margin size.

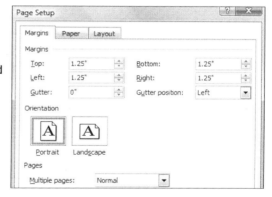

Figure 7-12 Margin options

 Changing The Default Margins
As you read earlier, the default margins are one inch on all four sides. If these margins do not meet the needs of the majority of new documents that you will create, you can change the default margins. Select the margins that you want on the Margins tab shown above in Figure 7-12. Click the **SET AS DEFAULT** button, then click Yes to change the default settings.

Changing Margins For Part Of The Document
If you need to change the margins for some text in the document, follow the steps below. The text will be placed on a page by itself. This is the default. If you want the text with different margins on the same page as the preceding text, I find it easier to put the text in a Text box.

1. Select the text that you want to change the margins for.
2. On the Margins tab shown above in Figure 7-12, select the margins that you want for the selected text.
3. Open the **APPLY TO** drop-down list and select Selected text, then click OK.

Mirror Page Margins

The **GUTTER** options are used to select how much of the page will be hidden by the binding.

The **BOOK FOLD** option in the Multiple pages drop-down list is similar to the two pages per sheet option because they both print two pages on one side of a piece of paper.

The difference is that the Book Fold layout option will let you fold the piece of paper down the middle to create a book with facing pages.

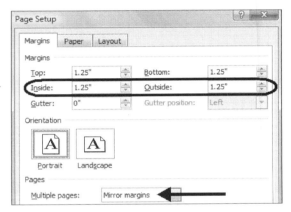

Figure 7-13 Mirror page margin options

If the **MULTIPLE PAGES** option illustrated at the bottom of Figure 7-13 is set to **MIRROR MARGINS**, you will see the margin options **INSIDE** and **OUTSIDE**, as illustrated at the top of Figure 7-13, instead of Left and Right, as shown earlier in Figure 7-12. You would use the mirror margins option when you need to print facing pages, like in a book or a document that will be bound. This sets up the inside margin (the side that the page is bound on) and outside margin (the side that is not bound) for printing a bound document.

Using The Ruler To Change The Margins

Like tab stops and paragraph alignment, you can set the margins for a document. In Chapter 5, you read how to change the paragraph indentation on the ruler. Changing the margins on the ruler is similar. The difference is that changing margins is for a section of the document or the entire document.

To change the margin, place the mouse pointer in one of the positions shown in Figure 7-14, then drag the mouse in the direction that you want to change the margin.

Figure 7-14 Margin options on the ruler

Page Breaks

Page breaks manually force the start of a new page, anyplace in the body of a document. This feature is useful when you want more control over where text will print on a page. The steps below show you how to add a page break.

1. Open the Term Paper document, then place the insertion point on the blank line below the first paragraph.

2. Page Layout tab ⇒ Page Setup group ⇒ Breaks ⇒ Page. The only part of the document on the first page should be the first paragraph.

 Pressing the **CTRL+ENTER** keys will create a page break without opening the Breaks drop-down list.

3. Insert a page break after the second paragraph on page 2. The second paragraph starts with the words "The American League".

4. Insert a page break after the third paragraph on page 3. The third paragraph starts with the words "Cy Young". Your document should now have four pages.

You can confirm this by looking in the lower left corner of the status bar, as shown in Figure 7-15.

Figure 7-15 Document page count

Creating Multi Column Documents

Multi column documents can be used to create brochures and newsletters. Multi column documents look like pages in a phone book, magazine or newspaper. This type of document is also known as a "snaking column" document. You can set the number of columns and the amount of space between the columns. Based on the number of columns that you select, the width of the columns can automatically be created for the entire document or for a section of the document. You can also manually set the width of the columns.

Columns Dialog Box

In addition to the options on the drop-down list shown in Figure 7-16, the **MORE COLUMNS** option opens the dialog box shown in Figure 7-17. The options on this dialog box provide a lot of options that will let you customize the columns.

 Columns can also be created using tables.

The **LEFT** and **RIGHT** column options shown in Figure 7-16 have one column that is narrower then the other.

Figure 7-16 Columns options

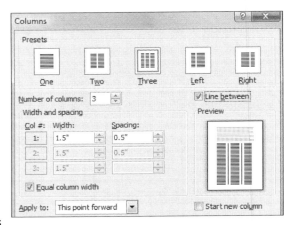

Figure 7-17 Columns dialog box

Columns Dialog Box Options

Presets Options The options in this section of the dialog box are used to select the number of columns. You can click on the image to select the number of columns or use the **NUMBER OF COLUMNS** spin button if you need more than three columns.

The **LINE BETWEEN** option is used to place a vertical line between the columns.

Width And Spacing Options The options in this section are used to select the width of each column and the amount of space between each column.

The **SPACING** field determines how much white space will be between each column.

EQUAL COLUMN WIDTH If checked, the width and spacing will automatically be calculated based on the number of columns that you select. Each column will be the same width. If you clear this option, you can select different widths for each column.

APPLY TO Is used to select what the column layout should be applied to, the entire document or from where the insertion point is to the end of the document.

The **START NEW COLUMN** option is only available if the **THIS POINT FORWARD** option is selected in the Apply to field. This option will start the columns where the insertion point is in the document.

How To Set Up Columns In A Document

1. Open a new document.

2. Page Layout tab ⇒ Page Setup group ⇒ Columns ⇒ More Columns. You should see the Columns dialog box.

3. Change the **NUMBER OF COLUMNS** to 3, then change the **SPACING** field to 0.25". You have to type this number in because it is not one of the default options in the list.

4. You can also add a line between the columns. Click OK. Your document will have three columns.

How To Copy And Paste Text From Another Document

Rather than have you type in information to see how the multi column document works, you can copy text from another document and paste it into this multi column document.

1. Open the Term Paper document.

2. Select the first three paragraphs in the document, then right-click on the selected paragraphs and select Copy.

3. Right-click in the first column of the multi column document and select the Paste option, Keep Source Formatting.

    Your document should look like the one shown in Figure 7-18.

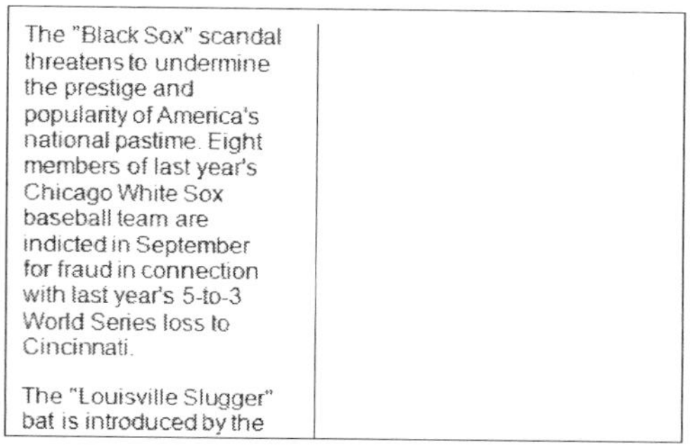

Figure 7-18 Text added to the first column

4. If you want to put text in the second and third columns of the document, place the cursor at the end of the text that you just pasted in the document and press the Enter key twice, then press the **CTRL+V** keys three times.

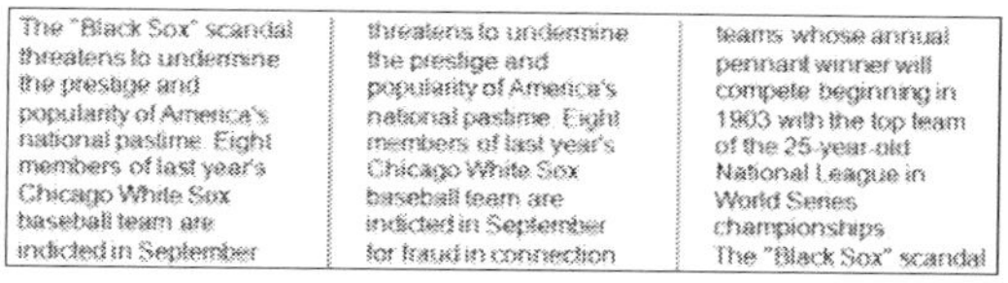

Figure 7-19 Multi column document with text

    Preview the document. It should look like the one shown in Figure 7-19.

Column Breaks Earlier in this chapter you read about page breaks. Column breaks are similar. Adding a column break causes the text after the insertion point to be moved to the top of the next column in the document.

How To Create Columns In An Existing Document

If you have already created a document and now have the need to change the layout to columns, you can do that by following the steps below.

1. Open the Term Paper document.

2. Follow the steps 2 to 4 earlier in the How To Set Up Columns In A Document section to add three columns to this document.

3. The Term Paper document should look like the one shown above in Figure 7-19. Save the document with a new file name.

How To Add An Image To A Multi Column Document

1. In the second column of the Term Paper document that you saved in the previous exercise, click on the blank line after the first paragraph, then press Enter.

2. Add the baseball1.tif file from the zip file.

3. Make the image larger, then center it in the column.

   Your document should look similar to the one shown in Figure 7-20.

   Save the document with a new file name.

| The "Black Sox" scandal threatens to undermine the prestige and popularity of America's national pastime. Eight members of last year's Chicago White Sox baseball team are indicted in September for fraud in connection with last year's 5-to-3 World Series loss to Cincinnati.

The "Louisville Slugger" bat is | The American League wins baseball's first All-Star Game July 6 at Chicago's Comiskey Field, defeating the National League 4 to 2.

Baseball's American | Boston Red Sox of the American League through 1908, the Cleveland Indians of the American League through 1911, and the Boston Braves of the National League for part of the 1911 season. Denton True "Cy" Young, 23, wins both games of a doubleheader in October and will be the first pitcher to win 500 games.

Baseball's two major |

Figure 7-20 Image added in the column

Multi Section Documents

So far all of the documents that you have created used the same section throughout the entire document. There may be times when only part of the document requires columns. The way to accomplish having part of a document have columns, requires creating sections in the document. Each section can have its own layout.

Create A Multi Section Document

The steps below show you how to create a document that has three sections. The first section will have two columns. The second section will display line numbers and the third section will have an orange background.

Create The First Section

1. Open a new document and press the Enter key once.

2. Page Layout tab ⇒ Page Setup group ⇒ Breaks ⇒ Next Page.

3. Click on the first page, then add two columns with a line between the columns.

4. Paste text from the Term Paper document into this section.

Create The Second Section

1. Paste the Term Paper document on the second page of the new document, then delete the third page of the document if it exists.

2. Add a Next page break on the line after the text that you just pasted into the document.

3. Click on the first line of page 2.

4. Page Layout tab ⇒ Page Setup group ⇒ Line Numbers ⇒ Restart Each Section. This should be the only section with line numbers.

Create The Third Section

1. Paste two paragraphs from the Term Paper document on the third page of the new document, then select the two paragraphs.

2. Home tab ⇒ Paragraph group ⇒ Borders ⇒ Borders and Shading.

3. On the Shading tab select a fill color, then click OK.

4. Save the document with a new file name.

Preview The Document

1. File tab ⇒ Print panel.

2. Lower the zoom percent in the lower right corner of the workspace so that all three pages are visible, as shown in Figure 7-21. Notice that the formatting that you created is only in the section that you placed it in.

Figure 7-21 Document with multiple sections

Change The Margins For A Section Of The Document
Earlier you read how to change the margins for the entire document. Changing the margins for a section of the document is similar. To change the margins for a section of the document, follow the steps below.

1. Click in the section of the document that you want to change the margins of.
2. Page Layout tab ⇒ Page Setup group ⇒ Margins.
3. Select the margins that you want or create custom margins for the section. As shown in Figure 7-22, the second section of the document shown above in Figure 7-21 has wider margins.

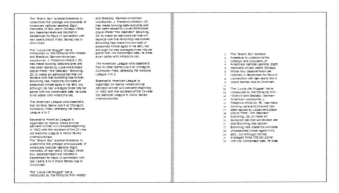

Figure 7-22 Wider margins in the second section of the document

Page Background Group

The options in this group are used to change the background (behind the text and objects) of the document. The options are explained in Table 7-3.

Option	Description
Watermark	The options shown in Figure 7-23 are used to add text or an image to the background of the document.
Page Color	The options are used to add a color or fill effect to the background of the document. This option is usually used for web pages more than printed pages.
Page Borders	Displays the Page Border tab on the Borders and Shading dialog box.

Table 7-3 Page Background group options explained

Watermarks

Watermarks are most often used to display an image or text, usually in gray scale, behind the text in the body of the document. You may have seen a document that has the word "draft" in gray scale on a document. Usually watermarks are used to provide the status of the document. They are only visible in the Print Layout view.

By default, the formatting and contents of a watermark are placed in the header section, even though the watermark is displayed in the body of the document. This causes the watermark to be displayed on every page of the document, even if the document has more than one section. That is because by default, the sections are linked. If the document only has one section, you can select specific pages to display the watermark on.

If the sections of the document are created after the watermark, the watermark will only be applied to the new sections. In Chapter 6 you read about the **LINK TO PREVIOUS** header and footer option. This option is also used to break the connection between sections.

Watermark Gallery Options

The **MORE WATERMARKS FROM OFFICE.COM** option is used to search the web site for more watermark image files.

The **CUSTOM WATERMARK** option opens the dialog box shown in Figure 7-24. The options are used to create a watermark that better meets your needs then the ones in the Watermark gallery.

The **REMOVE WATERMARK** option will remove the watermark that you added to the document.

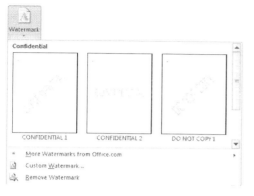

Figure 7-23 Watermark gallery

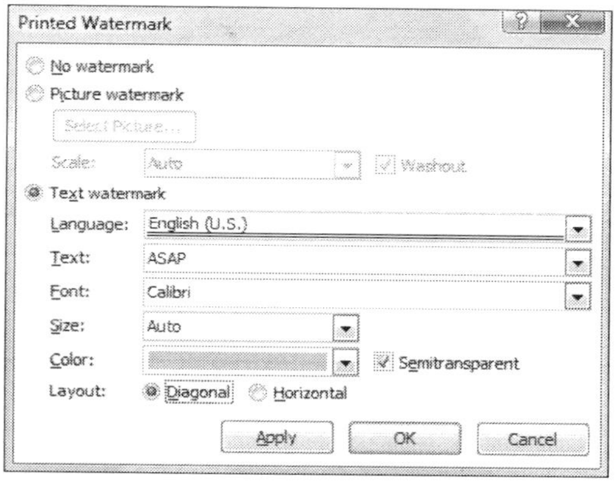

Figure 7-24 Printed Watermark dialog box

Create A Text Watermark In addition to using the built-in watermarks and image files for watermarks, you can create a text watermark by typing what you want in the Text field shown above in Figure 7-24. Use the Font, Size, Color and Layout options to customize the text that you entered.

Using Built-In Watermarks

The steps below show you how to add a built-in watermark to a document.

1. Open the Term Paper document.

2. Page Layout tab ⇒ Page Background group ⇒ Watermark ⇒ Select the **DRAFT 1** option.

3. Select the Custom Watermark option on the Watermark gallery.

4. Open the Color drop-down list and select the color orange on the first row, then clear the **SEMI TRANSPARENT** option.

   Click OK. The document should look like the one shown in Figure 7-25.

The "Louisville Slugger" bat is introduced by the Kentucky firm Hillerich and Bradsby. German-American woodturner J. Frederick Hillerich, 50, has made bowling balls and pins and has been asked by Louisville Eclipse player Peter "the Gladiator" Browning, 26, to make an ashwood bat that will replace one that Browning has broken. Browning has made his own bats of seasoned timber aged in his attic, but although he had averaged three hits per game with his homemade bats, he does even better with Hillerich's bat.

The American League wins baseball's first All-Star Game July 6 at Chicago's Comiskey Field, defeating the National League 4 to 2.

Baseball's American League is organized by teams whose annual pennant winner will compete beginning in 1903 with the top team of the 25-year-old National League in World Series championships.

Baseball's curve ball pitch is invented by Brooklyn, N.Y., pitcher William Arthur Cummings.

Cy Young signed with the Cleveland team of the National League to begin an outstanding pitching career that will continue for nearly 23 years: with Cleveland through 1898, the St. Louis Cardinals through 1900, the Boston Red Sox of the American League through 1908, the Cleveland Indians of the American League through 1911, and the Boston Braves of the National League for part of the 1911 season. Denton True "Cy" Young, 23, wins both games of a doubleheader in October and will be the first pitcher to win 500 games.

Baseball's two major leagues split into eastern and western divisions with two new expansion teams each. The National League adds the Montreal Expos and the San Diego Padres, the American League adds the Kansas

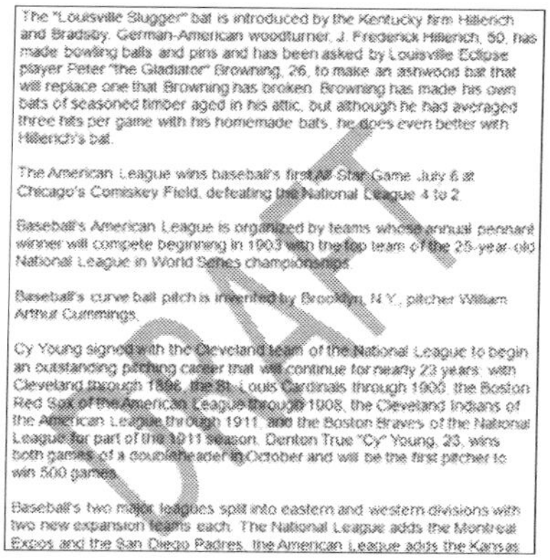

Figure 7-25 Text watermark added to the document

5. Save the document with a new file name if you want to keep it.

Using An Image As A Watermark

While Word allows you to type text and use it as a watermark, being the nice person that I am, I created a graphic with the word "Draft", that you can use to complete this exercise. The steps below show you how to use an image file as a watermark.

1. Open the Term Paper document.

2. Page Layout tab ⇒ Page Background group ⇒ Watermark ⇒ Custom Watermark.

3. Select the **PICTURE WATERMARK** option, then click the Select Picture button.

4. Navigate to the folder that has the image that you want to use. For practice, you can use the draft_watermark.gif file in your folder. Double-click on the file.

5. Click OK. You will see the image file in the background of the document.

Paragraph Group

The options in this group were covered in Chapter 5.
Indent Options [See Chapter 5, Indentation Options]
Spacing Options [See Chapter 5, Before And After Paragraph Spacing Options]

Arrange Group

The options in this group are the same as the options in the Arrange Group on the Picture Tools Format tab. [See Chapter 6, Table 6-6]

THE MAILINGS TAB

Overview

The mail merge feature is most often used to merge names and addresses into a document, as well as, other information to make the document personalized. Mail merge can also be used to create and print envelopes and mailing labels. In this chapter you will learn how to do the following:

☑ Merge fields into a document
☑ Sort and filter records for the merge
☑ Print envelopes
☑ Print labels

Mail Merge Basics

A mail merge can be used to print generic or customized letters, labels and envelopes. If you need to send the same welcome package to 20 new customers, or a cover letter and resume to 50 potential employers, you could open the letter, type in the name and address, print it or these days, email it, and repeat this process for each letter, or your could create a mail merge. To create a mail merge letter, you need two things, as discussed below.

① A list of names and addresses.

② A document with fields, like names and addresses that will be filled in from the list.

 A mail merge is not limited to adding names and addresses to a document. You can merge any information that is stored in a list.

There are two ways to create a mail merge, as discussed below.

① Use the options on the Mailings tab.

② Use the Mail Merge Wizard.

What Is A Data Source?

A data source is the file that has the data that will be used in the mail merge is saved in. Word refers to the data source as a "list". Examples of data sources are text files, electronic address books, spreadsheets and databases. In addition to these data source formats, Word can also connect to **.csv** files. If you have data that you need to use for a mail merge that is in a format that Word does not support, bring it into a format that Word supports.

 CSV Files
CSV stands for comma separated values. This type of file is most often created in a spreadsheet package.

Using Data Sources

It is not a requirement to use a data source to create a mail merge. More then likely you will though, if the names and addresses or other types of information that you want to merge already exists in a file. You can type the information in when you create the mail merge.

Mailings Tab

The options shown in Figure 8-1 are used to create mail merge documents, envelopes or labels.

Figure 8-1 Mailings tab

Create Group

The options in this group are used to select what you want to create. The options are explained below.

ENVELOPES Is used to create envelopes.

LABELS Is used to create labels.

Start Mail Merge Group

The options in this group are used to start the process of creating a mail merge and selecting the recipients for the mail merge. The options are explained in Table 8-1.

Option	Description
Start Mail Merge	The options are used to select the type of merge to create. You can also select to use the **MAIL MERGE WIZARD** to create the mail merge.
Select Recipients	The options are used to select the source of the recipients.
Edit Recipient List	Opens the Mail Merge Recipients dialog box, which is used to add, modify, sort and filter the recipient list, as well as, check for duplicates and validate addresses in the list.

Table 8-1 Start Mail Merge group options explained

Write & Insert Fields Group

The options in this group are used to create the merge document and add merge fields to the document. The options are explained in Table 8-2.

Option	Description
Highlight Merge Fields	Clicking this button will add a background color to the merge fields in the document, as shown in Figure 8-2. This is helpful if you need to be able to easily see the merge fields in the document. Clicking the button a second time removes the background color from the merge fields in the document.
Address Block	Opens the dialog box shown in Figure 8-3. The options on this dialog box are used to select the location to place the address fields in the document and to select the formatting for the address fields.
Greeting Line	Opens the dialog box shown in Figure 8-5, which is used to select a greeting for the recipients.
Insert Merge Field	The options in this list are the fields that are most often added to a merge document.
Rules	The options shown in Figure 8-6 are used to create criteria that the records in the data source must meet to be included in the merge. The options are explained in Table 8-3.
Match Fields	Opens the dialog box shown in Figure 8-4.
Update Labels	Is used to copy the layout and fields from the first label to the other labels on the sheet and update the data in the fields on the labels.

Table 8-2 Write & Insert Fields group options explained

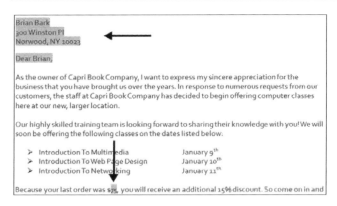

Figure 8-2 Merge fields illustrated

Using The Address Block

The **ADDRESS BLOCK** field is a combination of fields including the first name, last name, address, city, state and zip code.

The Address Block works like a single field. If you add this field to the document, the fields listed above are added to the document.

A comma is automatically added after the city field.

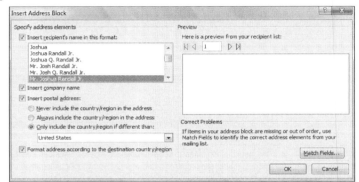

Figure 8-3 Insert Address Block dialog box

The options on this dialog box are used to map fields in the data source to the fields used by the merge.

The fields in the drop-down list on the right of the Match Fields dialog box, are the fields from your data source. To match the fields, open the drop-down list and select the field that has the data for the field on the left.

Using this dialog box is helpful when the field names in the database are not the same as the ones in the Address Block.

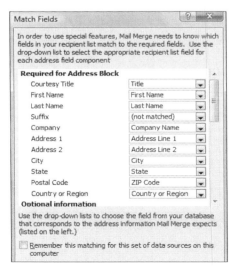

Figure 8-4 Match Fields dialog box

The **GREETING LINE** field shown in Figure 8-5 works like the Address Block because it combines several fields into one.

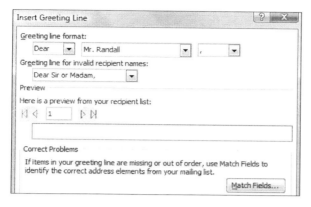

Figure 8-5 Insert Greeting Line dialog box

Figure 8-6 Rules options

Merge Rules

The options explained in Table 8-3 are used to create criteria (rules) to reduce the number of records in the data source that will be used in the merge. If you want to include all records in the data source, you can skip this step in the merge process.

Option	Description
Ask	Opens the dialog box shown in Figure 8-7. Select this option when the response needs to be used more than once in the merge document. If you need to change the value, change it on this dialog box and it will be changed throughout the mail merge document. (1)
Fill-in	Opens the dialog box shown in Figure 8-8. Select this option when the response will only be used once in the merge document. (1)
If ... Then ... Else	Opens the dialog box shown in Figure 8-9. The options are used to add additional text to the mail merge document based on a condition. For example, you have upcoming events in a specific state and only want to let recipients of the mail merge in that state know about the events. You can enter as much information as needed in the Insert this text field.
Merge Record #	Adds the record number of the recipient to the mail merge document where the insertion point is. This is a counter of the number of records in the data source that will be printed during the merge.
Merge Sequence #	This option is similar to the Merge Record #. The difference is this number does not exclude records in the data source that are excluded during the merge process. This is a counter of the number of records in the data source.
Next Record	Is used to print an entire page of address labels or another type of document that the data for several records should appear on the same page, like a directory that you will read about later in this chapter.

Table 8-3 Rules options explained

Option	Description
Next Record If	Opens the dialog box shown in Figure 8-10. The options are used to compare the value in a data source field to the criteria. If the value matches the criteria, the record is skipped. This option is used to determine if the data in the next record should be merged into the current document (because the data is the same) or merged into a new document.
Set Bookmark	Opens the dialog box shown in Figure 8-11. The options are used to store a value in a bookmark that will be used as a reference. You can add the bookmark field to the merge document.
Skip Record If	Opens the dialog box shown in Figure 8-12. The options are used to create criteria for records in the data source that you do not want included in the mail merge.

Table 8-3 Rules options explained (Continued)

(1) This option is used to create a prompt for the person running the mail merge to enter information, based on the question that you enter in the Prompt field on the dialog box. The answer will be added to the merge document.

Figure 8-7 Ask dialog box

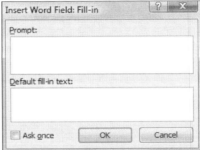

Figure 8-8 Fill-In dialog box

Figure 8-9 If Then Else dialog box

Figure 8-10 Next Record If dialog box

Figure 8-11 Set Bookmark dialog box

Figure 8-12 Skip Record If dialog box

Preview Results Group

The options in this group are used to view the mail merge output before it is printed or emailed. The options are explained in Table 8-4.

Option	Description
Preview Results	Replaces the merge fields in the document with data from the data source.
Navigation buttons	Are used to display the merge information for each record in the data source that meets the criteria.
Field Recipient	Opens the dialog box shown in Figure 8-13, which is used to find a specific record in the data source.
Auto Check For Errors	Opens the dialog box shown in Figure 8-14. The options are used to select how errors are handled during the merge. You can also run the merge to see if there are any errors.

Table 8-4 Preview Results group options explained

Figure 8-13 Find Entry dialog box

Figure 8-14 Checking and Reporting Errors dialog box

Finish Group

The options on the Finish & Merge drop-down list shown in Figure 8-15 are used to select the output format of the merge. The options are explained in Table 8-5.

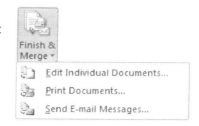

Figure 8-15 Finish & Merge options

Option	Description
Edit Individual Documents	Opens the dialog box shown in Figure 8-16. The options are used to select which merge records you want to edit.
Print Documents	Opens the Merge to Printer dialog box, which has the same options as the Merge To New Document dialog box shown in Figure 8-16.
Send E-mail Messages	Opens the dialog box shown in Figure 8-17. The options are used to create the subject line, select the mail format and select the records that you want to send the email to. Each recipient receives an email with their custom information, opposed to every recipient receiving a generic email.

Table 8-5 Finish & Merge options explained

Figure 8-16 Merge To New Document dialog box

Figure 8-17 Merge to E-mail dialog box

Mail Merge Process

The order of the buttons starting with the Start Mail Merge group to the end of the tab are the order that the tasks should be completed in to create a mail merge document. These options are used to create the mail merge without any help. If you want some guidance, you can use the Mail Merge Wizard. The mail merge process takes data from fields like names and addresses and puts the data into a document to make it personalized. During the merge process a copy of the document is created for each recipient in the list that meets the criteria. This tool is often used to customize a letter. Creating a mail merge is a six step process, as discussed below.

Step 1: Select The Document Type

There are five document types, as shown on the first wizard panel in Figure 8-18 that you can select from, as discussed below.

① **LETTERS** This is usually a form letter.
② **E-MAIL MESSAGES** This option works the same as the letter option. The difference is that you do not have to print anything.
③ **ENVELOPES** You can print the recipients name and address information on the envelope.
④ **LABELS** You can print any type of information that you want when selecting this option, including name tags for a convention.
⑤ **DIRECTORY** Is used to print a list (data source) of contact information, as shown in Figure 8-19. The list can also include email address, phone numbers and anything you want. You create the layout for the directory. Unlike the options listed above, the directory option merges the data into one document instead of creating individual documents.

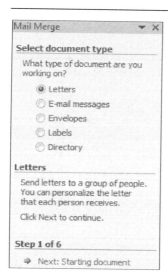

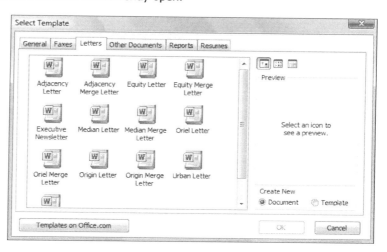

Tina Jones 30 Long St Ft Laud, FL 32991
Jamie Walker 997 Lenox Dr Reno, NV 32883
Stuart Thomas 90A Jersey Ave Orlando, FL 32761
Todd Green 41 Jefferson Rd Tampa, FL 32672

Figure 8-19 Directory list

Figure 8-18 Mail Merge Step 1 panel

Step 2: Select The Starting Document

You can create the body of the mail merge document during the mail merge process or you can create the document before you start the mail merge process. The three options discussed below are the types of documents that can be used for the merge.

① **USE THE CURRENT DOCUMENT** If you open the document that you will use for the merge before selecting the Start Mail Merge option, you can select this option.

② **START FROM A TEMPLATE** This option is used to select a template on your computers hard drive, as shown in Figure 8-20 or on www.office.com.

③ **START FROM EXISTING DOCUMENT** Select this option when you have a document that you want to use, but the document is not currently open.

Notice that some of the templates state that they are for a mail merge.

Figure 8-20 Select Template dialog box

Step 3: Select The Recipients

There are three options for selecting the list that has the recipients for the mail merge, as discussed below.

① **USE EXISTING LIST** Select this option if the list of recipients is in a format that the mail merge tool can use. You will see the Select Data Source dialog box. Figure 8-21 shows the data source formats that you can select from.

② **SELECT FROM OUTLOOK CONTACTS** Select this option if the recipient list is in Microsoft Outlook.

③ **TYPE NEW LIST** Select this option if the list of recipients does not exist. This option will save the data that you enter in a Microsoft Access database. You will see the dialog box shown in Figure 8-22. The options are used to create the names and addresses.

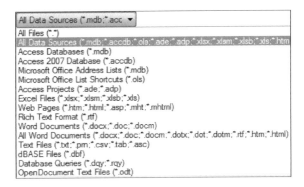

Figure 8-21 List of acceptable data source formats

Using A Microsoft Works Database
The ability to create a mail merge from a Microsoft Works database has been removed from Word. To use data from a Works database, you have to export the data to a format that Word recognizes.

New Address List Dialog Box

The buttons on this dialog box are explained in Table 8-6.

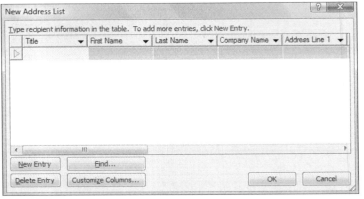

Figure 8-22 New Address List dialog box

Option	Description
New Entry button	Is used to add another recipient to the list.
Delete Entry button	Is used to delete the selected recipient from the list.
Find button	Opens the Find Entry dialog box shown earlier in Figure 8-13.
Customize Columns button	Opens the dialog box shown in Figure 8-23. The options are used to add, delete and rename the fields in the table. The order that the fields appear in can be changed.

Table 8-6 New Address List dialog box options explained

Figure 8-23 Customize Address List dialog box

Step 4: Write The Letter

Depending on the type of document that you selected in Step 1, this step will have a different name. In addition to creating the letter in this step, the Address Block, Greeting Line and merge fields are added to the document and edited as needed. If you are printing envelopes and have an electronic postage account, you can also select the options to print postage.

Step 5: Preview The Letter

This step is used to view the document and the merge fields to make sure the document is exactly how you want it. You can view each document that will be created.

Step 6: Finish The Merge

This step creates the actual merge documents that will be printed or sent via email.

Other Mail Merge Features

In addition to being able to create the list in the mail merge, there are other features that you can use to get the merge data just the way that it needs to be. This includes editing, sorting and filtering the data. If your data already exists in a spreadsheet or database, you can edit, sort and filter the list before starting the merge process.

Using The Mail Merge Recipients Dialog Box

The dialog box shown in Figure 8-24 is used to edit the data for the mail merge.

Mailings tab ⇒ Start Mail Merge group ⇒ Edit Recipient List, opens this dialog box.

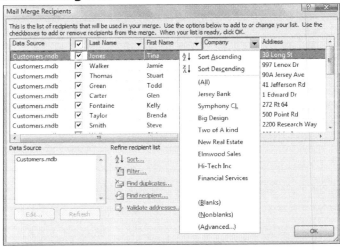

Figure 8-24 Mail Merge Recipients dialog box

EDIT BUTTON Opens the Edit Data Source dialog box, which looks like the New Address List dialog box shown earlier in Figure 8-22. This dialog box is used to change the data in the data source.

REFRESH BUTTON If changes have been made in the data source, click this button, so that the changes will be part of the mail merge.

Sorting Records If you only need to sort the data on one field, open the drop-down list on the Mail Merge dialog box for the field that you want to sort on and select how you want to sort the data. If you need to sort on more than one field, use the sort option discussed in the next section.

Refine Recipient List Options

In addition to editing data, there are several options that you can use. The five Refine recipient list options shown above in Figure 8-24 are explained below.

① **SORT** Selecting this option on the Mail Merge Recipients dialog box opens the dialog box shown in Figure 8-25.

The options are used to sort the data in the list. The data can be sorted on up to three fields.

The options selected in Figure 8-25 will sort the data by the country or region and then by state.

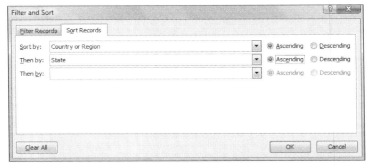

Figure 8-25 Sort Records tab on the Filter and Sort dialog box

Selecting Records If there are a few recipients in the list that you do not want to include in the merge, clear the check box after the Data Source field at the top of the Mail Merge Recipients dialog box shown earlier in Figure 8-24. If there are more than a few records that you do not want included in the mail merge, you need to create a filter.

② **FILTER** Selecting this option opens the dialog box shown in Figure 8-26. The options are used to create criteria that will reduce the number of records in the list that will be used in the mail merge. The filter criteria shown in the figure will select records that have the zip code 90210 or 90049. All other records in the list will not be included in the mail merge.

Figure 8-26 Filter Records tab (Filter and Sort dialog box)

And/Or Operators These operators are used to combine the criteria rows on the Filter Records tab shown above. Using **AND** means that both conditions must be met, meaning the condition on the row above the operator and the condition on the row with the operator. Using **OR** means that either condition can be met for the record to be included in the mail merge. For records to be included in the mail merge based on the criteria shown in Figure 8-27, the State must be TX and the Title must be Office Manager or Director.

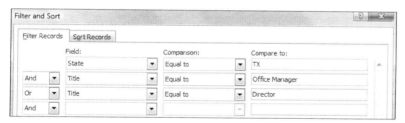

Figure 8-27 And/Or operators

③ **FIND DUPLICATES** Opens the dialog box shown in Figure 8-28. The options on this dialog box display duplicate records in the list. Clear the check mark for any record that you do not want included in the merge, then click OK.

Figure 8-28 Find Duplicates dialog box

④ **FIND RECIPIENT** Opens the Find Entry dialog box shown earlier in Figure 8-13.

⑤ **VALIDATE ADDRESSES** Is used to verify the recipients addresses. You need to have address validation software installed to use this option.

Create A Mail Merge Letter Using A Database

The steps below show you how to create a mail merge letter with names and addresses in a database. If you have names and addresses in a spreadsheet, instead of selecting a database, you would select the spreadsheet. I think it is easier to already have the body of the letter created that you want to use for the mail merge before adding the fields. This is how you will complete this exercise. On your own, you are free to create the letter at the same time that you create the merge.

1. Open the Mail Merge document and save it as My mail merge.

2. Mailings tab ⇒ Start Mail Merge group ⇒ Start Mail Merge ⇒ Step by Step Mail Merge Wizard. You should see the Mail Merge wizard task pane.

3. The letter document type is already selected. Click the Next link at the bottom of the panel. Because you already opened the document that you want to use for the mail merge, click Next on the step 2 panel.

4. Click the Browse link on the Step 3 panel so that you can select the list, which in this case is a database. Navigate to your folder on the Select data source dialog box, then double-click on the Customers.mdb database.

Create Filter Criteria For The Mail Merge

As you read earlier, the Mail Merge Recipients dialog box is used to refine the list. If the database has thousands of names and addresses, you may not want to send the letter to everyone in the database. The way to narrow down the names in the database that you send the letter to is to create a filter.

The filter that you will create will be for all customers that have purchased computer books. The Customers database has a field that contains the type of book that was purchased, as illustrated in Figure 8-29.

ID	First Name	Last Name	Phone	Company	Address	City	State	Zip Code	Category
1	Tina	Jones	(609)364-2500		30 Long St	Ft Laud	FL	32991	Computer
2	Jamie	Walker	(908)652-9609		997 Lenox Dr	Reno	NV	32883	Mystery
3	Stuart	Thomas	(718)503-0331		90A Jersey Ave	Orlando	FL	32761	Sports
4	Todd	Green	(203)452-1300		41 Jefferson Rd	Tampa	FL	32672	Biography
5	Glen	Carter	(407)471-0159		1 Edward Dr	Las Vegas	NV	60022	Sports
6	Kelly	Fontaine	(702)825-9787	Jersey Bank	272 Rt 64	Cherry Hill	NJ	07458	Computer
7	Brenda	Taylor	(610)967-7308	Symphony C&L	500 Point Rd	Ft Lee	NJ	08663	Sports
8	Steve	Smith	(702)947-8701	Big Design	2200 Research	Bronx	NY	11201	Computer
9	Clair	Walker	(215)909-8882	Two of A kind	892 Main St	Menden	CT	06403	Mystery
10	Tina	Walker	(702)703-0101		123 Main St	Stamford	CT	06402	Computer
11	Tom	Smith	(215)909-1885		45 Jericho Ave	Wilton	CT	06405	Sports
12	Fred	Amos	(215)327-7079		19 Rodney	Westwood	CT	06403	Biography
13	Amy	Gardner	(610)664-4646		132 W Park Ave	Wilson	NJ	07403	Mystery
14	Louis	Riker	(702)667-3053		23 Essex Pl	Tappan	CT	06402	Biography
15	Brian	Bark	(610)554-3002		300 Winston Pl	Norwood	NY	10023	Computer
16	Robert	Emerson	(908)587-6422	New Real Estat	200 Mountain A	Ft. Laud	FL	32847	Mystery
17	Peter	Young	(718)505-4259	Elmwood Sales	188 William St	Bogota	NV	32881	Sports
18	Randi	Sherwood	(718)505-3388	Hi-Tech Inc	777 Broad Ave	Ramsey	PA	19001	Computer
19	Carrie	Downing	(407)987-4563	Financial Servic	63 Maple Ave	Glen Rock	NV	32888	Computer

Figure 8-29 Database categories illustrated

1. Click the Filter link. You will see the Filter Records tab on the Filter and Sort dialog box.

2. Open the **FIELD** drop-down list and select Category.

The **COMPARISON** options or operators as I call them, are used to select how you want the information in the field that you select, in this example the Category field, to compare to what you enter in the **COMPARE TO** field. The comparison options are explained in Table 8-7.

Comparison	Selects Records That . . .
Equal to	Are equal to (the same as) the value that you specify.
Not equal to	Are not equal to the value that you specify.
Less than	Are less than the value that you specify. If you want to see products that have a reorder level of less then 10 items in stock, enter 10 in the Compare to field and the filter will retrieve products with a reorder level of nine or less.
Greater than	Are greater than the value that you specify. If you want to see all orders with an order amount over $500, enter $500 in the Compare to field and the filter will retrieve records with an order amount of $500.01 or more.
Less than or equal	Works similar to "Less Than". The difference is that this operator will also select records that have the value that you specify. In the less than example above, the filter would not retrieve records with a reorder level of 10 items. The less than or equal to operator will.
Greater than or equal	Works similar to "Greater Than". The difference is that this operator will also select records that have the value that you specify. In the greater than example above, the filter would not retrieve records with an order amount of exactly $500. The greater than or equal to operator will.
Is blank	Have no data in the field.
Is not blank	Have data in the field.
Contains	Match at least one of the values that you specify. If the criteria is NY, NJ or PA for the State field, any record that has one of these values in the State field would appear in the merge.
Does not contain	Are not one of the values that you specify. This operator works the opposite of the "Contains" operator.

Table 8-7 Comparison options explained

3. The only records that you want to have this filter retrieve are ones that have "Computer" in the Category field. Based on the information in Table 8-6, you want to select **EQUAL TO** in the Comparison field.

4. Type `Computer` in the Compare to field. Your dialog box should have the options selected that are shown in Figure 8-30. Click OK.

Figure 8-30 Filter options

If you scroll to the right on the Mail Merge Recipients dialog box and look in the Category column, you will only see records with Computer in the Category column.

5.   Click OK to close the dialog box, then click Next.

Checking For Duplicates

I think that it is always a good idea to check for duplicates. The records shown in Figure 8-31 may be duplicates. Clear the check box of any record that you do not want included in the mail merge.

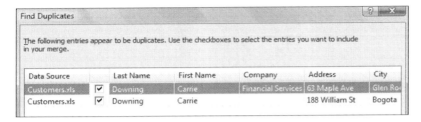

Figure 8-31 Find Duplicates dialog box

Add The Fields To The Document

Step 4 is where you add fields to the letter to create the merge. The recipient information can be added as a block by clicking the Address Block link or the fields can be added one by one, by clicking the **MORE ITEMS** link.

1.   Place the insertion point two lines above the word Dear in the letter, then click the Address block link.

2.   In the scroll box on the left, select the recipient name format that you want to use.

3.   Use the navigation buttons in the Preview section to view how your list will be displayed or printed. Once you have the information the way that you want it, click OK.

4.   As you can see, the font for the address block is different then the rest of the document. Select the Address Block field in the document. Change the font to Corbel, size 12, no bold, so that it matches the rest of the document.

5.   Delete the word Dear and the comma, then click the Greeting line link.

6.   Open the second drop-down list at the top of the Insert Greeting Line dialog box, scroll down and select Joshua.

7.   Click OK to close the dialog box. Press the Enter key to add a blank line after the Greeting Line field, then click Next twice on the Mail Merge panel.

View The Merge Documents

If you want to view the entire document with the merge fields and other changes that you may have made, you can, by clicking the navigation buttons at the top of Figure 8-32.

If you need to change the data in the list, click the **EDIT RECIPIENT LIST** link, which opens the Mail Merge Recipients dialog box.

If you decide that you do not want the recipient shown in the body of the letter to be part of the merge, click the **EXCLUDE THIS RECIPIENT** button.

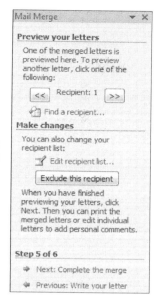

Figure 8-32 Mail Merge Step 5 panel

Complete The Merge

In this step, you can print the merge document and edit individual letters. The Print button opens the Merge to Printer dialog box.

1. On the Step 6 panel, click the Edit individual letters link. Select All on the Merge To New Document dialog box, then click OK.

You will see a document with the name Letters 1. If needed, you can change one of the letters if needed and the changes will not be applied to the other letters. When you have finished making the changes, save the document, then print the document.

Create A Personalized Mail Merge Letter

In the previous exercise, you created a mail merge letter than only included computer book buyers. Now you will take the filter process one step further.

Have you ever received a letter in the mail that had information about your last purchase or some other personal information besides your name and address? This is also done in the mail merge process and is what the steps below show you how to do. You will create a mail merge that will print the dollar amount of the customers last order in the body of the letter. You only want to send this letter to customers whose last order was $50 or more. You will use an existing letter as the basis for this personalized letter, because it already has the database attached that you need to use.

1. Open the My mail merge document that you created. Click Yes when prompted to run the SQL command.

2. Mailings tab ⇒ Start Mail Merge group ⇒ Edit Recipient List.

3. Click the Filter link on the dialog box. You will see the criteria from the previous merge.

Create The Order Amount Filter

As stated earlier, this filter will only select customers whose last order was $50 or more. The database field that contains the comparison information is the Order Amount field.

1. Open the first Field drop-down list and select Order Amount.

2. Open the Comparison drop-down list and select **GREATER THAN OR EQUAL**, then type `50.00` in the Compare to field. Click OK. On the Mail Merge Recipients dialog box, there should be five records displayed. These are the records with an order amount of $50.00 or more.

3. Click OK.

Personalize The Letter

The next task is to modify the body of the letter to let each customer know what their last order amount was, which is why they are receiving this offer.

1. Click in front of the third paragraph in the letter and type `Because your last order was $`.

2. Click the Insert Merge Field button on the Mailings tab and select Order_Amount.

3. Change the font size of the Order Amount field to 12.

4. Type a comma after the Order Amount field, then press the space bar.

5. Type `you will receive an additional 15% discount`. Press the space bar. The paragraph should look like the one shown in Figure 8-33. Save the changes.

> Because your last order was $ 75, you will receive an additional 15% discount. So come on in and see what we have to offer. Be on the lookout for gift certificates that we will be mailing soon that can be applied to any of our classes.

Figure 8-33 Order Amount field and text added to the letter

From here you can open the Mail Merge wizard and complete the remaining steps. You can also select the option on the Mailings tab for the task that you need to complete. When you are finished, you will see that each letter has the customers last order amount.

Earlier in this chapter you read about merge rules. In the exercise that you just completed, the letter included a discount. The next time that this mail merge is run, you or someone else that is using the document may want to offer a different discount. You could set up a Fill-In merge rule to prompt the person running the merge to type in the discount that they want to offer customers.

Printing Envelopes

There are two ways to print envelopes. The option that you select depends on how many envelopes you need to print.

Clicking the **ENVELOPES** button on the Mailings tab opens the dialog box shown in Figure 8-34. The options on the Envelopes tab are used to print envelopes one at a time because you have to enter the delivery address (recipient) information.

If the address information is in a document like a letter, open the document, then open this dialog box. Word will pick up the delivery address information from the document.

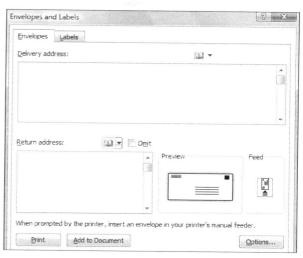

Figure 8-34 Envelopes and Labels dialog box

The **ADD TO DOCUMENT** button is used to save the envelope with the document. A blank page is inserted at the beginning of the document and the envelope is added there. This will let you print the envelope later. This button toggles and will display the **CHANGE DOCUMENT** button, which is used to edit the information right on the label in the document.

The **OPTIONS** button displays the dialog box shown in Figure 8-35. The options on this dialog box are used to customize the envelope.

Figure 8-35 Envelope Options dialog box

> **Delivery Address Tips**
> The Post Office claims that the tips listed below will help get mail delivered quicker.
> ① The address block should be in all capital letters.
> ② The last two lines of the address block should be for the street address, city, state and zip code.
> ③ The address block should not have any punctuation except the hyphen when using a nine digit zip code. This includes removing periods from the title like after Mr and the comma between the city and state.

Using The Mail Merge Wizard To Print Envelopes

If you need to print a lot of envelopes, this may be the easiest option. The steps below show you how to use the Mail Merge Wizard to print envelopes.

1. Open a new document. Mailings tab ⇒ Start Mail Merge group ⇒ Start Mail Merge button ⇒ Select the Mail Merge Wizard option.

2. On the Step 1 panel, select the Envelopes option, then click Next.

3. On the Step 2 panel, click the Envelope options link if you are going to print envelopes that are not size 10 or if you want to change the default font options, otherwise, click Next. You will see the Envelope Options dialog box. Click OK. You will see an envelope template.

4. On the Step 3 panel, click the **BROWSE** link. Navigate to and double-click on the file that has the names and addresses. In this exercise, double-click on the Customers.xlsx file in your folder.

5. Select the Category List table on the dialog box shown in Figure 8-36, then click OK .

> If you are unsure whether or not the first row of a spreadsheet has column headings, clear the check mark for the **FIRST ROW OF DATA CONTAINS COLUMN HEADERS** option shown in Figure 8-36. When you preview the data you can check the spreadsheet to see if the first row does have header information. If it does, you can select not to include it in the merge.

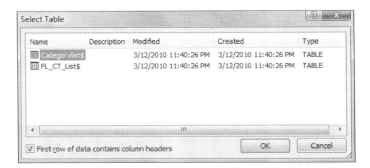

Figure 8-36 Select Table dialog box

6. If you need to sort, filter or check for duplicates, you can select the option on the Mail Merge Recipients dialog box, then click OK. Click Next on the Step 3 panel.

Just like you learned how to add the Address Block and Greeting line fields to a document, you can add them to an envelope. If you click in the center of the lower half of the envelope, you will see a square frame, as shown in Figure 8-37.

Figure 8-37 Address block added to the envelope

This is where you would add the Address Block. If you entered your mailing address information on the Word Options dialog box, it will automatically be added to the upper left corner of the envelope.

7. On the Step 4 panel, add the necessary fields to the envelope, then click Next.

8. Preview the envelopes and make any changes that are needed, then click Next.

9. On the Step 6 panel, click the **PRINT** link, then select the number of envelopes that you want to print. Click OK. The Print dialog box will open. Select the options that you need, then print the envelopes.

10. If you want to save the envelope, click the Save button on the Quick Access toolbar, then type in a file name.

Changing The Font For Envelopes And Labels
If you need to change the font for the text that will print on an envelope or label, select the text on the Envelopes and Labels dialog box (shown earlier in Figure 8-34), then right-click and select Font. You can change the font, style, size and color.

Create Mail Merge Labels

There are two types of labels that you can create. You can create a sheet of the same information on every label or a sheet of a different information on each label.

Creating labels via mail merge is very similar to creating mail merge envelopes. The steps below show you how to create mail merge labels.

1. Open a new document, then click the Start Mail Merge button on the Mailings tab and select the Mail Merge Wizard option.

2. On the Step 1 panel, select the Labels option, then click Next.

3. On the Step 2 panel, click on the Label options link.

   You will see the dialog box shown in Figure 8-38.

   The **LABEL VENDORS** drop-down list contains the brands of labels that have built in support.

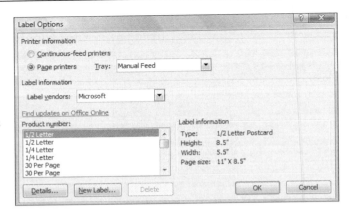

Figure 8-38 Label Options dialog box

4. Select the label brand that you will use.

5. In the **PRODUCT NUMBER** list, select the number of your labels. If you are not sure of the number, look on the box of labels.

6. If you need to customize the label, click the **DETAILS** button.

7. Click OK to close the Label Options dialog box. You will see a grid on the document. This represents the labels that will print on the page. Click Next.

> **Table Tools Contextual Tabs**
> Notice that these tabs are available. That is because in Word, the sheet of labels is in a table. That means that you can add borders and shading, as well as, change the direction of the text on the labels. [See Chapter 9, Table Tools Contextual Tabs]

8. On the Step 3 panel, click the **BROWSE** link. Navigate to and double-click on the file that has the names and addresses. In this exercise, double-click on the Customers.xlsx file in your folder.

9. Select the FL_CT_List table on the Select Table dialog box, then click OK.

10. If you need to sort, filter or check for duplicates, open the Mail Merge Recipients dialog box like you did for letters, then click OK. Click Next on the Step 3 panel.

If the information that you want to print is names and addresses, click on the Address Block link. If you want to add other fields from the data source, click the More Items link on the Step 4 panel.

11. In this exercise, click the Address Block link, then select the appropriate options on the Insert Address Block dialog box. Most of the time, the default options are what you will use. Click OK.

On the label layout, you should see the Address Block field on the first label and <<Next Record>> on the other labels. The **UPDATE ALL LABELS** button will copy the layout from the first label to the other labels.

12. Click the Update All Labels button. The label layout should look similar to the one shown in Figure 8-39.

Figure 8-39 Label layout

13. If you need to add anything else to the labels, select the appropriate options on the Step 4 panel and make the changes, then click Next.

14. Preview the labels and make any changes that are needed. The change in this exercise that you may want to make it to change the spacing before (paragraph) option to zero, then click Next on the Step 5 panel.

15. On the Step 6 panel, click the **PRINT** link to print the labels or click the **EDIT INDIVIDUAL LABELS** link to edit the labels.

16. If you want to save the label layout, click the Save button, then type in a file name.

Create A Sheet Of The Same Label

The steps below show you how to create a sheet of labels that have the same information on each label. This is often used to create return address labels.

1. Open a new document, then click the **LABELS** button on the Mailings tab. You will see the dialog box shown in Figure 8-40.

The **USE RETURN ADDRESS** option is used to add your address information to the Address box if you have entered it on the Word Options dialog box.

[See Chapter 2, Figure 2-34]

The **OPTIONS** button opens the Label Options dialog box shown earlier in Figure 8-38.

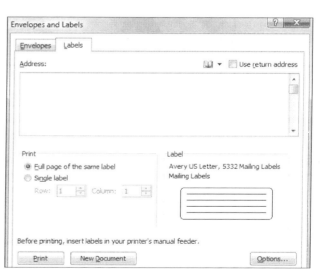

Figure 8-40 Labels tab options

2. Check the Use return address option if you want to use your address or type the name and address information in the Address box.

3. Click the **NEW DOCUMENT** button to view the labels. If any changes are needed, make them now. If you know that you will need to print more sheets of the same label at another time, save the document.

4. Print the labels like you would only other document. Just don't forget to put the sheet of labels in the printer.

Printing A Single Label

There may be times when you only need to print one label or there are a few labels on the sheet of labels that you don't want to waste.

The **SINGLE LABEL** option on the dialog box shown above in Figure 8-40 is used to print one label. The row and column options are used to select which label on the sheet, the address information will be printed on. This will keep you from wasting labels.

Figure 8-39 shown earlier shows a partial sheet of labels. If the third label in the second row is the label that you wanted to use, you would select 2 for the **ROW** option and 3 for the **COLUMN** option.

CREATING TABLES IN WORD

Overview

This chapter covers everything that you wanted to know about creating tables in Word and then some. You will learn how to do the following:

- ☑ Create a free style table
- ☑ Apply styles to tables
- ☑ Use the eraser option
- ☑ Merge and split cells in a table
- ☑ Sort data in a table
- ☑ Convert text to a table
- ☑ Convert data in a table to text
- ☑ Create formulas

Overview

Tables are similar to spreadsheets because they are used to organize large amounts of data in an easy to read format. You can also put images in a table. If the data that you need to organize does not require a lot of calculations that a spreadsheet provides, using a table in Word is easier then setting up a spreadsheet and linking or embedding it in the word processing document.

In addition to being able to organize large amounts of information, tables can be used for page layout. Tables are still used to create web pages. I use tables for the page layout of the books that I write. I find it easier, especially when I have to rearrange parts of a chapter. I also use **NESTED TABLES**, which is one table in the cell of another table. Many of the table formatting options like borders, line styles and auto format work the same way that they do for text.

How To Create A Free Style Table

The **DRAW TABLE** option (on the Borders button in the Paragraph group) is used to create what I call a free style table. This provides a lot of flexibility in the layout of the table. If you prefer to create a table by pointing and clicking, that option is available in the Tables group on the Insert tab. The steps below show you how to create a free style table.

1. Open the document that you want to add the table to, then display the section of the document where you want to place the table.

2. Home tab ⇒ Paragraph group ⇒ Borders ⇒ Draw Table.

3. The mouse pointer will change to a pencil. Draw three boxes (cells), as shown in Figure 9-1.

Figure 9-1 Three cells of a table created

Free Style Table Cells
You do not have to make all of the cells that you draw the same width and height.

4. In each of the three cells, draw two horizontal lines and three vertical lines, as shown in Figure 9-2.

Figure 9-2 Horizontal and vertical rows added to the table

Table And Cell Shortcut Menus

Like text and images, tables and cells have shortcut menu options, as shown in Figures 9-3 and 9-4. The options just for tables and cells are explained in Table 9-1.

Figure 9-3 Table shortcut menu

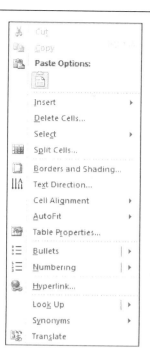

Figure 9-4 Cells shortcut menu

Table And Cell Shortcut Menu Options

Option	Description
Insert	Adds rows, columns or cells above or below the selected row.
Delete Table	Deletes the selected table. (1)
Merge Cells	Combines two or more cells. For this option to be enabled, two or more cells have to be selected. (1)
Distribute Rows Evenly	Makes the selected rows the same height. (1)
Distribute Columns Evenly	Makes the selected columns the same width. (1)
Draw Table	[See How To Create A Free Style Table, earlier in this chapter] (1)
Delete Cells	Deletes the cells that are selected.
Select	Is used to select a cell, entire column, row or table. (2)
Split Cells	Opens the dialog box shown in Figure 9-5. The options are used to divide one cell into two or more cells, in a row or column. (2)
Text Direction	Opens the Text Direction - Table Cell dialog box. The options are used to change the direction of the text in the selected cells. (2)
Cell Alignment	Displays options to select how the text in the selected cells should be aligned.
AutoFit	Displays the options shown in Figure 9-6. They are explained in Table 9-2.
Table Properties	Opens the dialog box shown in Figure 9-7.

Table 9-1 Table and cell shortcut menu options explained

(1)   This option is only available for tables.
(2)   This option is only available for cells.

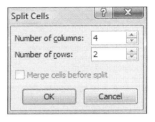

Figure 9-6 AutoFit options

Figure 9-5 Split Cells dialog box

The options on the Table tab are used to set precise alignment, row height, column width, cell width and alternate text for the table.

You may not have the need for this much precision if you are creating a basic table.

If you want to wrap text around a table, select the appropriate options on this tab.

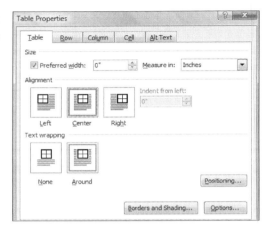

Figure 9-7 Table Properties dialog box

AutoFit Options

These options are used to select how the content in a table will be displayed.

Option	Description
AutoFit to Contents	The width of all cells in the table are automatically adjusted to accommodate the cell with the most content. This option is similar to the Distribute rows and Distribute columns evenly options.
AutoFit to Window	This option is mostly used for documents that will be viewed in a web browser (which can be any size). This option causes the table to automatically resize to fit the browser window.
Fixed Column Width	Is used to limit the width of columns.

Table 9-2 AutoFit options explained

Table Tools Contextual Tabs

When a table is added to a document or a table in a document is selected, the Table Tools Design and Layout tabs appear. These tabs contain options for customizing tables. Many of the options on these tabs can be applied to part of the table in addition to being applied to the entire table, by selecting part of the table before selecting an option on these tabs.

Design Tab

Figure 9-8 shows the Design tab options. These options are used to create and add styles to the table. The options are explained below.

Figure 9-8 Table Tools Design tab

Table Style Options Group

The options in this group are used to modify the table style. As an option in this group is selected or cleared, you will see that the styles in the Table Styles gallery change. This is one way to modify the style that will be applied to the table. The options are explained in Table 9-3.

Option	If Selected . . .
Header Row	The first row in the table will be formatted differently then the rest of the table.
Total Row	The total row in the table (which is usually the last row in the table) will be formatted differently then the rest of the table. (3)
Banded Rows	The odd numbered rows will be formatted differently then the even numbered rows the table.
First Column	The first column in the table will be formatted differently then the rest of the table.
Last Column	The last column in the table will be formatted differently then the rest of the table. (3)
Banded Columns	The odd numbered columns will be formatted differently then the even numbered columns in the table.

Table 9-3 Table Style Options group options explained

(3)   The cells in this section of the table usually sum the values in the other cells in the same row or column.

Table Styles

The purpose of table styles is to make the content easier to read. As you will see, there are a variety of styles. You should select a style for the type of content. Figures 9-9 to 9-11 show the same data with different table styles applied. Once a table style is applied, you can change parts of the style if needed.

College	New students	Graduating students	Change
Undergraduate			
Cedar University	110	103	+7
Elm College	223	214	+9
Maple Academy	197	120	+77
Pine College	134	121	+13
Oak Institute	202	210	-8
Total	998	908	90

Figure 9-9 Colorful shading - Accent 2 style

College	New students	Graduating students	Change
Cedar University	110	103	+7
Elm College	223	214	+9
Maple Academy	197	120	+77
Pine College	134	121	+13
Oak Institute	202	210	-8
Total	998	908	90

Figure 9-10 Dark list - Accent 3 style

College	New students	Graduating students	Change
Cedar University	110	103	+7
Elm College	223	214	+9
Maple Academy	197	120	+77
Pine College	134	121	+13
Oak Institute	202	210	-8
Total	**998**	**908**	**90**

Figure 9-11 Light grid - Accent 5 style

Table Styles Group

The options in this group will be applied to the table that you have selected.

You can scroll through the built-in table styles or click the More button to display the style gallery shown in Figure 9-12.

The three options at the bottom of the gallery are explained in Table 9-4.

The other options in the group are explained below.

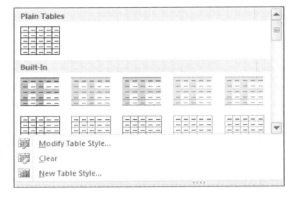

Figure 9-12 Table Styles gallery

SHADING The options on this drop-down list are used to add colors to the background of the entire table or the part of the table that you select. These are the same options that are on the Shading drop-down list in the Paragraph group on the Home tab.

BORDERS The options on this drop-down list are used to add borders to the entire table or the part of the table that you select. These are the same options that are on the Borders and Shading drop-down list in the Paragraph group on the Home tab.

Option	Description
Modify Table Style	This option is only available after a style has been applied to a table. This option displays the dialog box shown in Figure 9-13.
Clear	Removes the formatting from the table or the part of the table that is selected.
New Table Style	Opens the dialog box shown later in Figure 9-17, which is used to create a new table style based on the formatting from the style that you created in the selected table.

Table 9-4 Table Styles group options explained

Modify Style Dialog Box

The options on this dialog box are used to modify the style that is applied to the table. You can modify a portion of the table style or the entire table style. Once you have made the changes to the style, select **ONLY IN THIS DOCUMENT** if you do not want to save the modifications as a new style template. To save the changes as a new style template, select the **NEW DOCUMENTS BASED ON THIS TEMPLATE** option.

The Format button displays the options shown at the bottom of Figure 9-13.

Each option opens a dialog box that you can use to add more customizations to the table style. The options are explained in Table 9-5.

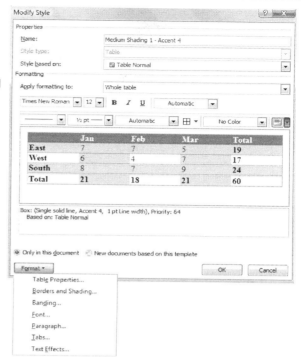

Figure 9-13 Modify Style dialog box

Option	Description
Table Properties	[See Figure 9-7 earlier in this chapter]
Borders and Shading	[See Chapter 5, Borders And Shading Dialog Box]
Banding	The options on the dialog box shown in Figure 9-14 are used to select the number of rows or columns that you want included in the background color. For example, Figure 9-15 shows the row and column banding set to 1. Figure 9-16 shows the row banding option set to 3.
Font	[See Chapter 5, Font Dialog Box]
Paragraph	[See Chapter 5, Paragraph Dialog Box]
Tabs	[See Chapter 5, Tab Stops]
Text Effects	[See Chapter 5, Format Text Effects Dialog Box]

Table 9-5 Format button options explained

Figure 9-14 Banding dialog box

Figure 9-15 Row and column banding set to 1

Figure 9-16 Row banding set to 3

Create New Style From Formatting Dialog Box

The options on the dialog box shown in Figure 9-17 are the same as the ones on the Modify Style dialog box, shown earlier in Figure 9-13.

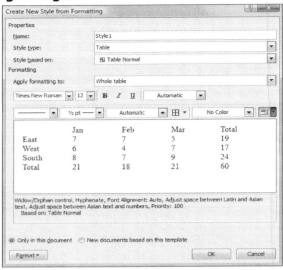

Figure 9-17 Create New Style From Formatting dialog box

Draw Borders Group

The options in this group provide additional customization options for borders. The options are explained in Table 9-6.

Option	Description
Line Style	Is used to select a line style for the line that is selected in the table.
Line Weight	Is used to select the size of the line style. This is similar to selecting the font size for a font.
Pen Color	Changes the color of the lines that are drawn (after this option is selected) to create a new table or to add lines to an existing table.
Draw Table	[See How To Create A Free Style Table, earlier in this chapter]
Eraser	Is used to remove part of a table.
Dialog Box Launcher	Opens the Borders and Shading dialog box.

Table 9-6 Draw Borders group options explained

Using The Eraser

This tool is used to remove part of the table. The steps below show you how to use this tool.

1. Click anywhere in the table that you want to remove a part of.

2. Design tab ⇒ Draw Borders group ⇒ Click the Eraser button.

3. Draw a box around the part of the table that you want to delete, as illustrated in Figure 9-18.

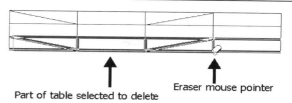

Part of table selected to delete

Eraser mouse pointer

Figure 9-18 Part of the table selected to delete

4. Release the mouse button. The part of the table that you selected should have been deleted from the table. Press the ESC key to turn the eraser off.

Layout Tab

The options shown in Figure 9-19 are probably the table options that you will use most. Many of the options on this tab are on another tab, but they are just not visible, like they are on this tab. Many of the options are also on the shortcut menus for tables and cells shown earlier in Figures 9-3 and 9-4, which you may find easier to get to. The other options are explained in Tables 9-7 to 9-12.

Figure 9-19 Layout tab

Table Group

The options in this group are used to view or select the table or part of the table.

Option	Description
Select	The options shown in Figure 9-20 are used to select a specific part of the table. What will be selected depends on where the insertion point is in the table before you select one of these options.
View Gridlines	Displays or hides the lines around the table and cells.
Properties	Opens the Table Properties dialog box. [See Figure 9-7, earlier in this chapter]

Table 9-7 Table group options explained

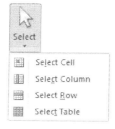

Figure 9-20 Select options

Rows & Columns Group

The options in this group are used to add rows and columns to a table.

Option	Description
Delete	The options shown in Figure 9-21 are used to remove part of the table. What is removed depends on where the insertion point is in the table before you select one of these options.
Insert Above	Adds a row above the row that the insertion point is in.
Insert Below	Adds a row below the row that the insertion point is in.
Insert Left	Adds a column to the left of the column that the insertion point is in.
Insert Right	Adds a column to the right of the column that the insertion point is in.
Dialog Box Launcher	Opens the dialog box shown in Figure 9-22. The options are used to move (shift) cells and add a row or column to the table.

Table 9-8 Rows & Columns group options explained

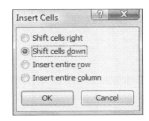

Figure 9-22 Insert Cells dialog box

Figure 9-21 Delete options

Merge Group

The options in this group are used to rearrange cells in the table. Select the cells that you want to change, then select one of the options explained in Table 9-9.

Option	Description
Merge Cells	Combines the selected cells into one cell. Figure 9-23 shows the original table. Figures 9-24 and 9-25 show different cells merged.
Split Cells	Opens the Split Cells dialog box shown earlier in Figure 9-5. The options on the dialog box are used to select the number of columns and/or rows that you want to add to the selected cells. The options shown in Figure 9-5 change a single cell to the one shown in Figure 9-26. The same options change two selected cells to the ones shown in Figure 9-27.
Split Table	Divides the table into two tables. The row that the insertion point is in becomes the first row of the second table.

Table 9-9 Merge group options explained

Figure 9-23 Original table

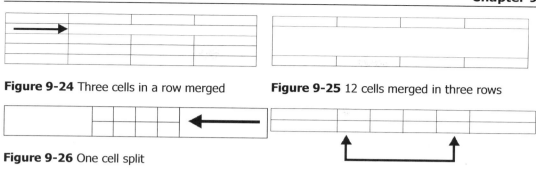

Figure 9-24 Three cells in a row merged

Figure 9-25 12 cells merged in three rows

Figure 9-26 One cell split

Figure 9-27 Two cells split

Cell Size Group

The options in this group are used to change the size of cells, rows or columns.

Option	Description
AutoFit	[See AutoFit Options, earlier in this chapter]
Width	Is used to change the width of the selected cells.
Height	Is used to change the height of the selected cells.
Distribute Rows	Is used to make the selected rows the same height.
Distribute Columns	Is used to make the selected columns the same width.
Dialog Box Launcher	Opens the Table Properties dialog box.

Table 9-10 Cell Size group options explained

Alignment Group

The options in this group are used to select how text is displayed in cells.

Option	Description
Align buttons	Each of the nine align buttons are used to change where the text in a cell is placed.
Text Direction	[See Table 9-1, earlier in this chapter]
Cell Margins	Opens the dialog box shown in Figure 9-28.

Table 9-11 Alignment group options explained

Table Options Dialog Box

The options on this dialog box are used to select cell spacing options. These options can be used for a single cell, some cells or the entire table.

The **CELL MARGIN** options are used to select the amount of space between the cell border and text in the cell.

The **CELL SPACING** options are used to add spacing between cells. The first spreadsheet in Figure 9-29 shows the spreadsheet without any cell spacing. The second spreadsheet shows cell spacing applied to the table.

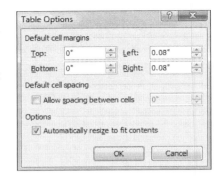

Figure 9-28 Table Options dialog box

North	South	East	West
$17,580	$110,023	$54,080	$64,926
$32,997	$10,001	$7,109	$29,478

North	South	East	West
$17,580	$110,023	$54,080	$64,926
$32,997	$10,001	$7,109	$29,478

Figure 9-29 Cell spacing applied to the table

Data Group

The options in this group are used to manage the data in the table. The options are explained in Table 9-12.

Option	Description
Sort	[See Chapter 5, Sort Options]
Repeat Header Rows	This option is used when the table needs to be printed on more than one page. Select the header rows in the table, then click this button. An example of this feature are the tables in this book that start on one page and end on the next.
Convert To Text	Opens the dialog box shown in Figure 9-30. The options on this dialog box are used to convert the data in a table to text.
Formula	Is used to create a formula in a cell. Clicking this button opens the dialog box shown in Figure 9-31.

Table 9-12 Data group options explained

Figure 9-30 Convert Table To Text dialog box

Figure 9-31 Formula dialog box

Handling Header Rows

By default, table rows can break across pages. This may not be what you want. There are two options to prevent this from happening, as explained below.

① Let the rows break across pages, but repeat the header row at the top of the table on the next page. The **REPEAT HEADER ROWS** option discussed earlier in Table 9-12 toggles on and off. Click in the header row of the table, then select this option. If the table needs to print on a second page, the header row will automatically be added to the top of the table on the second page. This option did not work for me.

② As stated earlier, the default is to let rows of a table print on different pages, if needed. If you do not want this to happen because you would prefer that the entire table print on the same page, you can turn the option off by clicking in the header row of the table. Then click the Properties button on the Table Tools Layout tab. On the Row tab, clear the **ALLOW ROW TO BREAK ACROSS PAGES** option.

Insert Tab Table Options

The options shown in Figure 9-32 are used to create tables, convert text and more.

The options are explained in Table 9-13.

Figure 9-32 Table options

Option	Description
Grid	The squares at the top of the drop-down list are used to select the number of rows and columns for the table that you want to create. A table with six columns and three rows will be created with the options that are selected above in Figure 9-32.
Insert Table	Opens the dialog box shown in Figure 9-33. The options are used to create a table. The benefit of using this dialog box over the grid is that there are a lot of options in one place. If you know that the majority of tables that you will create will have the same number of rows and columns that you select on the Insert Table dialog box, check the **REMEMBER DIMENSIONS FOR NEW TABLES** option.
Draw Table	[See How To Create A Free Style Table, earlier in this chapter]
Convert Text to Table	Opens the dialog box shown in Figure 9-34. The options on this dialog box are used to convert the selected text in the document to table format.
Excel Spreadsheet	Is used to add an empty Excel spreadsheet to the document, as shown in Figure 9-35. This allows you to use Excel functionality in a Word document. The Excel Ribbon replaces the Word Ribbon at the top of the workspace, as shown at the top of the figure.
Quick Tables	Displays the menu shown in Figure 9-36. The pre-formatted tables on this menu can be added to the document and then customized.

Table 9-13 Table options explained

Figure 9-33 Insert Table dialog box

Figure 9-34 Convert Text To Table dialog box

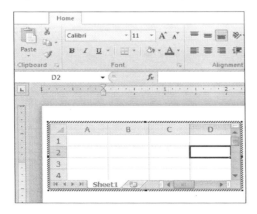

Figure 9-35 Embedded Excel spreadsheet

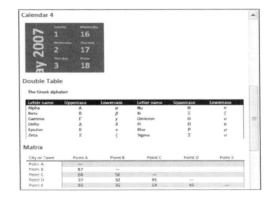

Figure 9-36 Quick Tables menu options

Create A Table

Earlier in this chapter you learned how to create a free style table. Before you create a table you should figure out how many rows and columns the table needs. If the table needs more rows or columns after it is first created, you can add them.

1. Open a new document, then press the Enter key once.

2. Insert tab ⇒ Tables group ⇒ Table ⇒ Insert Table.

3. Change the Columns option to 4 and the Rows option to 5, then click OK.

    Your table should look like the one shown in Figure 9-37.

Figure 9-37 Basic table

4. Save the document as Basic table.

Selecting Rows And Columns

To select an entire row, click outside of the row that you want to select on the left side of the table, as illustrated in Figure 9-38.

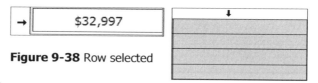

Figure 9-38 Row selected

To select an entire column, click above the column that you want to select, as illustrated in Figure 9-39.

Figure 9-39 Column selected

How To Select Cells Using The Keyboard

The easiest way to select cells without using a mouse is to follow the steps below.

1. Using the arrow keys, place the mouse pointer in the first cell of the range that you want to select, then press and hold down the **SHIFT** key.

2. Use the arrow keys on the keyboard to move to the right and then down to select the cells in the range that you need. After you have selected all of the cells, release the Shift key.

Adding Rows And Columns To A Table

The easiest way to add rows and columns to an existing table are discussed below.

How To Add Rows Right-click in a cell in the row where you want to add a row and select Insert. You will see the menu shown in Figure 9-40. Select where you want the row to be added, above or below the current row.

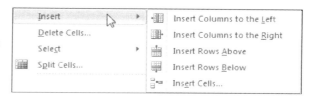

Figure 9-40 Insert menu options

How To Add Columns Right-click in a cell in the column where you want to add a column and select Insert. You will see the menu shown above in Figure 9-40. Select where you want the column to be added, to the left or right of the current column.

Resizing Rows And Columns

By default, tables are created as wide as the page margins. All of the rows have the same height and all of the columns have the same width. Most of the time you do not want a table with these dimensions, which means that the rows and columns need to be resized. There are several ways to resize a table, as discussed below.

Resize The Rows And Columns Manually

This is probably the easiest way to resize the table because you can see the outcome of the change immediately.

Resize A Row

1. Place the mouse pointer between two rows, as shown in Figure 9-41.

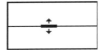

Figure 9-41 Mouse pointer in position to resize a row

2. Drag the mouse pointer down to make the row above wider or drag the mouse pointer up to make the row below wider.

Resize A Column

There are several ways to resize the column width. The easiest way is to drag the column border to resize the column. Another way is to use the Table Properties dialog box which is used to type in the width for each column in the table.

1. Place the mouse pointer between two columns, as shown in Figure 9-42.

Figure 9-42 Mouse pointer in position to resize a column

2. Drag the mouse pointer to the left or right to resize the column.

Merging Cells

Merging cells is used to combine two or more cells into one cell. There are two ways to merge cells, as discussed below, after selecting the cells to merge.

① Right-click on the selected cells and select Merge Cells.
② Layout Tab ⇒ Merge group ⇒ Merge Cells.

Splitting Cells

Splitting cells is used to split one cell into two or more cells. After selecting any of the options below, you will see the Split Cells dialog box shown earlier in Figure 9-5. The options on the dialog box are used to select how many cells to split the cell into. There are two ways to split cells, as discussed below, after selecting the cell to split.

① Right-click in the cell that you want to split and select Split Cells.

② Layout Tab ⇒ Merge group ⇒ Split Cells.

Merging And Splitting Tables

Just like cells can be merged and split, tables can be merged and split. Two tables can be merged into one table. One table can be split into two tables horizontally. This means that the top rows of the table will be in one table after the split and the bottom rows will be placed in another table.

Merging Tables

Figure 9-43 shows two tables that will be merged. The tables that you merge do not have to have the same number of columns or rows.

Figure 9-43 Tables to be merged

Use the **DELETE** key to remove any blank lines between the two tables.

The tables shown above in Figure 9-43 will look like the one shown in Figure 9-44 after they are merged.

Figure 9-44 Merged tables

Splitting A Table

The table that you split does not have to have the same number of columns or rows. The steps below show you how to split a table.

1. Click in a cell in the row that you want to be the start of the second table.

2. Layout Tab ⇒ Merge group ⇒ Split Table.

In Figure 9-44 above, the mouse pointer was placed in a cell in the fourth row from the top of the table to create the two tables shown in Figure 9-45.

Figure 9-45 Table split into two tables

Splitting Tables Vertically

You may have a need to split tables vertically so that two tables are side by side. Word does not have an option that will do this for you automatically, but you can create the effect of having side by side tables.

Create Side By Side Tables

1. Open the Side By Side Tables document.

2. Highlight the column in the table that does not have any data, then open the **BORDERS** drop-down list on the mini toolbar.

3. Click the Bottom Border option, then click the Top Border option shown in Figure 9-46.

   This will remove the line at the top and bottom of the selected cells.

Figure 9-46 Border button options

4. Select the Inside Borders option. The document should look like the one shown in Figure 9-47.

North	South
$17,580	$110,023
$32,997	$10,001

East	West
$54,080	$64,926
$7,109	$29,478

Figure 9-47 Side by side table effect

5. If you wanted to make the space between the two tables smaller, select the middle column, then on the Layout tab, change the **WIDTH** field to a smaller number.

Nested Tables

A nested table is a table in the cell of another table. The steps below show you how to create nested tables.

1. Click in the cell that you want to add a table to.

2. Insert tab ⇒ Tables group ⇒ Table ⇒ Insert Table. You will see the Insert Table dialog box.

   At a minimum, select the number of rows and columns for the second table, then click OK.

   You should see the second table in one cell of the original table, as illustrated in Figure 9-48.

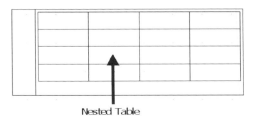

Nested Table

Figure 9-48 Nested table example

Sorting Data

The data in a table can be sorted, just like it can in a spreadsheet. Sorting is used to arrange the data in a more meaningful way. For example, if you are entering names and addresses in a table of people that want to sign up for various classes, more than likely you will enter the names in the table in the order that people sign up for a class and not in the order of the class they are signing up for. If you sort the table by the class each person signed up for, the names will be sorted (grouped) by class. Tables can be sorted on up to three columns at one time.

To sort data in a table you have to select the data that you want to sort. Tables that have split or merged cells cannot be sorted. When selecting the data, you should select the entire row of data. Otherwise, the data that is not selected in the row will not be sorted, which will cause the data in the rows to be in a different order, which is not what you want to have happen.

Sorting Data In A Table

The steps below show you how to sort the data in the table by the last and first name fields.

1. Open the Table To Sort document.

2. Highlight all of the rows in the table except the header row.

3. Layout tab ⇒ Data group ⇒ Sort, will open the dialog box shown in Figure 9-49.

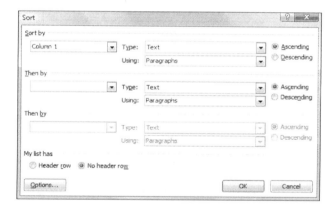

Figure 9-49 Sort dialog box

4. Open the Sort by drop-down list and select Column 2.

5. Open the Then by drop-down list and select Column 1. Because you selected the rows to sort, you do not have to select the **HEADER ROW** option.

6. Click OK. The customers with the last names Smith and Walker should be sorted as shown in Figure 9-50. Notice that customer Steve Smith comes before Tom Smith, which is what should happen because the table was sorted on the Last Name column first and then on the First Name column.

Steve	Smith	Big Design	2200 Research Way	Bronx	NY	11201	Computer	$12.95
Tom	Smith		45 Jericho Ave	Wilton	CT	06405	Sports	$25.00
Brenda	Taylor	Symphony C&L	500 Point Rd	Ft Lee	NJ	08863	Sports	$44.95
Stuart	Thomas		90A Jersey Ave	Orlando	FL	32761	Sports	$75.00
Jamie	Walker		997 Lenox Dr	Reno	NV	32883	Mystery	$21.95
Tina	Walker		123 Main St	Stamford	CT	06402	Computer	$50.00

Figure 9-50 Data sorted by last and first name

Converting Text And Table Data

Word has two options for converting a document. The options are used to convert text to table format and to convert data in a table to text format.

Converting Table Data To Text

Follow the steps below to convert the data in a table to text.

1. Click in a table that has data that you want to convert to text. You can use the Table To Sort document to practice.

2. Layout tab ⇒ Data group ⇒ Convert to Text. You will see the Convert Table To Text dialog box.

3. Select how the data should be separated on the dialog box. Click OK. The data will now be converted to text format.

> **Convert Text To Table Data**
> This feature works the opposite of the **TABLE TO TEXT** option. It will convert text to a table. The text that you want to convert must be separated by a character, like tabs or a comma. Select the text that you want to convert to table format, then Insert tab ⇒ Tables group ⇒ Table ⇒ Convert Text To Table. You will see the dialog box shown earlier in Figure 9-34. Select the options to convert the text to table format, then click OK.

Formulas

Word has some spreadsheet functions that you can use in tables. Like a spreadsheet, a table in Word uses rows and columns. You will not see the cell reference (row and column headings across the top and down the left side of the table) like you will in a spreadsheet, but the cells in a Word table have the same cell names. Tables can perform many of the calculations that spreadsheets can. The formulas shown below can be created in Word.

= Sum(Above)   = C5+C6+C7   = Sum(C5:C7)   = Count(C5:C7)

Referencing Cells In A Table

Cells in a table in Word are referenced like they are in a spreadsheet. Figure 9-51 shows how cells are referenced.

	A	B	C
1	A1	B1	C1
2	A2	B2	C2
3	A3	B3	C3

Figure 9-51 Cell references

Create Formulas In A Table

The steps below show you how to create a table that has three formulas. The first formula that you create will sum the quantity field. This formula will go in the last cell in the QTY column.

The second formula that you create will multiply the quantity times the price, which will calculate the total value for the product. This formula will go in the **TOTAL** column.

The third formula that you create will sum the Total column.

1. Open a new document.

   Press the Enter key a few times.

   Create the table shown in Figure 9-52.

Qty	Price	Total
10	7.50	
20	5.00	
15	3.99	

Figure 9-52 Table for the formulas

2. Click in cell A5, then click the Formula button on the Layout tab. You will see the dialog box shown in Figure 9-53.

   This formula will add the values in cells A2, A3 and A4.

   The **PASTE FUNCTION** drop-down list has more formulas that you can use.

Figure 9-53 Sum formula

3. Open the Number format drop-down list and select the first format, then click OK.

4. Click in cell C2, then click the Formula button on the Layout tab. Type $= (A2) * (B2)$ in the Formula field. This formula will multiply the value in cell A2 times the value in cell B2 and place the result in cell C2.

5. Open the Number format drop-down list and select the third format, as shown in Figure 9-54, then click OK.

Figure 9-54 Multiplication formula

6. Click in cell C3 and type = (A3) * (B3) in the formula field, then select the third number format. Click in cell C4 and type = (A4) * (B4) in the formula field, then select the third number format. Click in cell C5 and select the third number format. The Sum Above formula is what this cell needs.

7. Click OK. Your table should look like the one shown in Figure 9-55.

   If you want to add more formatting to the table, you can.

   Save the document as
   Table with formulas.

Qty	Price	Total
10	7.50	$ 75.00
20	5.00	$ 100.00
15	3.99	$ 59.85
45		$ 234.85

Figure 9-55 Completed table with formulas

CREATING CHARTS

Overview

This chapter covers creating and editing charts in Word documents. The following topics are covered.

☑ Chart types
☑ Parts of a chart
☑ How to create column, area and pie charts

Overview

In addition to being able to format data in tables in documents, charts are used to present data in a graphical format which often makes the data easier to understand by visually displaying the relationship between the data. Charts also allow data to be presented in formats that text-only reports cannot do as well. For example, charts can show trends over time, relationships or how one set of data compares to another set of data.

Chart Types

The Insert Chart dialog box is used to select the type of chart and what the chart will look like. There are 11 chart types that you can select from, as shown down the left side of Figure 10-1. These chart types have variations that you can select on the right, which give you more chart options. The chart types are explained in Table 10-1.

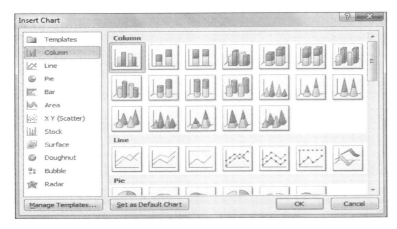

Figure 10-1 Insert Chart dialog box

The **MANAGE TEMPLATES** button opens the chart template folder, which by default is empty. This is where chart templates that you create are saved.

The **SET AS DEFAULT CHART** button is used to change the default chart, which is a column chart, to what you want. If you create a lot of charts with a different chart type, click on that chart type, then click this button.

Chart Type	Description
Column	Column charts, as shown in Figure 10-2, show differences between items and relationships between grouped data in columnar format.
Line	Line charts show trends and changes over a period of time. The markers at the bottom of the chart indicate the exact values. In Figure 10-3, the data is represented with lines. A good use of **3-D LINE CHARTS** is when the data lines cross each other often. This makes a line chart easier to read. (1)
Pie	Pie charts only show information for one point in time. Figure 10-4 shows the various types of income for July. Each slice of the pie represents the percent for the item. (2)

Table 10-1 Insert Chart dialog box options explained

Chart Type	Description
Bar	Bar charts, as shown in Figure 10-5, show differences between items and relationships between grouped data. This is probably the most used chart type. Stacked bar charts show each item as a percent of the total.
Area	Area charts show how the data has changed over a period of time. Figure 10-6 shows how the four types of income (mail order, store, kiosk and Internet) make up the total income and how the income changes over the months. Area charts are almost identical to stacked line charts. The difference is that area charts are filled in below the trendline. Area charts are probably best suited for a few groups of data. (1)
XY (Scatter)	XY Scatter charts show how two values are related (like month of year and order amount) and how a change in one value affects the other value, as shown in Figure 10-7. This chart type is used to show the correlation between the items. The X and Y axis must display numeric data. If data like dates or months can be converted to numeric data, it can be used in this chart type.
Stock	This chart type is similar to bar charts. The difference is that the bars in stock charts do not have to touch the bottom of the chart. This type of chart is often used to display the minimum and maximum of stock prices, where each bar represents a different stock. Stock charts plot the first and last trade of the day or the high and low values for each element.
Surface	This is the 3-D version of area charts. This chart type uses three sets of data. The surface of the chart has a curve and shows trends in relation to time.
Doughnut	This chart type is similar to pie charts. The difference is that there is a hole in the center of the chart. (2)
Bubble	This chart type is similar to XY Scatter charts because it plots individual points. The difference is that bubble charts use different size plot points based on the data value. The larger the data value, the larger the size of the plot point.
Radar	Radar charts compare sets of data relative to a center point and shows how far the data value is from the standard (the center point value). The values that are often used in this chart type are group subtotals. The data from the X axis is usually plotted in a circle and the Y values are plotted from the center of the circle out.

Table 10-1 Insert Chart dialog box options explained (Continued)

(1) This chart type requires at least two sets of data.
(2) This chart type only uses one value because it shows how the whole (100%) is divided.

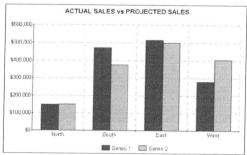

Figure 10-2 Column chart

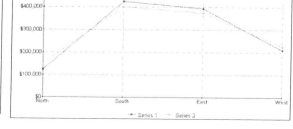

Figure 10-3 Line chart

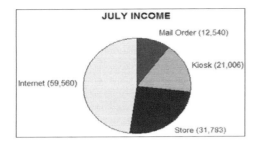

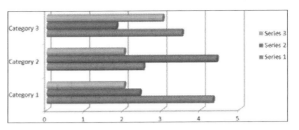

Figure 10-5 Bar chart

Figure 10-4 Pie chart

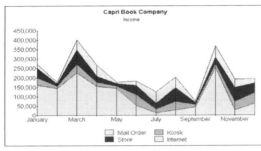

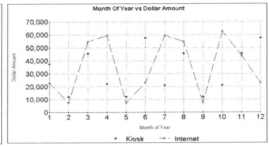

Figure 10-6 Area chart

Figure 10-7 XY Scatter chart

As you learn more about charts, it is probably a good idea to experiment with the chart variations to see which one displays the data in the best layout. As shown earlier in Figure 10-1, chart types have **VARIATIONS**. Figure 10-8 shows two variations of a bar chart that use the same data. Figure 10-9 shows two variations of a line chart that use the same data.

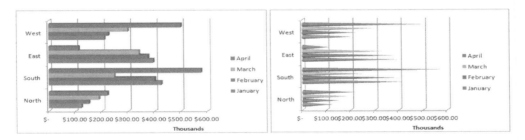

Figure 10-8 Clustered 3-D bar chart and Clustered horizontal cone chart that use the same data

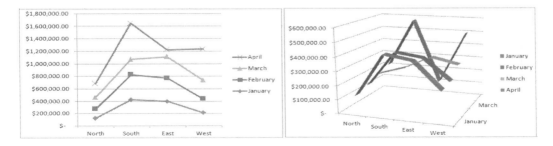

Figure 10-9 Stacked line with markers chart and 3-D line chart that use the same data

Chart Mini Toolbar And Shortcut Menu

Figure 10-10 shows the mini toolbar for charts. Figure 10-11 shows the shortcut menu for charts.

Figure 10-10 Chart mini toolbar

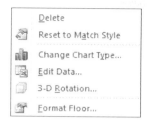

Figure 10-11 Chart shortcut menu

Axis Locations

The **HORIZONTAL AXIS** (also known as the X Axis) is at the bottom of the chart. The **VERTICAL AXIS** (also known as the Y Axis) is on the left side of the chart.

Parts Of A Chart

Each part of a chart is called an element. Charts can contain all or any of the elements discussed below. These elements can be added or deleted as needed. Figures 10-12 and 10-13 illustrate many of the elements of a chart. These elements can be customized individually. The easiest way to select an element is to click on it in the chart. The parts of the chart that are illustrated, are explained below.

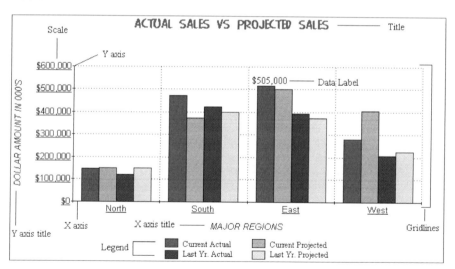

Figure 10-12 Parts of a chart illustrated

TITLE is a description of what type of data is displayed in the chart.

X and **Y AXIS** represent the vertical and horizontal axis of the chart. The X axis often represents quantities or percents. Both axes are used to determine the scale.

GRIDLINES make the chart easier to read if the values are close in range. You can have horizontal and vertical gridlines.

SCALE shows the unit of measurement. The scale range is taken from the data that is displayed on the chart. The scale is automatically created for you, but you can change it.

The **LEGEND** is used to help make the chart easier to read. Legends are color coded representations of different data elements on the chart. Legends can be difficult to understand when printed. They are in color on the computer screen but print in gray scale, unless you are using a color printer. Each series of data is represented in the legend.

A **DATA SERIES** is one set of data plotted on the chart. Figure 10-13 shows three data series.

A **DATA POINT** is one value in a data series.

The **PLOT AREA** is the background portion of the chart and includes the gridlines and everything inside of the grid on the chart.

The **SIDE WALL** is on the left on the Figure 10-13 next to the vertical axis.

The **BACK WALL** is behind the data.

The **FLOOR** is at the bottom of the plot area.

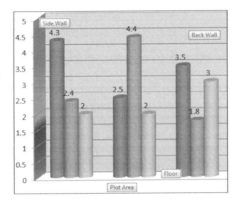

Figure 10-13 Parts of a column chart

Chart Tools Contextual Tabs

The options on these three chart tabs are used to create and format charts. The options on the tabs are explained in Tables 10-2 to 10-9.

Design Tab

The options on the tab shown in Figure 10-14 are used to change the chart type, select the data, layout and style for the chart.

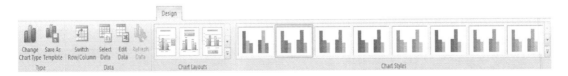

Figure 10-14 Chart Tools Design tab

Type Group

The options in this group are used to select a chart type or save an existing chart as a template.

Option	Description
Change Chart Type	Opens the Change Chart Type dialog box, which looks like the Insert Chart dialog box shown earlier in Figure 10-1. This will let you replace the existing chart type.
Save As Template	Opens the Save Chart Template dialog box, which is used to save the current chart as a template that you can apply to other charts.

Table 10-2 Type group options explained

Data Group

The options in this group are used to select and configure the data for the chart.

Option	Description
Switch Row/Column	Moves the data in the rows to columns and the data in columns to rows.
Select Data	Is used to select different data for the chart or add another series of data to the chart.
Edit Data	Displays the data for the chart so that the data can be modified.
Refresh Data	Select this option when the data in the spreadsheet for the chart has changed. This will update the data that is displayed in the chart.

Table 10-3 Data group options explained

Chart Layouts Group

The gallery in this group is used to select a different layout for the chart.

Chart Styles Group

The gallery in this group is used to select a different style for the chart.

Layout Tab

The options shown in Figure 10-15 are used to customize individual parts of the chart.

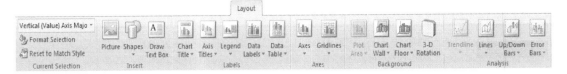

Figure 10-15 Layout tab

Current Selection Group

The options in this group are used to select and modify a specific part of the chart. The options are explained in Table 10-4.

Option	Description
Chart Elements	Is used to select a specific part of the chart. You can also click on the part of the chart that you want to select to modify. Depending on the chart type, the options in the drop-down list shown in Figure 10-16 will vary.
Format Selection	Once you have selected a part of the chart to modify, click on this option. The corresponding format section of a dialog box will open, based on the part of the chart that is selected, as shown in Figure 10-17. The corresponding format option for the part of the chart that is selected is also on the shortcut menu.
Reset to Match Style	Select this option when you want to remove the changes that you made to the part of the chart that is selected.

Table 10-4 Current Selection group options explained

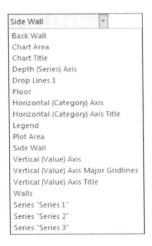

Figure 10-16 Chart Elements options

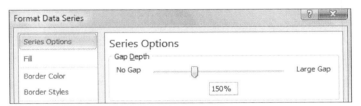

Figure 10-17 Format Data Series dialog box

Insert Group

The options in this group are used to add objects to the chart. The options are explained in Table 10-5.

Option	Description
Picture	Adds an image to the chart.
Shapes	Adds a shape to the chart.
Draw Text Box	Adds a Text box to the chart.

Table 10-5 Insert group options explained

Labels Group

The options in this group are used to add labels to different parts of the chart, as well as, modify labels. Each of the options in this group has a dialog box that is used to customize a specific part of the chart. The options are explained in Table 10-6.

Option	Description
Chart Title	The options shown in Figure 10-18 are used to position the charts title. The **MORE TITLE OPTIONS** option opens the dialog box shown in Figure 10-19. These options are used to format the charts title.
Axis Titles	The options are used to change the position of the horizontal and vertical axis titles.
Legend	The options are used to change the position of the legend.
Data Labels	The options are used to display or hide the labels next to the data in the chart. Each data point in a series has a data label. They are used to identify information in the chart. The dialog box shown in Figure 10-20 provides more options.
Data Table	This option is used to display the data that was used to create the table below the chart, as shown in Figure 10-21.

Table 10-6 Labels group options explained

Figure 10-19 Format Chart Title dialog box

Figure 10-18 Chart Title options

The options in the **LABELS CONTAINS** section are used to select the information that appears in the label.

Individual data labels can be added by clicking twice on the data point that you want to create the label for, then right-click and select Add Data Label.

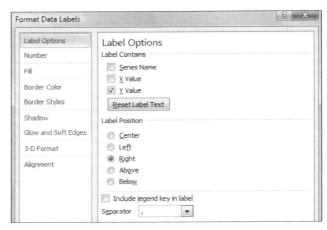

Figure 10-20 Format Data Labels dialog box

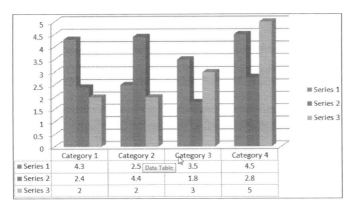

Figure 10-21 Data table below chart

The options on the dialog box shown in Figure 10-22 are used to customize the data table that is added to the bottom of a chart, as shown above in Figure 10-21.

Figure 10-22 Format Data Table dialog box

Axes Group

The options in this group are used to modify the X and Y axis. The options are explained in Table 10-7.

Option	Description
Axes	The options are used to change the formatting of text and numeric values on the X and Y axis.
Gridlines	The options are used to display or hide the gridlines on the X and Y axis.

Table 10-7 Axes group options explained

Background Group

The options in this group are used to change the background of different parts of the chart. The options are explained in Table 10-8.

Option	Description
Plot Area	The options are used to change the background color of the entire chart.
Chart Wall	The options are used to add color to the charts walls.
Chart Floor	The options are used to add color to the charts floor.
3-D Rotation	This option is used to rotate the chart. This option is only available for charts that have a 3-D layout.

Table 10-8 Background group options explained

Analysis Group

The options in this group are used to display trends in the data. These options are not available for all chart types. The options are explained in Table 10-9.

Option	Description
Trendline	Adds a line to the chart to better illustrate trends in the data. The trendline is also used to analyze problems. (3)
Lines	The options are used to display drop lines on line and area charts, as well as, high-low lines on a 2-D line chart.
Up/Down Bars	Is used to display up/down bars on a line chart. Figure 10-23 shows the up/down (white) bars.
Error Bars	Are used to graphically display the range of error the values in a data series can have. Each data series can have their own set of error bars using the options shown in Figure 10-24. When my local news reports on a survey, they will give the finding, then say with an error of plus or minus a percent. This percent would come from the error bars on a chart. (3)

Table 10-9 Analysis group options explained

(3) This option can be applied to a data series in an area, bar, bubble, column, line and XY (Scatter) chart.

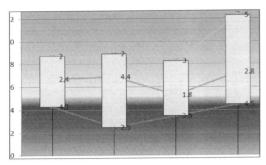

Figure 10-23 Up/Down bars

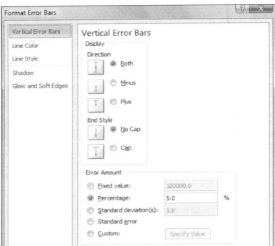

Figure 10-24 Format Error Bars dialog box

Format Tab

The options shown in Figure 10-25 are used to apply styles to different parts of the chart. They are explained below.

Figure 10-25 Format tab

Current Selection Group

The options in this group are the same as the ones on the Layout tab. [See Table 10-4 earlier in this chapter]

Shape Styles Group

The options in this group are used to apply and modify shape styles on the chart. The options are the same as the ones on the Insert tab. [See Chapter 6, Table 6-10]

The Dialog box launcher in the Shape Styles group opens the dialog box shown in Figure 10-26 if the vertical axis is selected or the dialog box shown in Figure 10-27 if the horizontal axis is selected.

The options on these dialog boxes are used to change the charts scale. This is helpful when there are a lot of data points in one part of the chart, which can make it difficult to distinguish one data point from another.

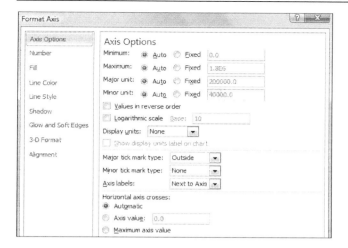

Figure 10-26 Format Axis dialog box (vertical axis)

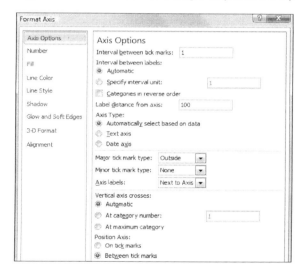

Figure 10-27 Format Axis dialog box (horizontal axis)

WordArt Styles Group

The options in this group are used to apply styles to text that is part of the chart. The options are the same as the ones on the Insert tab. [See Chapter 6, Table 6-11]

Arrange Group

The options in this group are used to change the location of parts of the chart. The options are the same as the ones on the Insert tab. [See Chapter 6, Table 6-6]

Size Group

The options in this group are used to resize the chart. The Shape Height and Shape Width options are useful if you need to make two or more charts the same size. The options are the same as the ones on the Insert tab. [See Chapter 6, Table 6-7]

Creating Charts Overview

The chart options in Word are quite remarkable in my opinion. The chart features probably provide more functionality then most of us will need to use in Word. That may be because the charts data is saved in an Excel spreadsheet. What I did find interesting is that there is no option to select the spreadsheet that has the data that you want the chart to be based on. Once you select a chart type, Excel opens automatically and displays a spreadsheet that has sample data, as shown on the right of Figure 10-28. You can type in the data for the chart that you want to create or you can paste the data in from another spreadsheet.

The other feature of charts in Word that I found interesting is that if you add a second chart to the document, a second spreadsheet with sample data will open. There are several things that need to be addressed when creating charts, as discussed below.

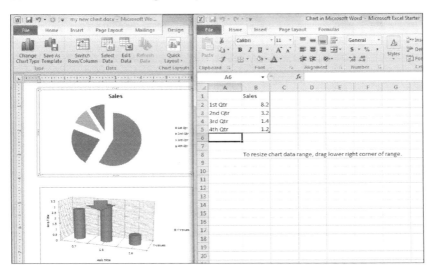

Figure 10-28 Sample chart in word from sample data in Excel

Data Layout Charts are created by plotting the data against the horizontal and vertical axis. To help make it easier to create a chart, keep the following in mind when creating the data for a chart.

① There should not be empty cells in the rows and columns of data that will be used to create the chart. For example, if the range of data for the chart is A3:H10, cells B5 and E8 should not be empty.
② The data should be in adjacent rows and columns for each data series.
③ Add the titles for the X and Y axis to the spreadsheet as needed. [See Axis Locations, earlier in this chapter]
④ If the chart needs titles, include them in the spreadsheet. Usually, the chart title is placed in cell A1.
⑤ Columns of data that are text should be in the left most columns of the spreadsheet.

Chart Placement Options There are two locations where charts can be placed in a workbook, as discussed below.

① **On the same sheet as the data** This is the most popular option. It enables you to see the chart update as the data for the chart is changed. This is known as an **EMBEDDED CHART**.

② **On a new worksheet** This option is useful if the chart is large. Many people use this option when they want to just print the chart, even though the chart can be printed by itself if it is on the same worksheet as the data. This is known as a **STANDALONE CHART**, which means that the chart is placed on it's own sheet in the workbook.

Chart Tips
Below are some tips that may help you make creating charts easier.

① While many people select the range of data on the spreadsheet for the chart, it is not a requirement. You can click in a cell that is in the range of data that will be used to create the chart or click in a cell that is in the range of the table. Tables are covered in Chapter 13.
② You can use the default chart style, column, without opening the Insert Chart dialog box by selecting the data and pressing the F11 key. The F11 key places the chart on its own sheet in the workbook, but you can copy the chart to the sheet with the data. If you changed the default chart type, the chart type that you selected as the default will be used when the F11 key is pressed.

Create A Column Chart

1. Open a new document.

2. Insert tab ⇒ Illustrations group ⇒ Chart. Select the first column chart option if it is not already selected, then click OK.

3. You should see a spreadsheet open in Excel. Delete all of the data in the spreadsheet.

4. In Excel, File tab ⇒ Open. Select the Chart data for Word spreadsheet.

5. Select the range A1 to C5. Right-click and select Copy.

6. In Excel, click on the Chart in Microsoft Word spreadsheet. Right-click in cell A1 and select Paste.

7. In Excel, File tab ⇒ Exit.

   In Word, you should see the chart shown in Figure 10-29.

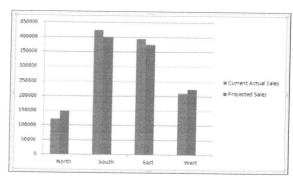

Figure 10-29 Column chart

Add Titles And Labels To The Chart

1. Layout tab ⇒ Labels group ⇒ Chart Title ⇒ Above Chart.

2. Select the chart title text, then type `Column Chart`.

3. Layout tab ⇒ Labels group ⇒ Legend ⇒ Show legend at bottom.

4. Layout tab ⇒ Labels group ⇒ Data Labels ⇒ Outside End.

5. Right-click on a data label in the chart and select Format Data Labels.

6. On the Label Options panel, select the Inside End label position option.

7. On the Number panel, select the Currency category option. You will see some of the numbers formatted in the chart.

8. On the Alignment panel, open the Text direction drop-down list and select Rotate all text 270°. If you wanted to change the data labels for the other series in the chart, click on it while the Format Data Labels dialog box is open. Click the Close button.

9. Your chart should look like the one shown in Figure 10-30.

   Save the document as `My charts`.

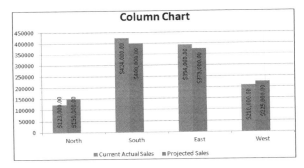

Figure 10-30 Column chart revised

Create A Pie Chart

1. Open the My charts document if it is not already open, then add a page break below the chart.

2. Insert tab ⇒ Illustrations group ⇒ Chart, then select the 5th pie chart option and click OK.

3. Close Excel.

4. Add the Outside End data labels option. The pie chart should look like the one shown in Figure 10-31.

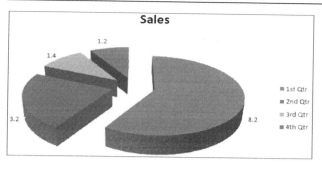

Figure 10-31 Pie chart

Create An Area Chart

1. Open the My charts document if it is not already open, then add a page break below the second chart.

2. Insert tab ⇒ Illustrations group ⇒ Chart, then select the 4th area chart option and click OK.

3. Delete the contents of the spreadsheet, then open the Bigger Balance Sheet spreadsheet.

4. Copy and paste the range A4 to C9 to the spreadsheet for the chart.

5. Delete rows 2 and 3, then close Excel.

6. Design tab ⇒ Data group ⇒ Select Data. Click the Switch Row/Column button, then click OK. Yes, I know that there is a Switch Row/Column option in the Data group, but for this chart it was not enabled for me, so I did the next best thing <smile>.

7. Design tab ⇒ Chart Layouts group. Select the second chart layout in the second row, then select a chart style.

8. Your chart should look similar to the one shown in Figure 10-32.

    Save the changes.

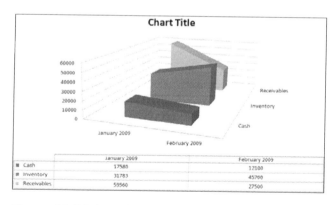

Figure 10-32 Area chart

Charting Data In Different Ways

What you may not have noticed while creating the charts in this chapter is that charts are created based on how the data is organized. Figure 10-33 shows the same data organized two different ways. If column charts were created based on the data, they would look like the ones shown in Figure 10-34.

As you can see, the chart on the left is grouped by month and the chart on the right is grouped by region. If you do not create the chart that you were looking for or expecting, you can try clicking on the Switch Row/Column button on the Chart Tools Design tab.

Keep in mind that if the data for the chart has more rows than columns, the first column of data will be used for the X axis. If the data for the chart has the same number of rows and columns or more columns then rows, the first row of data will be used for the X axis.

If the data for April was deleted, both charts would have grouped the charts the same way. While the charts shown in Figure 10-34 resemble each other, if another chart type like the Scatter chart was selected, the charts would be harder to read.

▲	A	B	C	D	E	F	G	H	I	J	K
1		January	February	March	April			North	South	East	West
2	North	$123,000.00	$150,000.00	$188,000.00	$220,500.00		January	$123,000.00	$424,000.00	$394,000.00	$210,000.00
3	South	$424,000.00	$400,000.00	$247,000.00	$575,000.00		February	$150,000.00	$400,000.00	$375,000.00	$225,000.00
4	East	$394,000.00	$375,000.00	$340,000.00	$112,500.00		March	$188,000.00	$247,000.00	$340,000.00	$299,000.00
5	West	$210,000.00	$225,000.00	$299,000.00	$499,000.00		April	$220,500.00	$575,000.00	$112,500.00	$499,000.00

Figure 10-33 Same data charted differently

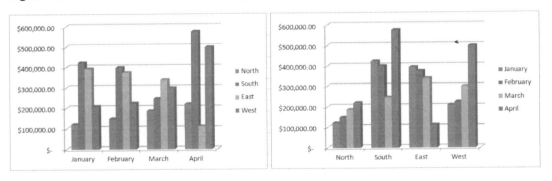

Figure 10-34 Column charts

THE FILE TAB

Overview This chapter covers the options on the File tab in Excel.
The following topics are also covered.

- ☑ Excel workspace
- ☑ Excel Options dialog box
- ☑ Parts of a spreadsheet explained
- ☑ Selecting cells, rows and columns
- ☑ Inserting and deleting rows and columns

Overview

Excel is primarily used to store raw numeric data that will be used for budgets or invoices for example. The spreadsheets often have formulas or functions for analysis purposes. Examples of formulas include costs by region, totals and averages. Excel is also used to create charts, which are a graphical presentation of the data. The other features that make Excel popular are it's pivot tables and goal seek analysis functionality. Sadly, these two features are not available in Excel Starter.

Figure 11-1 shows a basic spreadsheet.

Figure 11-2 shows an intermediate level spreadsheet. Hopefully, these figures let you know that spreadsheets can be basic or have some flair and still get the job done.

	A	B	C	D	E	F
1						
2						
3						
4						
5	Name Of Book	Quantity	Cost	Markup %	Sale Price	Book Profiit
6						
7	Learning Multimedia	8	$12.00	0.05	12.60	0.60
8	The New Way To Surf	7	$6.98	0.04	7.26	0.28
9	Excel Made Easy	9	$9.95	0.09	10.85	0.90
10	Learning Excel	4	$7.98	0.075	8.58	0.60
11	Surfing The Net	12	$5.95	0.03	6.13	0.18
12						
13	# Of Titles On Hand	5				
14						
15	Average Markup			0.057		

Figure 11-1 Basic spreadsheet

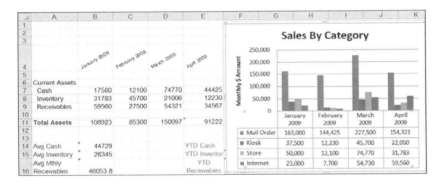

Figure 11-2 Intermediate level spreadsheet

Workbook vs Sheet vs Worksheet vs Spreadsheet

These are terms that are often used interchangeably, even though they refer to different things.

A **WORKBOOK** is the entire Excel file, which includes the tabs and sheets of information.

A **SHEET** or **WORKSHEET** is the information on one tab in the workbook. You can put data on each worksheet. The data on each worksheet does not have to be related or similar to data on any other worksheet in the workbook.

A **SPREADSHEET** is another name used for a workbook, but many people including yours truly use the term spreadsheet instead of sheet or worksheet.

What's New In Excel Starter 2010

What you will notice that's new, depends on the previous version of Excel that you used, if any. The older the version that you are upgrading from, the more new features you will notice. The following list does not include all of the new features in the full version of Excel 2010, just some of those that are available in Excel Starter.

Conditional Formatting provides more control for formatting data.

Sparklines are charts in the background of a cell that represents the data from other cells on the spreadsheet. Sparklines can help you see trends or patterns in the data.

Search Filter Is used to help find specific data in a workbook.

Paste with live preview Is used to see how the various paste options will display the data being copied.

Backstage View, Recover documents and **Share and access documents online**
[See Chapter 1, What's New In Word Starter 2010]

Getting Started With Excel Starter

If you have used Excel 2007, the look and feel of Excel Starter will not be that much different and this chapter will be a refresher. If the last version of Excel that you used was version 2003 or if you have never used Excel, you need to read this chapter. The majority of the features that you have used in prior versions are still in Excel Starter, they are just in a different place.

Excel Starter 2010 vs Excel 2010

Below are some of the features that are not in Excel Starter that are available in the full version of Excel. If you open a spreadsheet that already has incorporated some of the options listed below, you may be able to view them, but you will not be able to create them from scratch.

① Cannot create SmartArt graphics and signature lines.
② Cannot create Pivot tables, Pivot charts and slicers.
③ The Freeze Panes option is not available.
④ Cannot add comments to cells.
⑤ Cannot create a connection to external data or create a data table.
⑥ Goal seek analysis is not available.
⑦ Cannot create macros or VBA code.

Excel Starter Workspace

Figure 11-3 shows the Excel Starter 2010 workspace. Table 11-1 explains the features illustrated in the workspace.

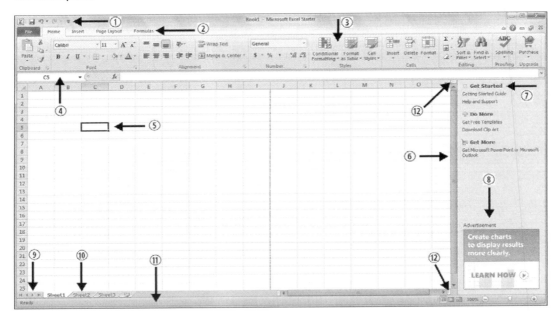

Figure 11-3 Excel Starter workspace (in Normal view)

Option	Description
1	The Quick Access toolbar. (1)
2	The **TABS** are used to navigate the Ribbon to display the options.
3	The **RIBBON** is the navigation tool in Excel.
4	**NAME BOX** Displays the first selected cell or Range Name of the selected cells.
5	The **CELL** is where you enter the data in the spreadsheet.
6	**SCROLL BAR** Right-clicking on the vertical scroll bar displays a shortcut menu. [See Chapter 1, Figure 1-5]
7	**HELP AND SUPPORT** opens the Microsoft Office support page on Microsoft's web site.
8	**ADVERTISEMENT SECTION** [See Chapter 1, Table 1-1]
9	**NAVIGATION BUTTONS** Are used to display tabs that are not currently visible in the workspace. If the workbook has a lot of worksheets, you may not be able to see all of the tabs. If that is the case, you can use the navigation buttons to display more tabs or you can display all of the tabs by right-clicking on any of the navigation buttons, as shown in Figure 11-4 and select the tab that you want to view.
10	**TABS** Are used to display different sheets in the workbook.
11	The **STATUS BAR** contains information about the spreadsheet. The spreadsheet view and Zoom percent can also be changed in the status bar.
12	The **HORIZONTAL** and **VERTICAL SPLITTER BARS** are used to divide the spreadsheet into two sections.

Table 11-1 Excel Starter workspace options explained

. . . .

(1) The right arrow on the Quick Access toolbar is called **REDO**, not Repeat, like it is in Word. The Redo option reapplies the last action that was undone. Unlike the Repeat option in word, the Redo option lets you select a specific action from the list to redo.

20		
21		Sheet1
22		Sheet2
23		Sheet3
24		Sheet4
25		Sheet5
26	✓	Sheet6

Figure 11-4 Navigation buttons shortcut menu

Status Bar

Figure 11-5 shows the status bar, which is at the bottom of the workspace. The options are explained in Table 11-2.

Figure 11-5 Status bar

Option	Description
1	**PAGE NUMBER** Displays the page number that the insertion point is on and the total number of pages that the worksheet has.
2	**VIEW** The options in this section are used to select how the spreadsheet is displayed in the workspace. The options are explained below.
3	**ZOOM** The options in this section are used to change the size of the cells displayed on the screen. The default is 100%. Sliding the button to the left will reduce the size of the cells on the screen to a minimum of 10%. Sliding the button to the right will increase the size of the cells to a maximum of 400%. Clicking on the zoom level (the percent) opens the dialog shown in Figure 11-8.

Table 11-2 Status bar options explained

View Options

There are several ways to view spreadsheets, as explained below.

①   **NORMAL** This is the default view when a spreadsheet is opened, as shown earlier in Figure 11-3.
②   **PAGE LAYOUT** Displays the spreadsheet as it will look when printed. This view displays the header and footer sections if the spreadsheet has them, as shown in Figure 11-6.
③   **PAGE BREAK PREVIEW** Displays the spreadsheet with page breaks, as shown in Figure 11-7.

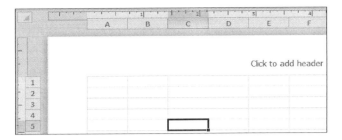

Figure 11-6 Page Layout view

	A	B	C	D	E	F	G	H	I	J	K	L	M
1	Current Assets												
2	Cash	17580	12100	74770	44425	74770	17580	44425	12500	343434	17580	74770	17580
3	Inventory	31783	45700	21006	12230	21006	37874	12230	45700	12230	31783	21750	31783
4	Receivables	59560	27500	54321	34567	54321	59560	44567	27500	34567	12345	54321	59560
5													
6	Total Assets	108923	85300	150097	91222	150097	115014	101222	85700	390231	61708	150841	108923
7													
8													
9	Avg Cash	44729			YTD Cash	223645							
10	Avg Inventory	26345			YTD Inventory	325075							
11	Avg Mthly Receivables	46053.8			YTD Receivables	522689							
12													
13	Income												
14	Mail Order	163,000	144,425	227,500	154,321	144,725	53,000	12,540	27,500	44,425	254,321	27,500	63,000
15	Kiosk	37,500	12,230	45,700	22,050	12,230	57,500	21,006	45,700	12,230	21,006	45,700	57,500
16	Store	50,000	12,100	74,770	31,783	12,100	50,000	31,783	74,770	12,100	31,783	74,770	50,500
17	Internet	23,000	7,700	54,730	59,560	7,700	23,000	59,560	54,730	7,500	62,600	43,850	23,000
18													
19	Total Income	273,500	176,455	402,700	267,714	176,755	183,500	124,889	202,700	76,255	369,710	191,820	194,000

Figure 11-7 Page Break Preview view

Zoom Dialog Box Options

The options shown in Figure 11-8 are used to select a pre-defined or custom percent.

The **FIT SELECTION** option is used when the spreadsheet has data that is not visible on the screen. Select the portion of the spreadsheet that you want to zoom in on, then select this option. For this option to work properly, you need to select a rather large portion of the spreadsheet.

Select the **CUSTOM** option if none of the preset options are what you need. You can type in the percent that you want.

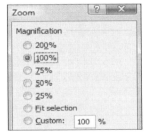

Figure 11-8 Zoom dialog box

Status Bar Customization Options

The status bar can be customized by right-clicking on an empty space on it and adding or removing the options shown in Figure 11-9. The items that are checked are enabled.

Splitting A Spreadsheet

As illustrated earlier in Figure 11-3, there are two splitter bars. This feature is used to split the spreadsheet horizontally, vertically or both. Doing this allows you to view different parts of the worksheet at the same time. For example, if you want to view rows 1-10 and rows 75-81 at the same time, you would split the worksheet horizontally.

Excel Starter does not have the Freeze Panes option, like the full version of Excel has, but you could use the splitter bars to emulate that functionality because the horizontal and vertical splitter bars can be used on the same worksheet.

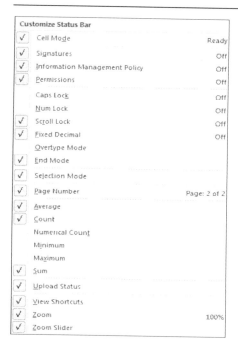

Figure 11-9 Status Bar customization options

Splitting A Spreadsheet Horizontally

The steps below show you how to split a spreadsheet horizontally.

1. Open the spreadsheet that you want to split.

2. Place the mouse pointer over the Horizontal Splitter bar, then drag the bar down to where you want to split the spreadsheet. As you are dragging the bar down you will see a gray bar, as illustrated in Figure 11-10.

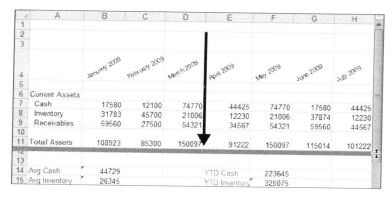

Figure 11-10 Horizontal Splitter bar illustrated

3. Release the mouse button.

The spreadsheet should look similar to the one shown in Figure 11-11.

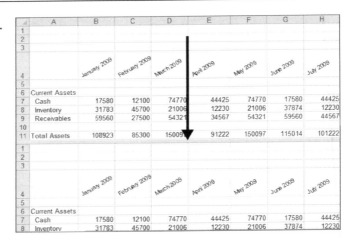

Figure 11-11 Spreadsheet split horizontally

 Changing The Location Of The Splitter Bar
If the splitter bar is not exactly where you need it, click on it and drag it in the direction that will give you the split that you need.

As you can see, the spreadsheet now has two panes, which work independently of each other. You can scroll in one pane and the other pane will not move. Each pane contains the entire spreadsheet. It is like have two copies of the spreadsheet open at the same time. Any change that you make in one pane is also applied to the spreadsheet in the other pane. If you save the spreadsheet with a splitter bar enabled, when you reopen the spreadsheet the splitter bar will still be there.

Removing The Split

There are two ways to remove the split, as explained below.

① Double-click on the splitter bar in the spreadsheet.
② Drag the splitter bar back to the location that you dragged it from.

Quick Access Toolbar

[See Chapter 1, Quick Access Toolbar]

The Ribbon

The Ribbon, as shown in Figure 11-12 is the heart of Excel. It is the navigation system. The Ribbon replaces the menu and toolbars in Excel 2003. The purpose of the Ribbon is to make it easier to find options because more options are visible by default.

Figure 11-12 The Excel Ribbon

Getting Help Using Excel Starter

[See Chapter 1, Getting Help Using Word Starter]

File Tab

The File tab (also called the **BACKSTAGE VIEW**) shown in Figure 11-13 replaces the File menu in Excel 2003 and the Microsoft Office Button in Excel 2007. The commands and panels are explained below.

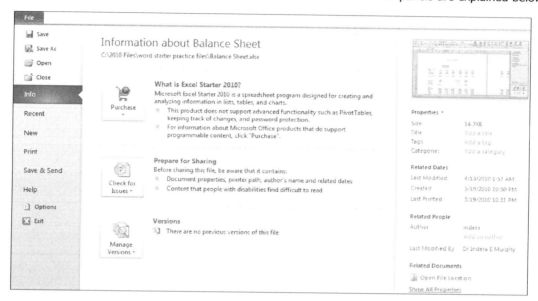

File 11-13 File tab

File Tab Commands

[See Chapter 2, File Tab Commands]

Saving Spreadsheets In Excel 97-2003 Format

If you save an Excel 2010 spreadsheet in the old file format, the **COMPATIBILITY CHECKER** will run automatically, unless you disable it. If there are features that are not supported, you will see the dialog box shown in Figure 11-14. The dialog box displays Excel 2010 features that are not supported in the old file format.

The **COPY TO NEW SHEET** button will display the summary information shown in Figure 11-14 on a new worksheet in the workbook, as shown in Figure 11-15.

This is similar to clicking on the **FIND** link on the Compatibility Checker dialog box, which highlights the row numbers that have a cell with a compatibility error.

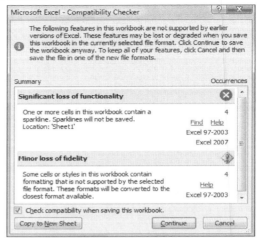

Figure 11-14 Compatibility Checker dialog box

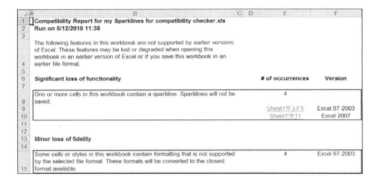

Figure 11-15 Compatibility report

File Tab Panels

[See Chapter 2, File Tab Panels]

Excel Options Dialog Box

Selecting the **OPTIONS** option on the File tab displays the dialog box shown in Figure 11-16. The options on this dialog box are used to customize the options that are set for Excel when Office Starter was installed. If you encounter a feature that is not working the way that you think it should, this would be a good place to look.

General Panel

The options shown in Figure 11-16 are used throughout Excel.

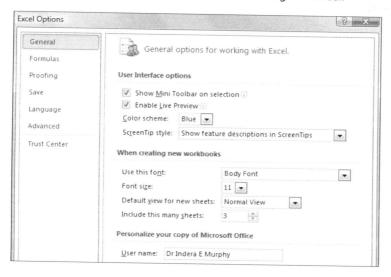

Figure 11-16 General panel

User Interface Options [See Chapter 2, General Panel]

When Creating New Workbooks

The options in this section are used to select the defaults for new workbooks that you create.

USE THIS FONT Select the font that you want to use as the default font in Excel for new spreadsheets.

FONT SIZE Select the font size that you want to be the default font size in Excel for new spreadsheets.

DEFAULT VIEW FOR NEW SHEETS [See View Options, earlier in this chapter]

INCLUDE THIS MANY SHEETS Select the number of sheets for new workbooks. If the majority of workbooks that you will create only use one sheet, select one because it will reduce the file size a little. If you need more sheets, you can add them in the workbook.

Personalize Your Copy Of Microsoft Office [See Chapter 2, General Panel]

Formulas Panel

The options shown in Figure 11-17 are used to customize formulas and error handling.

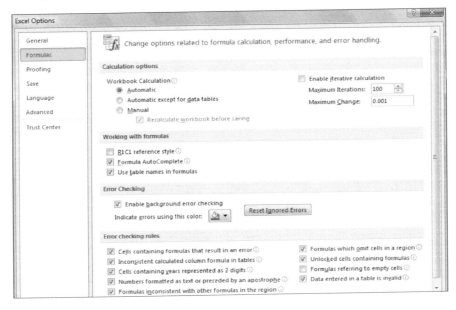

Figure 11-17 Formulas panel

The **Calculation Options** are used to select when and how formulas are recalculated.

The **AUTOMATIC** option recalculates the formulas each time the data is changed.

The **MANUAL** option forces you to use the Calculate Now command or to press the F9 key to recalculate the formulas.

The **WORKING WITH FORMULAS** options are used to select how formulas are created and displayed.

If checked, the **R1C1 REFERENCE STYLE** option causes the rows and columns to be referenced by numbers. For example, R3C2 is row 3, column 2, which references cell B3.

When this option is enabled, the column headers are numeric, as shown in Figure 11-18, instead of letters.

Figure 11-18 R1C1 reference style option enabled

This option probably is not used often. The one time that it may be helpful is for spreadsheets that have a lot of columns. The first 26 columns use one letter. Column 27 is AA. Can you imagine trying to figure out what letters column 75 uses? If this option is enabled, you will see R10C75.

> **R1C1 Reference Style Option**
> This option is spreadsheet specific. This means that if you save a spreadsheet with the option enabled and email the spreadsheet to someone, they will see the R1C1 format, even if that is not the reference style that they normally use.

FORMULA AUTO COMPLETE turns on the AutoComplete functionality.

USE TABLE NAMES IN FORMULAS If checked, you can use the name of the table in a formula.

Error Checking Options The options in this section are used to enable error checking and select the color that the error symbols should be displayed in.

Error Checking Rules The options in this section are the formula errors that you can select to be notified of in the spreadsheet.

Proofing Panel

The options shown in Figure 11-19 are used to select default spell check and AutoCorrect options. [See Chapter 2, Proofing Panel]

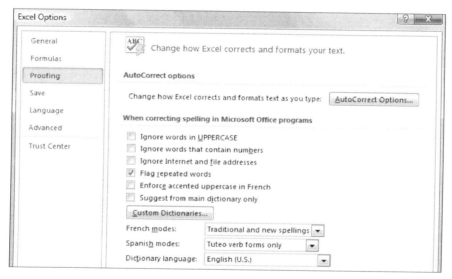

Figure 11-19 Proofing panel

Save Panel

The options shown in Figure 11-20 are used to select options for saving and recovering workbooks.

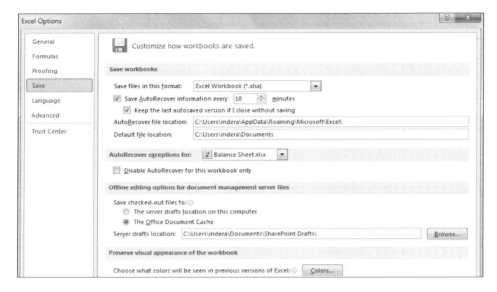

Figure 11-20 Save panel

Save Workbooks Options [See Chapter 2, Save Panel]

SAVE DATE AND TIME VALUES USING ISO 8601 DATE FORMAT If checked, XML files will be saved in ISO 8601 format. [See http://en.wikipedia.org/wiki/ISO_8601 for more information on this standard]

Auto Recover Exceptions For Options

DISABLE AUTO RECOVER FOR THIS WORKBOOK ONLY If checked, the Auto Recover functionality will be disabled for the workbook that is selected in the drop-down list.

Offline Editing Options For Document Management Server Files

[See Chapter 2, Offline Editing Options For Document Management Server Files]

Preserve Visual Appearance Of The Workbook Options

CHOOSE WHAT COLORS WILL BE SEEN IN PREVIOUS VERSIONS OF EXCEL If an Excel 2010 workbook is opened in a previous version of Excel, the colors will be mapped to the closest color match available in the previous version of Excel. Clicking the **COLORS** button shown above in Figure 11-20 opens the dialog box shown in Figure 11-21, which has the map color options.

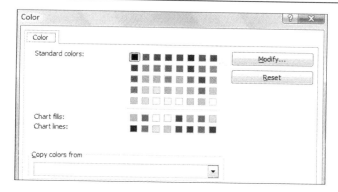

Figure 11-21 Color (mapping) dialog box

Language Panel

The options shown in Figure 11-22 are used to select language preferences. [See Chapter 2, Language Panel]

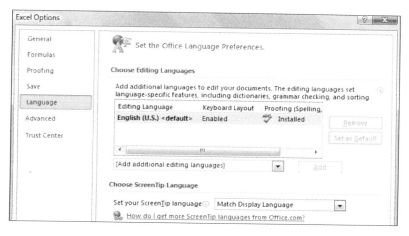

Figure 11-22 Language panel

Advanced Panel

The options shown in Figures 11-23, 11-25 to 11-28 are used to set defaults for options that you may use and are not aware that they can be changed.

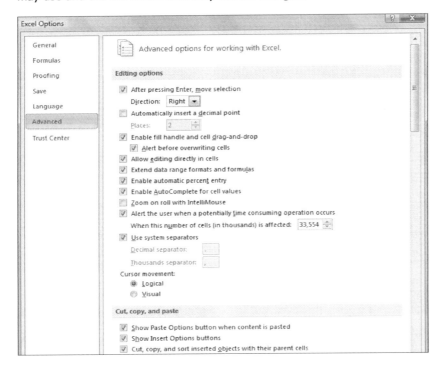

Figure 11-23 Advanced panel

Editing Options

AFTER PRESSING ENTER, MOVE SELECTION If checked, open the Direction drop-down list and select which cell you want the cursor in after you press Enter in the spreadsheet.

AUTOMATICALLY INSERT A DECIMAL POINT If checked, in the Places field select how many digits from the left of the number that you want the decimal point to be placed. This means that all numbers that you enter in spreadsheets will have a decimal point, which may not be what you want.

ENABLE FILL HANDLE AND CELL DRAG-AND-DROP
If checked, this option allows you to fill cells by dragging the handle (the square in the lower right corner of the cell) illustrated in Figure 11-24 to adjacent cells.

Figure 11-24 Fill handle

Cut, Copy And Paste Options The options in this section provide additional functionality for the clipboard.

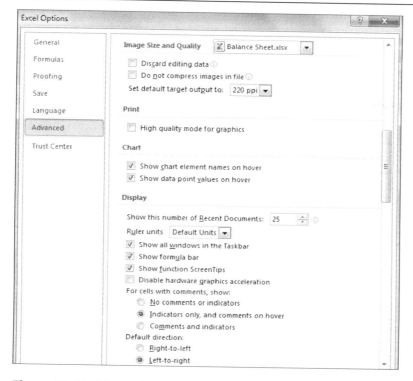

Figure 11-25 Advanced panel (Continued)

Image Size And Quality Options The options in this section are used to select image options. If the majority of spreadsheets that have images are printed, you should select the highest layout output. By design you cannot save the option selected in this drop-down list or any other drop-down list like this one.

Display Options
The options in this section are used to select the non document items that are displayed in the workspace.

SHOW THIS NUMBER OF RECENT DOCUMENTS [See Chapter 2, Advanced Panel Display Options]

RULER UNITS Is used to select the unit of measurement for the ruler.

FOR CELLS WITH COMMENTS, SHOW Is used to select how you want comments in cells displayed on the spreadsheet.

Display Options For This Workbook The options in this section are used to select the features that you want displayed in the workbook.

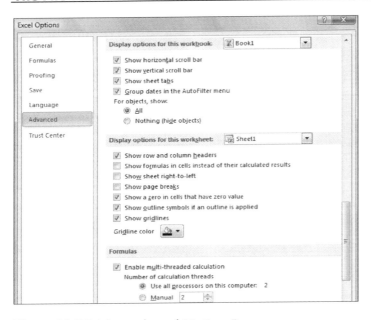

Figure 11-26 Advanced panel (Continued)

Display Options For This Worksheet

The options in this section are used to select worksheet features that you want displayed in the workspace.

The **SHOW FORMULAS IN CELLS INSTEAD OF THEIR CALCULATED RESULTS** option would be more useful on a tab because it would be easier to enable/disable.

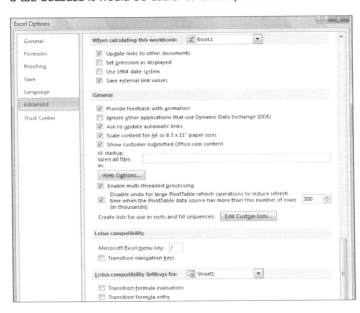

Figure 11-27 Advanced panel (Continued)

When Calculating This Workbook The options in this section are used to select how values in the spreadsheet are updated.

General Options

SCALE CONTENT FOR A4 OR 8.5x11 PAPER SIZES [See Chapter 2, Print Options]

AT STARTUP, OPEN ALL FILES IN If there are spreadsheets that you use almost daily, put them in the same folder and enter the full folder path in this field. Every time that you open Excel, the spreadsheets in the folder will open automatically.

EDIT CUSTOM LISTS This option (button) opens the Custom Lists dialog box, which is used to create new lists and edit existing ones.

Trust Center Panel

[See Chapter 2, Trust Center Panel]

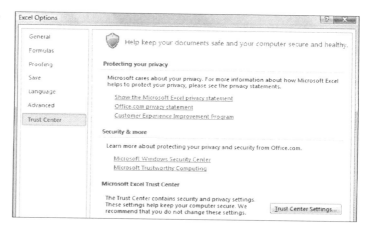

Figure 11-28 Trust Center panel

Excel File Format Options

When Office 2007 was launched, so were new file formats for Excel. Like Word, if you are going to save a spreadsheet in an old file format, you should also save a copy in the new file format because the old file formats do not support the new features and functionality in Excel 2010. Table 11-3 explains the file formats.

Format	Description
.xlsx	This is the format used for most spreadsheets. It replaces the **.XLS** format in Excel 2003. It reduces the file size because it uses zip file compression. This compression creates several files, mostly XML files, from your spreadsheet.
.xltx	This format is for templates. It replaces the **.XLT** format in Excel 2003.
.xltm	This format is for a template that has macros.
.xlsm	This format is for workbooks that have macros.
.xlsb	This file format is similar to the .xlsx format. The difference is that it doesn't use XML. Date is saved in binary format. Select this file format for really large spreadsheets that take a long time to open.

Table 11-3 Excel file formats explained

Parts Of A Spreadsheet

Figure 11-29 illustrates the parts of a spreadsheet. Table 11-4 explains each option that is illustrated.

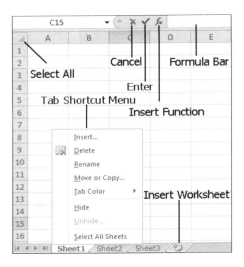

Figure 11-29 Parts of a spreadsheet illustrated

Option	Description
Select All	Clicking in this square will select (highlight) the entire spreadsheet.
Formula Bar	Is used to view, create and edit formulas or data. Using this field is the same as typing in a cell. When you click in the formula bar, the Cancel and Enter buttons appear.
Cancel	Deletes the information that you just entered in the spreadsheet.
Enter	Works the same as pressing the Enter key.
Insert Function	Is used to select a function from the Insert Function dialog box to add to the cell.
Tab Shortcut Menu	The options on this menu are explained in Table 11-5.
Insert Worksheet	Click this button to add a worksheet to the workbook.

Table 11-4 Parts of a spreadsheet explained

Spreadsheet Tab Shortcut Menu

 Many of the options on the Tab shortcut menu are also on the Home tab.

Option	Description
Insert	Opens the dialog box shown in Figure 11-30.
Delete	Deletes the selected tab from the workbook. This option cannot be undone, unless you close the workbook and do not save the changes.
Rename	Is used to give the selected sheet a new name. When selected, the current name of the sheet will be highlighted. Type in the new name that you want. Worksheet names can be up to 31 characters.

Table 11-5 Spreadsheet tab shortcut menu options explained

Option	Description
Move or Copy	Opens the dialog box shown in Figure 11-31. The options are used to reorder and copy sheets in the workbook. Worksheets that are copied are automatically given the same name as the one it was copied from plus a number in parenthesis. For example, if you copy Sheet 5, the name of the copied sheet is Sheet 5(2). You can rename sheets that are moved or copied.
Tab Color	Opens the color palette so that you can select or create a background color for the tab.
Hide	Hides the selected worksheets.
Unhide	Displays the hidden worksheets.
Select All Sheets	Select this option when you want to make the same change to all of the sheets in the workbook.

Table 11-5 Spreadsheet tab shortcut menu options explained (Continued)

The options on this dialog box are used to add objects to the spreadsheet.

The options on the **SPREADSHEET SOLUTIONS** tab are templates. When you select one, a new worksheet is added to the workbook with the template.

Figure 11-30 Insert dialog box

The **TO BOOK** drop-down list contains all open workbooks, plus an option to create a new workbook. Select the workbook that you want to move or copy the selected worksheet(s) to.

The **BEFORE SHEET** options are used to select which sheet you want to put the selected sheet before in the workbook that you selected.

The **(MOVE TO END)** option will move or copy the selected sheet after all of the other sheets in the workbook that you selected.

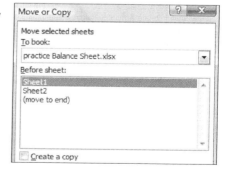

Figure 11-31 Move or Copy dialog box

The **CREATE A COPY** option will create a copy of the selected sheet and place it where you specified in the Before Sheet section.

Moving Sheets In The Workbook
Instead of opening the Move or Copy dialog box to rearrange the sheets in the workbook, click on the tab for the sheet that you want to move, then drag the tab to a new location.

Grouping Sheets

If you use more than one sheet in a workbook, in addition to moving the sheets, you may have the need to make the same change on more than one sheet. The types of changes that you can make include adding and formatting text, hiding and moving sheets, copying and pasting content, and adding header and footer content.

To group sheets, click on the first tab that you want to group.

Press and hold down the CTRL key, then click on the other tabs that you want in the group.

The Title bar will have [Group] in it, as shown in Figure 11-32. The tabs in the group will have a white background.

When you are finished changing the content on the sheets, click on a tab that is not in the group or right-click on a tab and select UNGROUP.

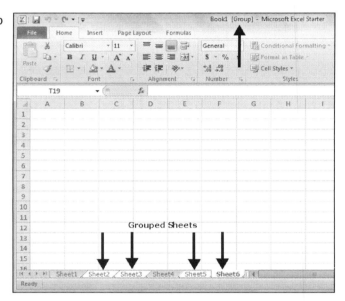

Figure 11-32 Grouped sheets illustrated

Selecting Cells, Rows And Columns

Selecting Cells

To select a cell, put the cursor in the cell that you want to enter new information in or edit existing information. This is sometimes called HIGHLIGHTING a cell.

In the upper left corner of the spreadsheet you will see the cell address, cell name or range name of what you have selected, as shown in Figure 11-33. In the figure, cell B3 is selected.

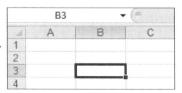

Figure 11-33 Cell selected and cell address

 A cell can contain up to 32,000 characters.

Selecting Rows

To select an entire row, click on the row number on the left side of the spreadsheet. Figure 11-34 shows that row 2 is selected.

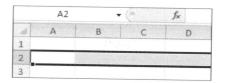

Figure 11-34 Row 2 selected

Selecting Columns

To select an entire column click on the column letter, which is also called the column heading, as shown in Figure 11-35.

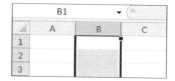

Figure 11-35 Column B selected

Select A Range Of Cells

You can select a group of adjacent cells. If you wanted to select the range A2 to D5, (which includes the following cells; A2, A3, A4, A5, B2, B3, B4, B5, C2, C3, C4, C5, D2, D3, D4 and D5) click in cell A2, hold down the left mouse button and drag the mouse across to column D and then down to row 5. Your spreadsheet would look like the one shown in Figure 11-36.

Throughout the Excel chapters, you will see instructions like: **SELECT THE RANGE A2 TO D5**. This means that you should select the cells that are in the range, similar to what is shown in Figure 11-36.

It would be nice if the cell range was displayed in the Name box so that you could double check to make sure that you selected the correct range.

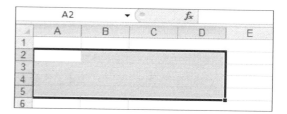

Figure 11-36 Cell range A2 to D5 selected

Select Cells Using The Keyboard

The easiest way that I know how to select cells without using a mouse is to follow the steps below.

1. Place the cursor in the first cell of the range that you want to select, then press and hold down the **SHIFT** key.

2. Use the arrow keys on your keyboard to move to the right and then down to select the cells in the range that you need. After you have selected all of the cells, release the Shift key.

(1)

Range Selection Shortcuts
This tips listed below are other ways that you can select a range of cells.
① In the instructions above, instead of holding down the Shift key, you can press the **F8** key. If you use the F8 key, you do not have to hold the F8 key down like you do the Shift key to select cells.
② Click in the top left cell of the range that you want to select. Press and hold down the Shift key, then click in the bottom right cell of the range that you want to select.

Create Your First Spreadsheet

Spreadsheets can have up to 1,048,576 rows and 16,384 columns. While not a requirement, it is good practice to only put one piece of information in each cell. For example, you can put a persons first and last name in the same cell, but the standard is to use one column for the first name and another column for the last name. You have thousands of columns at your disposal, so you might as well use them <smile>. Another reason to put each piece of information in it's own cell is it may make it easier to sort and filter the information.

1. Open a new spreadsheet if one is not already open.
   Type Actual Sales vs Projections in cell A1, then press Enter.

2. Type Actual in cell B3, then type Projected Sales in cell C3.

In addition to entering or modifying existing data in a cell, you can add or modify data in the Formula bar which was illustrated earlier in Figure 11-29.

3. Add the data in Table 11-6 to the spreadsheet. When you are finished, your spreadsheet should look like the one shown in Figure 11-37.

Cell	Data
A4	North
A5	South
A6	East
A7	West
B4	123000
B5	424000
B6	394000
B7	210000
C4	150000
C5	400000
C6	375000
C7	225000

Table 11-6 Data to add to the spreadsheet

	A	B	C
1	Actual Sales vs Projections		
2			
3		Actual	Projected Sales
4	North	123000	150000
5	South	424000	400000
6	East	394000	375000
7	West	210000	225000

Figure 11-37 Actual Sales vs Projections spreadsheet

Change The Column Width

You may often find that the default column width size does not meet your needs. The Projected Sales title in cell C3 is an example of this. There are several ways to adjust the column width. The easiest way is to drag the column border to the right to make the column wider. Another way is to open the Column Width dialog box. You can type in the width that you want.

1. Place the mouse pointer on the line between columns C and D, as illustrated above in Figure 11-37. The mouse pointer will change to a double headed arrow. Hold down the left mouse button and drag the mouse to the right until it is past the end of the Projected Sales title.

2. Save the spreadsheet. Type `Actual Sales vs Projected` as the file name.

Change The Row Height

Just like the column width can be changed, the row height can also be changed.

1. Place the mouse pointer on the line between rows 3 and 4, as illustrated in Figure 11-38.

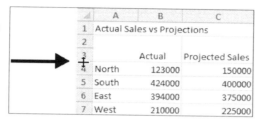

Figure 11-38 Mouse pointer in position to change the row height

2. Hold down the left mouse button and drag the mouse pointer down to the middle of row 4.

Insert Rows

1. Right-click on row 4 (in the light blue area on the left) and select **INSERT**. There should be a blank row between the column titles and the first row of data.

Insert Columns

1. Right-click on column B and select **INSERT**. There should be a blank column after column A.

Delete A Column

1. Right-click on the column heading (in this example, column B) that you want to delete and select **DELETE**. Deleting a row works the same way.

Number Formats

When you enter numbers in a spreadsheet, no formatting is applied by default. You can add commas, dollar and percent signs. You can also format dates and times. The numbers in columns B and C would look better and be easier to read if they were formatted.

1. Select the range B5 to C8, as shown in Figure 11-39, then right-click on the highlighted cells and select Format Cells. You will see the dialog box shown in Figure 11-40.

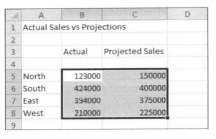

Figure 11-39 Cells selected to format

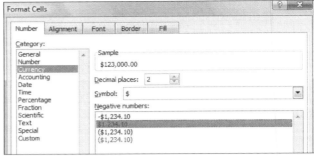

Figure 11-40 Format Cells dialog box

 Home tab ⇒ Cells group ⇒ Format ⇒ Format Cells, will also open the Format Cells dialog box.

The default number of decimal places is two. It is probably a good idea to show negative numbers in red on the spreadsheet in case you enter negative numbers or create formulas that could produce negative numbers. Selecting the second option in the Negative numbers section forces negative numbers to appear in red on the spreadsheet.

2. Click on the Currency category, then select the second option in the Negative Numbers section, as shown above in Figure 11-40.

3. The Format Cells dialog box also allows you to modify alignment, font, border and fill options. Click on each of the tabs now so that you can become familiar with the options. The options selected on each tab are the default formatting options.

4. Click OK. You may see the pound sign in column B, as shown in Figure 11-41.

   The pound signs let you know that the data in the cell is too large for the width of the cell.

	A	B	C
1	Actual Sales vs Projections		
2			
3		Actual	Projected Sales
4			
5	North	#########	$150,000.00
6	South	#########	$400,000.00
7	East	#########	$375,000.00
8	West	#########	$225,000.00

Figure 11-41 Cell width that is too small

5. Place the mouse pointer between columns B and C, then double-click. Save the changes.

Entering Content Into Cells

If you have used Excel before, you may have noticed some or all of the topics covered in this section. If you have not used Excel before, you may find this section interesting. Keep the following in mind to help understand how Excel interprets what is entered in a cell.

① If you type an apostrophe in the cell and then type a number, the number is treated as text. A green triangle is displayed in the upper left corner of the cell, as shown in the top left corner of Figure 11-42. You will see a button with an exclamation point. If you click on the arrow on the button, you will see the drop-down list shown. The options are used to select what if anything you want to do about the content in the cell. The green triangle is Excels way of letting you know that the content in the cell may have an error.

② If you type an apostrophe in the cell and then type a date like 9-8-01, you will see the menu options shown in Figure 11-43.

③ Cells with a single comma or decimal point are treated as a number. If you enter 9,8,7 or 9.8.7 in a cell, the cell will be treated as text.

④ If you enter A61 or 61A in a cell, it is treated as text.

⑤ Cells with a dash or slash are treated as a date. Therefore, typing 9-8-1 or 9/8/1 will automatically be displayed as the date 9/8/2001.

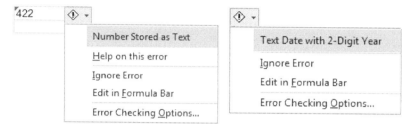

Figure 11-42 Cell content numeric warning fix options

Figure 11-43 Cell content text warning fix options

Replacing And Editing Data

As good as we think we are, from time to time we all make typos and need to change the data. There are two options for changing data as discussed below.

① **Replace Data** Use this option when the data in the cell is not what you want. To replace the data, click in the cell and start typing. The existing data in the cell will automatically be deleted.

② **Edit Data** Use this option when you only need to change some of the data in a cell. To edit the data in a cell, click in the cell, then press the F2 key or double-click in the cell. The other option is to click in the formula, select the data that you want to change and start typing. When you are finished editing, press the Enter key. If you do not want to keep the changes and want the original content back, press the ESC (Escape) key.

Using The Arrow Keys For Editing
When in edit mode, you can use the arrow keys to move around in the cell or move around in the formula bar.

THE HOME TAB

Overview

In addition to learning about the options on the Home tab, you will learn about the following:

- ☑ Spreadsheet mini toolbar and shortcut menu options
- ☑ Conditional formatting
- ☑ Sorting data in a spreadsheet

Overview

The options on the Home tab are used to format and edit spreadsheets. Many of the options on this tab are the same as the ones on the Home tab in Word.

Spreadsheet Mini Toolbar And Shortcut Menu

The toolbar shown in Figure 12-1 appears when you right-click on a cell. Unlike the mini toolbar in Word that first appears transparent, the mini toolbar in Excel does not.

Many of the options on the Home tab are on the shortcut menu shown in Figure 12-2. To access this shortcut menu, right-click on the spreadsheet. The first section of the menu has options from the Clipboard group that you will learn about later in this chapter. The other options are explained in Table 12-1.

Figure 12-1 Spreadsheet mini toolbar

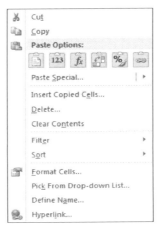

Figure 12-2 Spreadsheet shortcut menu

Spreadsheet Shortcut Menu Options

Option	Description
Insert Copied Cells	Adds cells to the row or column that is selected and then pastes the cells that were copied into the new cells. This option does not over write existing data. If no cells are selected prior to opening the shortcut menu, you will see the **INSERT** option on the shortcut menu instead. This option opens the dialog box shown in Figure 12-3. The options are used to move cells to the right, down or add rows or columns.
Delete	Deletes the contents of the selected cells and opens the Delete dialog box. The options on the dialog box are used to shift cells, delete a row or column, similar to the options on the Insert dialog box shown in Figure 12-3.
Clear Contents	Deletes the information in the selected cells but not the formatting that has been added to the cell.

Table 12-1 Spreadsheet shortcut menu options explained

Option	Description
Filter	Displays the options shown in Figure 12-4. The options are used to display a subset of all of the data on the spreadsheet, by temporarily hiding data that does not meet the filters criteria.
Sort	The options shown in Figure 12-5 are used to rearrange the order of the data.
Format Cells	Opens the Format Cells dialog box. [See Cells Group, later in this chapter]
Pick From Drop-Down List	This option is suppose to display a drop-down list in the selected cell. I could not get an answer on whether or not this option is disabled in Excel Starter.
Define Name	Is used to create a range name for the selected cells.
Hyperlink	Is used to create a link to an image, web page or document.

Table 12-1 Spreadsheet shortcut menu options explained (Continued)

If you select more than one row or column before opening this dialog box, that is the number of rows or columns that will be added to the spreadsheet.

Figure 12-3 Insert dialog box

Figure 12-4 Filter options

Figure 12-5 Sort options

Keyboard Shortcuts

There are some keyboard shortcuts that you may find useful when navigating around a worksheet. They are explained in Table 12-2.

Shortcut Key	Description
Home	Places the cursor in the first cell in the current row.
CTRL+Home	Place the cursor in cell A1.
Page Up	Moves up one screen.
Page Down	Moves down one screen.
CTRL+End	Places the cursor in the last column and row that has data. For example, if there is data in columns A to I and rows 1 to 24, the cursor will move to cell I24.

Table 12-2 Keyboard shortcuts explained

Shortcut Key	Description
↑	Moves up one cell.
↓	Moves down one cell.
→ or Tab key	Moves one cell to the right.
←	Moves one cell to the left.

Table 12-2 Keyboard shortcuts explained (Continued)

Home Tab

The options shown in Figure 12-6 are used to edit and format data in the spreadsheet.

Figure 12-6 Home tab options

Clipboard Group

The options in this group are used to cut, copy and paste content into the spreadsheet. The options are explained in Table 12-3.

Option	Description
Paste	Displays the options or a subset of the options shown in Figure 12-7.
Cut	Deletes the contents of the selected cell and places the contents in the clipboard.
Copy	Displays the options shown in Figure 12-8.
Format Painter	[See Chapter 4, Using The Format Painter]
Dialog Box Launcher	[See Chapter 4, Clipboard Task Pane]

Table 12-3 Clipboard group options explained

Paste Button Options

As you hold the mouse pointer over these options, look in the status bar to the left of the view section, you will see a representation of the formatting that will be applied when numeric data is pasted.

These options are explained in Table 12-4.

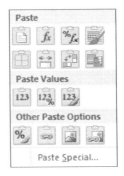

Figure 12-7 Paste button options

Option	Description
Paste	Copies what is in the clipboard to the spreadsheet.
Formulas	Only pastes the formula into the selected cell.
Formulas & Number Formatting	Only pastes the formula and number formatting. (1)
Keep Source Formatting	Will paste the cut or copied cells with the same formatting as the original cells.
No Borders	Pastes everything that is copied to the clipboard except border formatting.
Keep Source Column Widths	Pastes the copied cells with the same column width as the original cells width.
Transpose	If the copied cells are in a row, they will be pasted in a column and vise versa.
Merge Conditional Formatting	Pastes conditional formatting that the copied cells have.
Values	Only pastes the contents of the copied cells, even if the cell has formatting or a formula. (1)
Values & Numbering Formatting	Only pastes the values and number formatting. (1)
Values & Source Formatting	Only pastes the values and formatting. (1)
Formatting	Only pastes the formatting from the copied cells. (1)
Paste Link	Creates a link to the copied cells. The linked cells can be used in a formula independently of the cells that they are linked to. If the values in the original cells change, the linked cells will be updated automatically.
Picture	Creates an image of the contents of the copied cells and pastes the image in the spreadsheet. The image can be formatted like graphic files that you add to a document or spreadsheet.
Linked Picture	Works the same as the Picture option. The difference is that if the values in the original cells change, the values in the Linked Picture cells will be updated automatically.
Paste Special	Opens the dialog box shown in Figure 12-10.

Table 12-4 Paste button options explained

(1) The content is not copied.

Copy Options

COPY Places a copy of the selected cells in the clipboard.

COPY AS PICTURE Places a copy of the selected cells in the clipboard, then opens the dialog box shown in Figure 12-9.

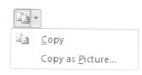

Figure 12-8 Copy options

Copy Picture Dialog Box

The options shown in Figure 12-9 are used to select how the selected cells will be created as a picture.

AS SHOWN ON SCREEN provides the best picture quality because it is pasted at 100%.

When the image is selected in the spreadsheet, the Picture Tools Format tab options are available.

Figure 12-9 Copy Picture dialog box

Paste Special Dialog Box

The options shown in Figure 12-10 are used to select what will be pasted.

The options in the Paste section are used to select the content that will be pasted. They are the most useful options on the dialog box and are explained in Table 12-5.

The Operation options are used to combine the numeric pasted cells with the content of the cells that they will be pasted in by adding, subtracting, multiplying or dividing two sets of numbers before pasting.

Figure 12-10 Paste Special dialog box

Option	What Is Pasted . . .
All	Formatting and numbers.
Formulas	Content and formulas.
Values	Content.
Formats	Formatting.
Comments	Comments in the cells. Keep in mind that you cannot create comments in Excel Starter.
Validation	Only cells that have validation.
All using Source theme	Cells that have a them applied to them.
All except borders	Everything except borders.
Column widths	Formatting and numbers. If necessary, the column width where the cells will be pasted will be adjusted to match the column width of the original location.

Table 12-5 Paste Special options explained

Option	What Is Pasted . . .
Formulas and number formats	Formulas and number formatting.
Values and number formats	Everything and number formatting.
All merging conditional formats	Formatting, numbers and conditional formatting.

Table 12-5 Paste Special options explained (Continued)

Copy And Paste Cell Options

After you copy and paste (opposed to cut and paste) content, you will see the button shown in Figure 12-11.

It has a subset of the Paste button options shown earlier in Figure 12-7. You can use these options as needed to modify the content that was pasted.

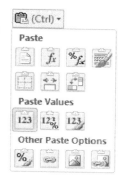

Figure 12-11 Copy and paste options

Font Group

The majority of options in this group are the same as the ones for text in Word. [See Chapter 5, Font Group] The options that are different are explained below.

BORDERS [See Chapter 5, Paragraph Group]

The **MORE BORDERS** option on the Borders drop-down list opens the dialog box shown in Figure 12-12.

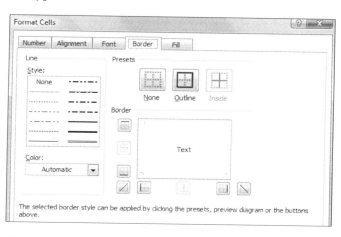

Figure 12-12 Border tab options

Alignment Group

Many of the options in this group are the same as the ones for text in Word. [See Chapter 5, Paragraph Group] The options that are different are explained in Table 12-6.

Option	Description
Top Align	Aligns at the top of the cell.
Middle Align	Aligns vertically in the middle of the cell.
Bottom Align	Aligns at the bottom of the cell.
Orientation	The options shown in Figure 12-13 are used to rotate the content in the cell.
Wrap Text	Wraps the content in the cell so that all of the content is visible in the cell.
Merge & Center	Displays the options shown in Figure 12-15, which are used to combine two or more cells into one cell.

Table 12-6 Alignment group options explained

Orientation Options

The picture next to each option on the drop-down list shown in Figure 12-13 shows the rotation direction. The **FORMAT CELL ALIGNMENT** option opens the dialog box shown in Figure 12-14.

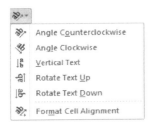

Figure 12-13 Orientation options

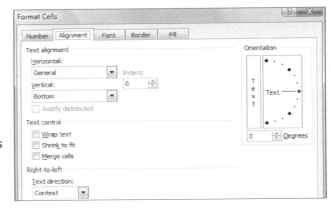

Figure 12-14 Alignment tab options

Merge & Center Options

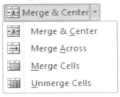

Figure 12-15 Merge & Center options

Formatting Text In A Spreadsheet

You can format text in a spreadsheet just like you can in a word processing document.

1. Open the Actual Sales vs Projected spreadsheet that you created in Chapter 11.

2. Select cells B3 and C3, then click the Bold button on the Home tab.

3. With the cells still selected, click the **CENTER** option in the Alignment group. The titles should be centered in the cells.

Center Text Across Cells

This option is used to spread the contents of one cell across several adjacent cells in additional rows and columns.

1. Select the range A1 to C1.

2. Home tab ⇒ Alignment group ⇒ Click the Merge & Center button.

3. In the Font group, click the Bold button. The title should now be centered across columns A, B and C.

   Your spreadsheet should look like the one shown in Figure 12-16. The title appears to be in cells A1, B1 and C1. Click in cell A1.

   Look in the **FORMULA BAR** and you will see that the title is only in this cell, as illustrated in Figure 12-16.

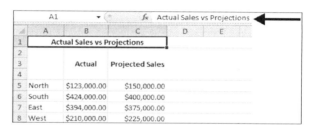

Figure 12-16 Text centered across cells and the contents of cell A1 are illustrated in the Formula bar

Adding Borders And Shading

1. Select the range A1 to C1, then click on the Font group dialog box launcher button. On the Font tab, change the size to 14.

2. On the Border tab, select the last option in the second column in the **LINE STYLE** section, then click the **OUTLINE** button in the Presets section, as illustrated in Figure 12-17.

   Change the **BORDER COLOR** to black.

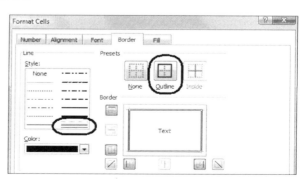

Figure 12-17 Line style and border location illustrated

3. On the Fill tab, change the **BACKGROUND COLOR** to Yellow.

4. Open the **PATTERN STYLE** drop-down list and select an option that you like, then click OK.

5. Your spreadsheet should look similar to the one shown in Figure 12-18.

    Save the changes and leave the spreadsheet open.

	A	B	C
1	Actual Sales vs Projections		
2			
3		Actual	Projected Sales
4			
5	North	$123,000.00	$150,000.00
6	South	$424,000.00	$400,000.00
7	East	$394,000.00	$375,000.00
8	West	$210,000.00	$225,000.00

Figure 12-18 Borders and shading added to the spreadsheet

How To Wrap Text In A Cell

The wrap text feature is useful when you have more information then will fit on one line in a cell. This feature is primarily used for text.

1. Click on cell C3. In the Alignment group, select the **WRAP TEXT** option.

2. Make column C smaller, then make row 3 longer.

    The text in cell C3 should now be on two lines in the cell, as shown in Figure 12-19. If not, adjust the width of column C.

    Save the changes.

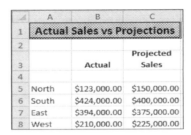

	A	B	C
1	Actual Sales vs Projections		
2			
3		Actual	Projected Sales
4			
5	North	$123,000.00	$150,000.00
6	South	$424,000.00	$400,000.00
7	East	$394,000.00	$375,000.00
8	West	$210,000.00	$225,000.00

Figure 12-19 Wrap text option applied to a cell

Number Group

The options in this group are used to format numeric values. The options are explained in Table 12-7.

Option	Description
Number Format	The options shown in Figure 12-20 are the number formats that you can select.
Accounting Number Format	Displays currency formats for different countries. The **MORE ACCOUNTING FORMATS** option displays the accounting category on the Number tab on the Format Cells dialog box.
Percent Style	Formats the selected cell as a percent.
Comma Style	Changes the format of the selected cell to the Accounting format without a currency symbol.
Increase Decimal	Moves the decimal point in the number one position to the left.
Decrease Decimal	Moves the decimal point in the number one position to the right.
Dialog Box Launcher	Opens the Format Cells dialog box shown in Figure 12-21.

Table 12-7 Number group options explained

Below the format name (in bold) on the Number Format drop-down list shown in Figure 12-20 is an example of the formatting. If the specific format that you need to apply is not shown on this drop-down list, select the **MORE NUMBER FORMATS** option, which displays the options shown in Figure 12-21.

As you can see, the categories on this tab are the same as the options shown in Figure 12-20. The custom category allows you to create your own format. The difference is that when you click on a category, additional formatting options are displayed, as shown in Figure 12-22.

When you need to enter a fraction, you should format the cell first, then type in the fraction. The reason I say this is because by default, Excel interprets a slash as part of a date.

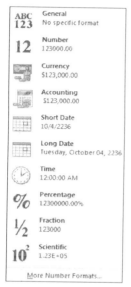

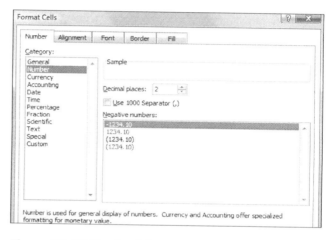

Figure 12-21 Number tab options

Figure 12-20 Number Format options

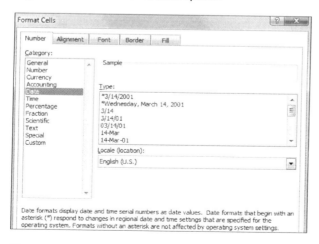

Figure 12-22 Date formatting options

Styles Group

The options in this group are used to apply auto formatting to cells and tables. The options are explained in Table 12-8.

Option	Description
Conditional Formatting	The options shown in Figure 12-23 are used to apply formatting based on the condition that you create.
Format As Table	The options are used to format the entire table or the selected cells.
Cell Styles	The options are used to apply a style to the selected cells.

Table 12-8 Styles group options explained

Conditional Formatting

Conditional formatting is used to highlight important information on a spreadsheet. The good thing is that after you set up the conditional formatting, Excel handles the rest because it automatically applies the conditional formatting to cells based on the criteria that you set up, even when data is added or changed in the spreadsheet.

A benefit of conditional formatting is that you do not have to know the exact cells that the formatting will be applied to.

Examples of conditional formatting include changing the background color of cells that have a value in the range that you select or apply formatting to the 10 best selling items.

The options shown in Figure 12-23 provide a variety of ways to create conditional formatting. The options are explained in Table 12-9.

If the default rules do not meet your needs, you can create your own rules, as you will see in the next section.

Figure 12-23 Conditional formatting options

Option	Description
Highlight Cells Rules	These rules are used to compare the data in a table to a value that you select. Based on the result of the comparison, the formatting is applied.
Top/Bottom Rules	These rules are used for tables that have a lot of data. They will format the top or bottom 10 cells by default or you can select the number of cells to format.
Data Bars	These options add bars to the cells to visually represent the value in the cell, as shown in Figure 12-24. The longer the bar, the higher the number in the cell.

Table 12-9 Conditional formatting options explained

Option	Description
Color Scales	These options are used to add a background colors to the selected cells to represent the value in the cell. The color scale is either low numbers have a lighter color then higher numbers or low numbers have a darker color then higher numbers.
Icon Sets	These options add an icon to each cell. The icon represents the value in the cell.
New Rule	Opens the dialog box shown in Figure 12-25.
Clear Rules	These options are used to delete the rule for the selected part of the table. Use this option when the spreadsheet was changed after a formatting rule was applied. Otherwise, you can use the Undo option.
Manage Rules	Opens the dialog box shown in Figure 12-26.

Table 12-9 Conditional formatting options explained (Continued)

$123,000.00	$150,000.00
$424,000.00	$400,000.00
$394,000.00	$375,000.00
$210,000.00	$225,000.00

Figure 12-24 Data Bars conditional formatting applied to cells

New Formatting Rule Dialog Box

The options on this dialog box are used to create the rule for when formatting should be applied.

When you select the **RULE TYPE** at the top of the dialog box, the corresponding options in the **RULE DESCRIPTION** section will be displayed.

Select the options to create the criteria that will format the appropriate cells.

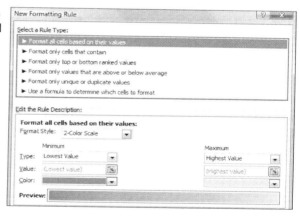

Figure 12-25 New Formatting Rule dialog box

Conditional Formatting Rules Manager Dialog Box

The options shown in Figure 12-26 are used to create, edit and delete conditional formatting rules.

There is no limit to the number of conditional formatting rules that can be created.

Figure 12-26 Conditional Formatting Rules Manager dialog box

The **STOP IF TRUE** option (on the dialog box shown above in Figure 12-26) is used to stop the remaining conditional formatting rules for the cells in the Applies to field from processing.

Checking For Duplicates

If the spreadsheet has a lot of data, it can be difficult to see duplicate entries. Sorting and filtering, which you will learn about in this chapter can be used to find duplicates, but it is possible that you may miss some duplicate entries using this technique.

The Duplicate Values conditional formatting option changes the background color of cells in a column that have duplicate values. Even better, as data is changed or new rows of data are added, the duplicate values option keeps working. The steps below show you how to use the duplicate checking feature.

1. Open the Products spreadsheet, then select the Product Number column.

2. Home tab ⇒ Styles group ⇒ Conditional Formatting ⇒ Highlight Cells Rules ⇒ Duplicate Values.

3. Open the second drop-down list shown in Figure 12-27 and select how you want the cells with duplicate values formatted. For this example, accept the default option.

Figure 12-27 Duplicate Values dialog box

4. Click OK. You should see six product numbers highlighted.

5. Add a row of data that has CH-101 as the product number. When the insertion point is moved from the Product Number column in the new row, you will see that the product number cell is highlighted with a red background.

6. Save the spreadsheet as `My duplicates`.

Create A Custom Format
If you do not like the conditional formatting options in the drop-down list on the right of Figure 12-27 above, you can create your own conditional formatting rule by selecting **CUSTOM FORMAT** at the bottom of the drop-down list. The Format Cells dialog box will open. You will see that some of the options are disabled, but you can select any of the other options to create your custom conditional formatting.

Cell Styles

The options in this gallery are similar to the other style galleries. One unique feature is that custom cell styles can be copied from one workbook to another. The steps below show you how to copy cell styles to another workbook.

1. Open the workbook that has the styles that you want to copy. Open the workbook that you want to copy the styles to.

2. In the workbook that the styles will be copied to, Home tab ⇒ Styles group ⇒ Cell Styles ⇒ Merge Styles.

3. On the dialog box shown in Figure 12-28, click on the workbook that has the styles that you want to copy to the active workbook (the one that you selected in Step 2), then click OK.

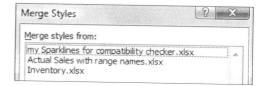

Figure 12-28 Merge Styles dialog box

4. When prompted to overwrite styles with the same name, click No, unless you are really sure that the styles that have the same name in both workbooks are the same.

5. Home tab ⇒ Styles group ⇒ Cell Styles. At the top of the gallery you will see a section called **CUSTOM**. The style that you created in the other workbook should be in this section.

Cells Group

The options in this group are used to add, delete and format cells, rows, columns and sheets. The options are explained in Table 12-10.

Option	Description
Insert	The options are used to add cells, rows, columns and sheets.
Delete	The options are used to delete cells, rows, columns and sheets.
Format	The options shown in Figure 12-29 are used to change the structure of a component of the sheet.

Table 12-10 Cells group options explained

Format Options

The options shown in Figure 12-29 are used to change the row height and column width. Rows, columns and sheets can be hidden.

The **AUTOFIT ROW HEIGHT** and **AUTOFIT COLUMN WIDTH** options are used to expand the row or column to display the content of the selected cell.

The three options in the **ORGANIZE SHEETS** section are used to rename the selected sheet, reorder and copy sheets using the Move or Copy dialog box and change the tab color.

Figure 12-29 Format options

> **Protect Cells**
> The tooltip for the Format button shown above in Figure 12-29 says that there is the ability to protect cells. This functionality is not available in Excel Starter.

Editing Group

The options in this group are used to create basic formulas, sort the data and find and replace content in the spreadsheet. The options are explained in Table 12-11.

Option	Description
Sum	The first five options shown in Figure 12-30 are used to create basic formulas. The **MORE FUNCTIONS** option opens the Insert Function dialog box. The Sum option is the same as the **AUTO SUM** option on the Formulas tab. [See Chapter 15, Auto Sum]
Fill	The options are used to select the direction of the adjacent cells that will be filled. [See Chapter 15, Auto Fill]
Clear	The options shown in Figure 12-31 are used to remove the content and formatting from the selected cells.
Sort & Filter	The options are used to sort and filter the selected data.
Find & Select	The options are used to search for specific information, formatting or formulas and replace them if necessary.

Table 12-11 Editing group options explained

As you read earlier in this chapter, when you delete the contents of the cell, the formatting is not deleted.

To remove the formatting, select the Clear Formats option shown in Figure 12-31 or if you want to delete everything, select Clear All.

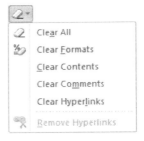

Figure 12-30 Sum options

Figure 12-31 Clear options

Sorting Data In A Spreadsheet

Sorting is used to arrange the data in a more meaningful way. If you are entering names and addresses in a spreadsheet of people that want to sign up for various classes, more than likely you will enter the names in the order that people sign up for a class and not in the order of the class that they are signed up for.

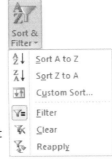

If you sort the spreadsheet by the class each person signed up for, the names will be grouped by class. You can sort on any column on the spreadsheet. Figure 12-32 shows the sort and filter options. The options are explained in Table 12-12.

Figure 12-32 Sort & Filter options

Option	Description
Sort A to Z	Sorts the information in ascending order (low to high, A to Z or 1 to 10).
Sort Z to A	Sorts the information in descending order (high to low, Z to A or 10 to 1).
Custom Sort	Opens the Sort dialog box shown later in Figure 12-35.
Filter	Turns on the filter option.
Clear	Removes the sort or filter.
Reapply	Adds the sort or filter back to the selected cells.

Table 12-12 Sort & Filter options explained

Sorting The Entire Spreadsheet

1. Open the Sort Customers spreadsheet, then select the range A1 to I20.

 Clicking on the empty square above row 1 will select the entire spreadsheet, which is quicker then highlighting the spreadsheet.

2. Home tab ⇒ Editing group ⇒ Sort & Filter ⇒ Custom Sort. You will see the Sort dialog box. Table 12-13 explains the sort options.

Option	Description
Add Level	Adds a new row to add more sort criteria.
Delete Level	Deletes the selected criteria row.
Copy Level	Duplicates the selected criteria row.
Up/Down buttons	Is used to change the order of the sort criteria.
Options	Opens the Sort Options dialog box, which is used to change the sort to left to right and create a case sensitive sort.
My data has headers	Select this option if the first row of the spreadsheet has column names. Selecting this option will not sort the first row, which is what you want most of the time. This means that the contents of row 1 will stay at the top of the spreadsheet. If the first row of the spreadsheet does not have column names or is not selected, do not select this option.

Table 12-13 Sort dialog box options explained

 If you select the **MY DATA HAS HEADERS** option, you will see the column heading names (the text in row 1) in the Sort by drop-down list instead of column A, column B etc. It will probably be easier to select the columns that you want to sort on by using this option.

3. Open the **SORT BY** drop-down list and select Last Name. This will sort the spreadsheet by the Last Name column.

4. Click OK. Your spreadsheet should look like the one shown in Figure 12-33. Figure 12-34 shows what the spreadsheet would look like if the My data has headers option was not selected. The column names are not in row 1, they are in row 10.

	A	B	C	D	E	F	G	H	I
1	First Name	Last Name	Phone	Company	Address	City	State	Zip Code	Category
2	Fred	Amos	(215)327-7079		19 Rodney	Westwood	CT	06403	Biography
3	Brian	Bark	(610)554-3002		300 Winston Pl	Norwood	NY	10023	Computer
4	Glen	Carter	(407)471-0159		1 Edward Dr	Las Vegas	NV	60022	Sports
5	Carrie	Downing	(407)987-4563	Financial Services	63 Maple Ave	Glen Rock	NV	32888	Computer
6	Robert	Emerson	(908)587-6422	New Real Estate	200 Mountain Ave	Ft. Laud	FL	32847	Mystery
7	Kelly	Fontaine	(702)825-9787	Jersey Bank	272 Rt 64	Cherry Hill	NJ	07458	Computer
8	Amy	Gardner	(610)664-4646		132 W Park Ave	Wilson	NJ	07403	Mystery
9	Todd	Green	(203)452-1300		41 Jefferson Rd	Tampa	FL	32672	Biography
10	Tina	Jones	(609)364-2500		30 Long St	Ft Laud	FL	32991	Computer
11	Louis	Riker	(702)667-3053		23 Essex Pl	Tappan	CT	06402	Biography
12	Randi	Sherwood	(718)505-3388	Hi-Tech Inc	777 Broad Ave	Ramsey	PA	19001	Computer
13	Steve	Smith	(702)947-8701	Big Design	2200 Research Way	Bronx	NY	11201	Computer
14	Tom	Smith	(215)909-1885		45 Jericho Ave	Wilton	CT	06405	Sports
15	Brenda	Taylor	(610)967-7308	Symphony C&L	500 Point Rd	Ft Lee	NJ	08663	Sports
16	Stuart	Thomas	(718)503-0331		90A Jersey Ave	Orlando	FL	32761	Sports
17	Clair	Walker	(215)909-8882	Two of A kind	892 Main St	Menden	CT	06403	Mystery
18	Jamie	Walker	(908)652-9609		997 Lenox Dr	Reno	NV	32883	Mystery
19	Tina	Walker	(702)703-0101		123 Main St	Stamford	CT	06402	Computer
20	Peter	Young	(718)505-4259	Elmwood Sales	188 William St	Bogota	NV	32881	Sports

Figure 12-33 Spreadsheet sorted in last name order

	A	B	C	D	E	F	G	H	I
1	Fred	Amos	(215)327-7079		19 Rodney	Westwood	CT	06403	Biography
2	Brian	Bark	(610)554-3002		300 Winston Pl	Norwood	NY	10023	Computer
3	Glen	Carter	(407)471-0159		1 Edward Dr	Las Vegas	NV	60022	Sports
4	Carrie	Downing	(407)987-4563	Financial Services	63 Maple Ave	Glen Rock	NV	32888	Computer
5	Robert	Emerson	(908)587-6422	New Real Estate	200 Mountain Ave	Ft. Laud	FL	32847	Mystery
6	Kelly	Fontaine	(702)825-9787	Jersey Bank	272 Rt 64	Cherry Hill	NJ	07458	Computer
7	Amy	Gardner	(610)664-4646		132 W Park Ave	Wilson	NJ	07403	Mystery
8	Todd	Green	(203)452-1300		41 Jefferson Rd	Tampa	FL	32672	Biography
9	Tina	Jones	(609)364-2500		30 Long St	Ft Laud	FL	32991	Computer
10	First Name	Last Name	Phone	Company	Address	City	State	Zip Code	Category
11	Louis	Riker	(702)667-3053		23 Essex Pl	Tappan	CT	06402	Biography
12	Randi	Sherwood	(718)505-3388	Hi-Tech Inc	777 Broad Ave	Ramsey	PA	19001	Computer
13	Steve	Smith	(702)947-8701	Big Design	2200 Research Way	Bronx	NY	11201	Computer
14	Tom	Smith	(215)909-1885		45 Jericho Ave	Wilton	CT	06405	Sports
15	Brenda	Taylor	(610)967-7308	Symphony C&L	500 Point Rd	Ft Lee	NJ	08663	Sports
16	Stuart	Thomas	(718)503-0331		90A Jersey Ave	Orlando	FL	32761	Sports
17	Clair	Walker	(215)909-8882	Two of A kind	892 Main St	Menden	CT	06403	Mystery
18	Jamie	Walker	(908)652-9609		997 Lenox Dr	Reno	NV	32883	Mystery
19	Tina	Walker	(702)703-0101		123 Main St	Stamford	CT	06402	Computer
20	Peter	Young	(718)505-4259	Elmwood Sales	188 William St	Bogota	NV	32881	Sports

Figure 12-34 Spreadsheet sorted without the My data has headers option selected

How To Sort On Two Columns

The steps below show you how to sort on the Last Name and First Name fields.

1. Select the range A2 to I20, then open the Sort dialog box.

2. Clear the My data has headers option.

3. Open the first Sort by drop-down list, select Column B, then click the Add Level button.

4. Open the Then by drop-down list, select Column A. Figure 12-35 shows the options that should be selected. Because the first row is not selected in the spreadsheet, you do not have to select the headers option. Notice that the options are the column letters instead of the column names.

Figure 12-35 Two column sort options selected

5. Click OK. Your spreadsheet should look like the one shown in Figure 12-36. Look at rows 17 to 19. The three people with the last name Walker are in alphabetical order by their last and first names.

	A	B	C	D	E	F	G	H	I
1	First Name	Last Name	Phone	Company	Address	City	State	Zip Code	Category
2	Fred	Amos	(215)327-7079		19 Rodney	Westwood	CT	06403	Biography
3	Brian	Bark	(610)554-3002		300 Winston Pl	Norwood	NY	10023	Computer
4	Glen	Carter	(407)471-0159		1 Edward Dr	Las Vegas	NV	60022	Sports
5	Carrie	Downing	(407)987-4563	Financial Services	63 Maple Ave	Glen Rock	NV	32888	Computer
6	Robert	Emerson	(908)587-6422	New Real Estate	200 Mountain Ave	Ft Laud	FL	32847	Mystery
7	Kelly	Fontaine	(702)825-9787	Jersey Bank	272 Rt 64	Cherry Hill	NJ	07456	Computer
8	Amy	Gardner	(610)664-4646		132 W Park Ave	Wilson	NJ	07403	Mystery
9	Todd	Green	(203)452-1300		41 Jefferson Rd	Tampa	FL	32672	Biography
10	Tina	Jones	(609)364-2500		30 Long St	Ft Laud	FL	32991	Computer
11	Louis	Riker	(702)667-3053		23 Essex Pl	Tappan	CT	06402	Biography
12	Randi	Sherwood	(718)505-3388	Hi-Tech Inc	777 Broad Ave	Ramsey	PA	19001	Computer
13	Steve	Smith	(702)947-8701	Big Design	2200 Research Way	Bronx	NY	11201	Computer
14	Tom	Smith	(215)909-1885		45 Jericho Ave	Wilton	CT	06405	Sports
15	Brenda	Taylor	(610)967-7308	Symphony C&L	500 Point Rd	Ft Lee	NJ	08663	Sports
16	Stuart	Thomas	(718)503-0331		90A Jersey Ave	Orlando	FL	32761	Sports
17	Clair	Walker	(215)909-3882	Two of A kind	892 Main St	Menden	CT	06403	Mystery
18	Jamie	Walker	(908)652-9609		997 Lenox Dr	Reno	NV	32883	Mystery
19	Tina	Walker	(702)703-0101		123 Main St	Stamford	CT	06402	Computer
20	Peter	Young	(718)505-4259	Elmwood Sales	188 William St	Bogota	NV	32881	Sports

Figure 12-36 Result of the two column sort

Custom Sorting

Earlier in this chapter you learned how to check for duplicate values. The steps below show you how to sort the spreadsheet based on color so that the duplicate values will be next to each other, which will make it easier to fix the duplicate values.

1. Open the My duplicates spreadsheet.

2. Home tab ⇒ Editing group ⇒ Sort & Filter ⇒ Custom Sort.

3. Open the Sort by drop-down list and select Product Number.
   Change the Sort on option to Cell color.
   Open the Order drop-down list and select the cell color.
   Open the last drop-down list and select On top.

4. Click the Add Level button.

5. Open the Then by drop-down list and select Product Number.

   You should have the options shown in Figure 12-37.

Figure 12-37 Options to sort by color

6. Click OK. Save the changes. The product numbers should be in ascending order and the duplicate values should be next to each other.

Filter Data

Filtering data is a way to only view the data that you need to see. The steps below show you how to filter data in a spreadsheet.

1. Open the Customers spreadsheet.

2. Home tab ⇒ Editing group ⇒ Sort & Filter ⇒ Filter. You should see down arrow buttons at the top of each column.

3. Open the Category filter and clear all of the options except Computer, as shown at the bottom of Figure 12-38, then click OK.

   You will only see customers that have Computer in the Category column. If you look in the left corner of the status bar, you will see **7 OF 19 RECORDS FOUND**, which is a count of records that meet the criteria and the total number of records on the spreadsheet.

   Notice that the Category filter button has the filter icon on it. This icon is used to let you know which columns the spreadsheet is filtered on.

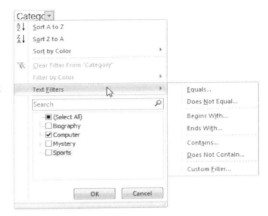

Figure 12-38 Filter options

4. Open the State filter and clear all of the options except NY, then click OK. You will see two records that meet the criteria of having Computer in the Category column and NY in the State column.

Filter Options

In addition to the filter options shown on the left of Figure 12-38 above, there are additional options shown on the right of the figure based on the type of data in the column.

Text Filters

Figure 12-38 above, shows text filters because the category column is text. The text filter options are used to find specific text in the column.

Number Filters

The options shown in Figure 12-39 are used to select specific numbers based on the number filter that you select. For example, select the **BETWEEN** option if you want to find rows of data that have a value between two numbers.

The **TOP 10** option shown in Figure 12-40 is used to select the X highest value items or the records in the top X percent. X defaults to 10, but you can select a different number. If you want the lowest values, select **BOTTOM** in the first drop-down list.

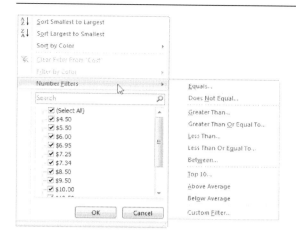

Figure 12-40 Top 10 AutoFilter dialog box

Figure 12-39 Number Filter options

Date Filters

These options are used to find rows of data that have a date in the range that you select from the options shown in Figure 12-41.

For example, if you wanted to only display rows that have a date from last month, select **LAST MONTH** from the Date Filter menu options on the right of the figure.

The last option on each of the filter lists is **CUSTOM FILTER**. Selecting this option also opens the dialog box shown in Figure 12-42, like most of the other options do.

Figure 12-42 Custom AutoFilter dialog box

Figure 12-41 Date Filter options

Find & Select Options

The options shown in Figure 12-43 are used to look for content in the spreadsheet. The options are explained in Table 12-14.

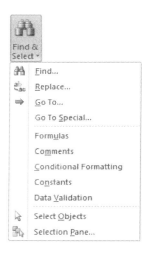

Figure 12-43 Find & Select options

Option	Description
Find	Is primarily used to search for content in the workbook. Opens the Find tab on the Find and Replace dialog box.
Replace	Is used to search for and replace content in the workbook. Opens the Replace tab on the Find and Replace dialog box.
Go To	Opens the dialog box shown in Figure 12-44, which is used to select a cell or range name that you want to display the contents of. The Special button opens the Go To Special dialog box.
Go To Special	Opens the dialog box shown in Figure 12-45, which is used to search for non content information in the spreadsheet.
Formulas	Selects cells in the spreadsheet that have a formula. It would be nice if the actual formulas were displayed.
Comments	Is used to search for cells that have comments. Because Excel Starter does not have the ability to add comments, this option is only helpful for spreadsheets that were created in a different version of Excel.
Conditional Formatting	Selects cells that have conditional formatting applied.
Constants	Selects cells that have a constant value.
Data Validation	Selects cells that have data validation applied.
Select Objects	Is used to select part of the sheet.
Selection Pane	[See Chapter 4, Selection and Visibility Task Pane]

Table 12-14 Find & Select options explained

Figure 12-44 Go To dialog box

Figure 12-45 Go To Special dialog box

Searching A Spreadsheet Or Workbook

Excel provides two search options: The Find command and the Replace command. As you will see, the Find command has some of the Replace command functionality. These commands have some search options that are the same, as explained in Table 12-15.

Common Find And Replace Search Options

Option	Description
Format button	Is used to select the search (or replace) formatting option. Selecting the **FORMAT** option opens the Find Format dialog box which looks like the Format Cells dialog box. The difference is that the Find Format dialog box has less options. Selecting the **CHOOSE FORMAT FROM CELL** option is used to select the format from a cell on the worksheet. The name of the format is placed in the box to the left of the Format button.
Within	Is used to select what is searched, the current sheet or the entire workbook.
Search	Is used to select the direction of the search, either by row or by column. It doesn't really matter which of these options is selected, because the entire sheet is searched.
Look In	Is used to select where to search, in formulas, the values or comments of each cell.
Match Case	If selected, only cells that have values exactly as you enter the search criteria will be retrieved.
Match entire cell contents	If checked, only cells that have everything that you are searching for will be retrieved. That means that cells that have part of the search criteria that you select will not be retrieved.

Table 12-15 Common Find and Replace search options explained

The Find Command

There are two ways to search for content in a spreadsheet using the Find command, as explained below.

① **FIND NEXT** Clicking this button causes Excel to highlight the next cell that has the content that you are searching for.

② **FIND ALL** Clicking this button will display a list of all of the cells that have the content that you are searching for, at the bottom of the dialog box shown in Figure 12-46.

If you wanted to change some of the values on the dialog box, click on the first cell that you want to change.

Press and hold down the CTRL key, then click on the other cells that you want to change, similar to what is shown in the figure.

Click in the Formula bar and type in the change.

Press the CTRL+Enter keys and the change will be applied to all of the selected cells.

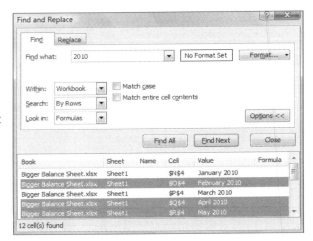

Figure 12-46 Find command options

 If you only want to search a specific portion of the spreadsheet, select the portion of the spreadsheet first, then select the Find or Replace command and select the options that you need.

Using The Replace Command

This command will search for what you specify and replace it with what you want. The Replace command in the Excel works very similar to how it works in Word.

1. Open the Actual Sales vs Projected spreadsheet.

2. Home tab ⇒ Editing group ⇒ Find & Select ⇒ Replace. You should see the Find and Replace dialog box.

3. In the **FIND WHAT** field, type Projections.

4. Press the Tab key, then type Projected in the Replace with field.

The options shown at the bottom of Figure 12-47 are used to select where in the workbook to search, the direction that the search will take, either row by row or column by column and where to look.

If you want to see each match before it is changed, click the Find Next button.

If you want the information replaced every place that it exists in the spreadsheet without being able to view each occurrence, click the Replace All button.

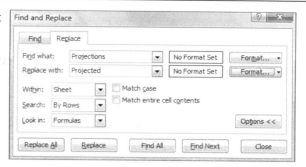

Figure 12-47 Replace options

5.   Click the Replace All button. The word **PROJECTIONS** should have been replaced with the word **PROJECTED** in the title of the spreadsheet.

6.   Click OK, then click Close. Save the changes.

How To Edit Text Or Data In A Cell

There are two ways to edit data in a cell. You can re-type the contents of the cell or you can only change the portion of data in the cell that needs to be changed.

1.   Open the Actual Sales vs Projected spreadsheet if it is not already open.

2.   Click in cell B3, then click in the Formula bar.

3.   Type `Current` before the word Actual, then press the space bar.

4.   Press the **END** key, then press the space bar. Type `Sales`, then press Enter.

Wrap the text in this cell.

Your spreadsheet should look like the one shown in Figure 12-48.

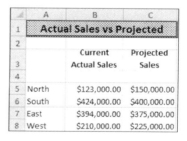

Figure 12-48 Completed spreadsheet

5.   Save the changes.

Proofing Group

The options in this group work the same as they do in Word. The one difference that I noticed is that there is no spell check option on the shortcut menu. [See Chapter 4, Proofing Group]

A lot of information in a spreadsheet is numeric. Row and column names are primarily text, which means that there can be typos. Numeric only fields are skipped during the spell check process. If you did check fields that had numbers, every numeric field would be considered a spelling error.

THE INSERT TAB

Overview

The options on the Insert tab are used to enhance spreadsheets. You will learn about the following.

- ☑ Create a basic table
- ☑ Create and modify charts
- ☑ Add sparklines to a cell
- ☑ Add content to the header and footer sections

Overview

The options on the Insert tab are used to add objects and functionality to spreadsheets that make them look more professional. The options on this tab are how you can customize spreadsheets. Figure 13-1 shows the Insert tab. The options are explained below.

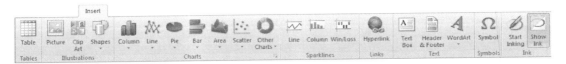

Figure 13-1 Insert tab

Tables Group

In appearance, a table looks like the filter options that you read about in Chapter 12. Prior to Excel 2007, tables were called **LISTS**. A table is a way to store information about items. Each item has its own row. This is similar to records in a database. The way to tell a table from a regular spreadsheet is that the column headings have bold white letters, filter buttons and a dark background. The other rows in the table have a shaded background with alternating colors. Some of the advantages tables have over a regular worksheet are discussed below.

① Tables can link to databases.

② As you add adjacent rows and columns the formulas automatically change to accommodate the new information.

TABLE Is used to create a table in the spreadsheet. This command selects all adjacent cells surrounding the cell that is selected.

Creating A Basic Table

The steps below show you how to create a table.

1. Save the Customers spreadsheet as `My customer table`.

2. Insert tab ⇒ Tables group ⇒ Table.

    The range A1 to I20 should be in the field on the dialog box shown in Figure 13-2. The **MY TABLE HAS HEADERS** option should be selected.

    If you wanted to increase or decrease the number of rows or columns in the table, click the button at the end of the field. The dialog box will minimize. Select the rows and columns for the table, then click the button again.

Figure 13-2 Create Table dialog box

3. Click OK. The table should look like the one shown in Figure 13-3.

Placing the mouse pointer in the lower right corner of the table will let you add or remove rows or columns, by dragging the mouse pointer up and to the left to remove rows or columns or down and to the right to add rows or columns.

Figure 13-3 Spreadsheet converted to a table

If a cell in the table is selected and you scroll down the page far enough so that the column headers are not visible, the column letters (A, B, etc) are replaced with the column header information, as shown in Figure 13-4.

	Last Name	Phone	Company
5	Green	(203)452-1300	
6	Carter	(407)471-0159	
7	Fontaine	(702)825-9787	Jersey Bank
8	Taylor	(610)967-7308	Symphony C&L
9	Smith	(702)947-8701	Big Design
10	Walker	(215)909-8882	Two of A kind

Figure 13-4 Column letters replaced with column headers

Table Tools Design Contextual Tab

When a cell in a table is selected, the tab shown in Figure 13-5 is available. The options are explained below.

Figure 13-5 Table Tools Design tab

Properties Group

TABLE NAME You can use the default name or type in a more descriptive name if the spreadsheet will have more than one table. Doing this is optional.

RESIZE TABLE Opens the Resize Table dialog box so that you can add or remove rows or columns.

Tools Group

CONVERT TO RANGE This button will remove the table functionality, but leaves the formatting.

Table Style Options Group

Table styles format different parts of the table. The options in this group are used to change the appearance of the table. The options are explained in Table 13-1.

Option	Description
Header Row	Displays or hides the header row.
Total Row	Adds or removes a total row. This row contains summary information.
Banded Rows	The odd numbered rows in the table will be formatted with a different background color then the even numbered rows. (1)
First Column	Applies different formatting (like bold) to the first column. (1)
Last Column	Applies different formatting to the last column. (1)
Banded Columns	Applies different formatting to every other column in the table. (1)

Table 13-1 Table Style Options group options explained

(1) This option is only supported if the selected table style uses it.

Table Styles Group

[See Chapter 9, Table Styles Group]

> **Table Styles**
> Table styles function like the cell styles that you read about in Chapter 12. The difference is that the table styles that come with Excel cannot be modified. You can modify table styles that you create.

The **NEW TABLE STYLE** option on the gallery opens the dialog box shown in Figure 13-6.

The options are used to create a new table style.

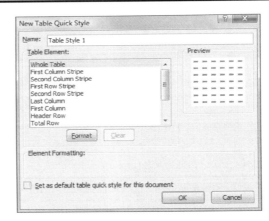

Figure 13-6 New Table Quick Style dialog box

Adding Data To A Table

To add data to a table, you can insert rows, type new data at the end of the table or paste data from another source. All of the data on the worksheet does not have to be part of the table. If there is data on the worksheet below the table for example and you add (or delete) rows in the table, the data outside of the table on the worksheet is not affected. To demonstrate this, you will paste data into the worksheet and then edit the table.

1. Open the My customer table and Products spreadsheets.

2. Copy the first four rows of data in the Products spreadsheet and paste them starting in cell A23 in the My customer table spreadsheet.

3. Add your name to columns A and B in rows 21 and 22. Notice that the two rows that you just created have the same formatting.

4. Leave the My customer table spreadsheet open to complete the next exercise.

How To Add A Column To A Table

The steps below show you how to add a column to a table without changing the structure of the data outside of the table.

1. Click in cell C2.

2. Right-click ⇒ Insert ⇒ Table columns to the left. The table should look like the one shown in Figure 13-7.

   Notice that the data below the table has not changed.

	A	B	C	D
1	First Name	Last Name	Column1	Phone
2	Tina	Jones		(609)364-2500
3	Jamie	Walker		(908)652-9609
4	Stuart	Thomas		(718)503-0331
5	Todd	Green		(203)452-1300
6	Glen	Carter		(407)471-0159

Figure 13-7 Column added to the table

3. If you want to save the changes, save the My customer table spreadsheet with a new file name.

Illustrations Group

[See Chapter 6, Illustrations Group]

Charts Group

The options in this group are used to create charts. Clicking on an option in this group displays different styles of the chart type. [See Chapter 10, Chart Types]

Resizing Charts The default size of the chart may fit most of your needs. When it doesn't, select the chart, then hold the mouse pointer near the dots on the frame closest to how you want to resize the chart. I tend to resize charts the same way that I resize images, by placing the mouse pointer in the lower right corner and dragging the frame up to the left to make the chart smaller or down and to the right to make the chart larger.

Create A Column Chart

1. Save the Actual Sales vs Projected spreadsheet as My column chart.

2. Delete rows 2 and 4.

3. Select the range A2 to C6.

4. Insert tab ⇒ Charts group ⇒ Column ⇒ Select the first 3-D Column chart option.

   The chart should look like the one shown in Figure 13-8.

   Save the changes.

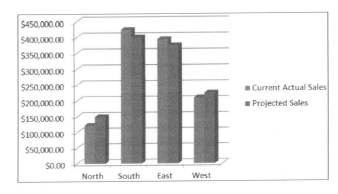

Figure 13-8 3-D column chart

Y Axis Scale By default, the Y axis scale starts at zero and ends at a value greater than the largest number that is plotted on the axis. This value is the next value in the interval used on the scale. As shown in Figure 13-8 above, the scale stops at $450,000.00.

If you changed a value in the spreadsheet to a number larger than that amount, the chart and Y axis scale range would be recalculated, as shown in Figure 13-9.

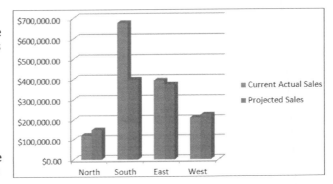

Figure 13-9 Chart with a larger value

Create A Pie Chart

1. Save the Bigger Balance Sheet spreadsheet as My pie chart.

2. Select the range A19 to B22.

3. Insert tab ⇒ Charts group ⇒ Pie ⇒ Select the first 2-D Pie chart option.

4. The chart should look like the one shown in Figure 13-10.

   Save the changes.

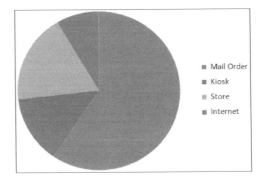

Figure 13-10 2-D pie chart

Create An Area Chart

1. Save the Bigger Balance Sheet spreadsheet as `My area chart`.

2. Copy the range B4:M4 to B18:M18.

3. Select the range A18 to M22.

4. Insert tab ⇒ Charts group ⇒ Area ⇒ Select the second 2-D Area chart option.

5. The chart should look like the one shown in Figure 13-11.

   Save the changes.

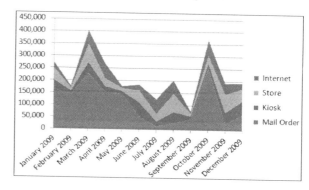

Figure 13-11 2-D area chart

Chart Tools Contextual Tabs

These tabs are available when a chart is selected in the spreadsheet. The majority of options on these three tabs are the same as the options for charts in Word. [See Chapter 10, Chart Tools Contextual Tabs] The options on these tabs that are different are explained below.

Design Tab

The options on the tab shown in Figure 13-12 are used to change the chart type, select the data, layout and style for the chart.

Figure 13-12 Design tab

Location Group

The **MOVE CHART** option is used to move the chart to another tab in the workbook by selecting the options shown in Figure 13-13.

The **OBJECT IN** option is used to move the chart to another sheet in the workbook and make the chart an object, like an image.

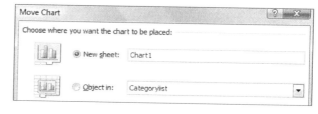

Figure 13-13 Move Chart dialog box

Layout Tab

The options shown in Figure 13-14 are used to customize individual parts of the chart.

Figure 13-14 Layout tab

Properties Group

CHART NAME is used to give the chart a name. Changing the default name is optional. The main reason to change the name is if there is more than one chart and you have the need to reference the charts by a more descriptive name.

Format Tab

The options shown in Figure 13-15 are used to apply styles to different parts of the chart.

Figure 13-15 Format tab

Enhancing Charts

So far in this chapter you have created basic charts. As you just read, the options on the Chart Tools tabs are used to enhance charts. The next few exercises demonstrate various ways to enhance a chart.

How To Change The Chart Type And Layout

The steps below show you how to change the area chart that you created to a column chart.

1. Open the My area chart spreadsheet, then click on the chart.

2. Design tab ⇒ Type group ⇒ Change Chart Type.

3. Select the first column chart option, then click OK.

4. Click the Select Data button, then change the data range to A18:E22, as shown at the top of Figure 13-16. Click OK.

The **HIDDEN AND EMPTY CELLS** button displays the dialog box shown in Figure 13-17. The options are used to select how Excel handles empty cells.

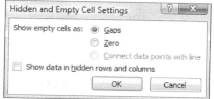

Figure 13-17 Hidden and Empty Cell Settings dialog box

Figure 13-16 Select Data Source dialog box

5. Open the Charts Layout gallery and select the second layout in the second row.

    The chart should look like the one shown in Figure 13-18.

    Save the spreadsheet with a new name.

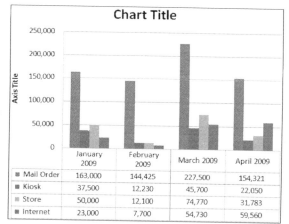

Figure 13-18 Changed chart layout

	January 2009	February 2009	March 2009	April 2009
Mail Order	163,000	144,425	227,500	154,321
Kiosk	37,500	12,230	45,700	22,050
Store	50,000	12,100	74,770	31,783
Internet	23,000	7,700	54,730	59,560

How To Change The Shape Of A Data Series

In the previous section you learned how to change the chart type. You can also change the shape of a data series by following the steps below.

1. Right-click on the shape in the chart that you want to change and select Format Data Series.

2. Display the Shape panel.

   On the right you will see the shapes that you can select from, as shown in Figure 13-19.

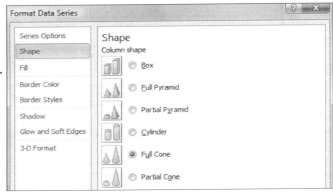

Figure 13-19 Shape options

3. Select the shape that you want, then click the Close button.

   Figure 13-20 shows a chart with a column shape changed to the full cone shape.

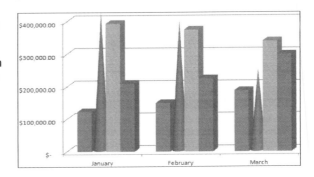

Figure 13-20 Column shape changed to the full cone shape

Adding Labels To Charts

Labels help to make the data easier to understand. The steps below show you how to add labels to a chart.

1. Open the My pie chart spreadsheet, then click on the chart.

2. Layout tab ⇒ Labels group ⇒ Chart title ⇒ Above chart.

3. Click in the chart title object on the chart, then type in a title.

4. Layout tab ⇒ Labels group ⇒ Legend ⇒ Show Legend at Bottom.

5. Layout tab ⇒ Labels group ⇒ Data Labels ⇒ Best fit.

   The chart should look like the one shown in Figure 13-21.

   Save the changes.

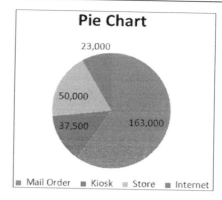

Figure 13-21 Labels added to a pie chart

Add A Border To A Pie Chart

There may be times when exploding a slice of a pie chart is too much, but you still want each section to be easily recognizable. This can be especially helpful when a pie chart is printed on paper in grayscale. Adding a thin border around each slice of the pie will make each slice stand out a little. The steps below show you how to add a border around each slice of a pie chart.

1. Open a spreadsheet that has a pie chart.

2. Right-click on any slice of the chart, then select Format Data Series.

3. Display the Border Color panel, then select the **SOLID LINE** option.

   You will see the Color option, as shown in Figure 13-22.

   If it is not set to white, select white now.

Figure 13-22 Format Data Series (pie chart options)

4. Display the Border Styles panel.

   Change the Width to 2pt, then click the Close button.

   Your pie chart should look similar to the one shown in Figure 13-23.

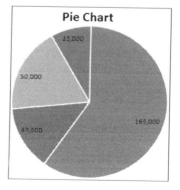

Figure 13-23 Pie chart with white border added

Adding A Data Series To A Chart

At some point you may have the need to add another series of data to the chart. If so, the steps below show you how.

1. Open the spreadsheet that has the chart that you want to add another series of data to.

2. Click on the chart, then Design tab ⇒ Data group ⇒ Select Data.

3. Click the Add button.

4. Click the button at the end of the Series name field, then select the cell that has the name of the series that you want to add.

5. Click the button at the end of the Series values field, then select the cells for the series. You should have options similar to those shown in Figure 13-24.

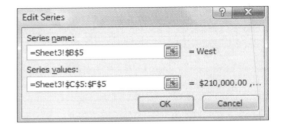

Figure 13-24 Edit Series dialog box

6. Click OK twice, then format the new series as needed.

Sparklines Overview

This is a new feature. A sparkline is a small chart that is placed in the background of a cell. Line, Column and Win/Loss are the types of sparklines that can be created. One big difference between a chart and a sparkline is that you can add text to the cell that a sparkline is in.

Like charts, sparklines have styles. Often, sparklines are used to show patterns in data. For example, showing the monthly sales for the quarter. Like charts, the data used to create a sparkline needs to be in adjacent cells. The sparkline can be next to or near the data that it is plotting, but it is not a requirement. When the data used in a sparkline is changed, the sparkline is updated. Unlike charts, you can create multiple sparklines at one time.

Sparklines Group

The options in this group are used to create a chart in the background of a cell in the worksheet. Sparklines are not objects like charts.

Links Group

[See Chapter 6, Links Group]

Text Group

The options in this group are used to add text boxes, headers, footers and WordArt to the worksheet. The options are explained in Table 13-2.

Option	Description
Text Box	[See Chapter 6, Text Group, Table 6-19]
Header & Footer	Displays the spreadsheet in the Page Layout view so that the header and footer sections can be modified.
WordArt	[See Chapter 6, Text Group, Table 6-19]

Table 13-2 Text group options explained

Symbols Group

[See Chapter 6, Symbols Group]

Ink Group

[See Chapter 6, Ink Group]

The **SHOW INK** option is used to show or hide annotation made in ink.

Sparkline Tools Design Contextual Tab

When a sparkline is added to a worksheet, the tab shown in Figure 13-25 is available to modify the sparkline.

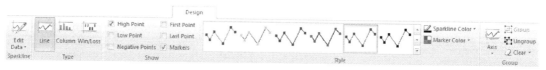

Figure 13-25 Sparkline Tools Design tab

Design Tab

The options on this tab are used to edit the data, change the sparkline type and select a style for the sparkline.

Sparkline Group

EDIT DATA This option is used to change the location or data source of the sparkline.

Type Group

The options in this group are used to change the sparkline type.

Show Group

The options in this group add features to the sparkline. The options are explained in Table 13-3.

Option	Description
High Point	Displays the highest value in each group in a different color.
Low Point	Displays the lowest value in each group in a different color.
Negative Points	Displays the negative values in each group in a different color.
First Points	Displays the first value in each group in a different color.
Last Point	Displays the last value in each group in a different color.
Markers	Plots each value (point) in each group.

Table 13-3 Show group options explained

Style Group

The options in this group are styles that can be applied to the sparkline. The options are explained in Table 13-4.

Option	Description
Style Gallery	Change the style for the sparkline.
Sparkline Color	Change the color for the line or bar on the sparkline.
Marker Color	Change the color for the points on the sparkline.

Table 13-4 Style group options explained

Group

The options in this group are used to change the axis options and group sparklines. The options are explained in Table 13-5.

Option	Description
Axis	Change the scale of each sparkline axis.
Group	Is used to group sparklines together so that they can share formatting and scaling options.
Ungroup	Removes the group functionality from the selected sparklines.
Clear	Removes the selected sparkline or sparkline group.

Table 13-5 Group options explained

How To Create A Sparkline

1. Open the Sparklines spreadsheet, then select the range B11 to E11.

2. Insert tab ⇒ Sparklines group ⇒ Column. You will see the dialog box shown in Figure 13-26.

3. Click the button at the end of the **LOCATION RANGE** field, then click in cell F11.

4. Click the button on the Create Sparklines dialog box, then click OK.

Figure 13-26 Create Sparklines dialog box

5. Make column F wider. If you want to save the sparkline, save the spreadsheet with a different name.

How To Modify A Sparkline

The options to modify sparklines are on the Sparkline Tools Design tab. You can use the spreadsheet that you created in the previous exercise.

1. Click on the sparkline.

2. On the Design tab, click the Line button.

3. Select the High Point and Low Point options.

4. Select a style that you like, then open the Sparkline Color drop-down list and select a color for the line.

5. Open the Marker Color drop-down list and select a color for the high point and low point markers.

How To Create Multiple Sparklines At One Time

The steps below show you how to create multiple sparklines at one time. The only downside to creating multiple sparklines at one time is that any changes that you make to one sparkline are applied to all sparklines that were created at the same time, unless you ungroup the sparklines.

1. Open the Sparklines spreadsheet.

2. Select the range B3 to E5.

3. Insert tab ⇒ Sparklines group ⇒ Line.

4. Click the button at the end of the **LOCATION RANGE** field, then select the range F3 to F5.

5. Click the button on the Create Sparklines dialog box, then click OK.

Drawing Tools Format Contextual Tab

When a text box is added to a spreadsheet or selected in a spreadsheet the tab shown in Figure 13-27 is available. The options are explained in detail in Chapter 6 as listed below.

Figure 13-27 Drawing Tools Format tab

Insert Shapes Group [See Chapter 6, Insert Shapes Group]
Shape Styles Group [See Chapter 6, Shape Styles Group]
WordArt Styles Group [See Chapter 6, WordArt Styles Group]
Arrange Group [See Chapter 6, Arrange Group]
Size Group [See Chapter 6, Size Group]

Moving Charts

Often, you may have a need to move a chart from its default location, especially if the chart is covering up data. There are two ways to move a chart, as discussed below.

① Select the chart then drag it to the new location on the worksheet.
② Use the **MOVE** command to place the chart on a new worksheet.

Using The Move Command

The steps below show you how to move a chart to a new worksheet.

 The **MOVE** command cannot be undone without closing the spreadsheet and not saving the changes. The chart cannot be resized.

1. Right-click on the chart and select Move Chart. You will see the Move Chart dialog box shown earlier in Figure 13-13.

2. Select the New Sheet option.

3. You can accept the default name for the new sheet, Chart1, or you can type in the name that you want, then click OK.

   The chart will be placed on the new tab, as shown in Figure 13-28.

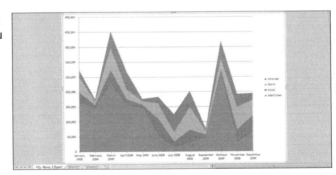

Figure 13-28 Chart moved to a new sheet

Adding Or Deleting Rows/Columns To Chart Data

Once you have created a chart, you have to be careful about changing the structure of the data. Adding or deleting rows or columns can cause the data in the chart to change in a way that you aren't expecting. For example, if you inserted a row after row 4 in the column chart that you created earlier, the chart would change and look like the one shown in Figure 13-29. Compare this to the chart shown earlier in Figure 13-8. To prevent this from happening follow the steps below.

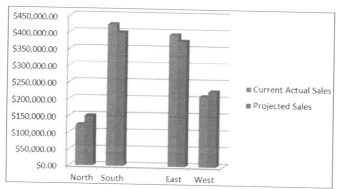

Figure 13-29 Chart automatically resized

1.   Select the chart.

2.   Format tab ⇒ Size group ⇒ Dialog box launcher.

3.   Select the Properties panel as shown in Figure 13-30. Select the option that best meets your needs, then click the Close button.

MOVE AND SIZE WITH CELLS is the default option, which causes the chart to change, as shown above in Figure 13-29.

MOVE BUT DON'T SIZE WITH CELLS Select this option if you want to be able to move the chart and not have it automatically resized.

DON'T MOVE OR SIZE WITH CELLS This option does not allow the chart to be moved or resized.

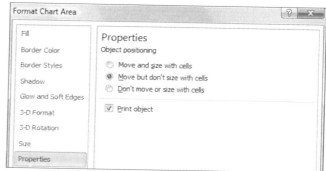

Figure 13-30 Format Chart Area dialog box

Printing Charts

As you read earlier, you can place the chart on its own worksheet. I suspect many people do this just so that they can print the chart on it's own sheet of paper because they don't know how to just print the chart when it is on the same worksheet as the data. There are three other options for printing a chart on its own sheet of paper if it is on the same worksheet as the data, as discussed below.

① Click on the chart, then open the Print panel on the File tab.

② Place the chart below the data, then insert a page break after the data.

③ Create a print area around the chart and print the print area.

Header & Footer Tools Design Contextual Tab

When the header or footer section of a spreadsheet is selected, the tab shown in Figure 13-31 is displayed. The options are explained below.

Figure 13-31 Header & Footer Tools Design tab

Header & Footer Group

The options in this group are used to select items commonly placed in the header or footer section of the spreadsheet, as shown in Figure 13-32.

Select the option that you want from the list.

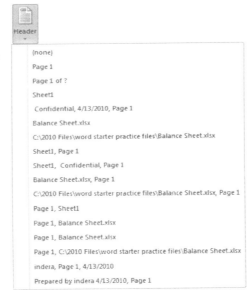

Figure 13-32 Header (or footer) options

Header & Footer Elements Group

The options in this group are used to add individual items to the header or footer section. The Font group options on the Home tab can be used to modify content in the header and footer sections of the spreadsheet. Many of the options in this group are the same as the options in the Header & Footer group. The difference is that you can select the placement of the item. The options are explained in Table 13-6.

Option	Description
Page Number	Adds the page number.
Number of Pages	Adds the total number of pages. This option is usually used after the Page Number option to create this page number style: Page 2 of 8, where 2 is the Page Number field and 8 is the Number of Pages field.
Current Date	Adds the date in this format: MM/DD/YYYY.
Current Time	Adds the time in this format: HH:MM AM or PM.
File Path	Adds the path (location) of the spreadsheet and file name, as shown in Figure 13-33.
File Name	Adds the file name.
Sheet Name	Adds the name of the tab.
Picture	Adds an image.
Format Picture	Opens the Format Picture dialog box. [See Chapter 6, Figure 6-13]

Table 13-6 Header & Footer Elements group options explained

C:\2010 Files\word starter practice files\Balance Sheet.xlsx

Figure 13-33 File Path option

Navigation Group

The options in this group are used to switch between the header and footer sections.

Options Group

The options in this group are used to format the layout of the content in the header and footer sections, as explained in Table 13-7.

Option	Description
Different First Page	[See Chapter 6, Table 6-17]
Different Odd & Even Pages	[See Chapter 6, Table 6-17]
Scale With Document	If checked, the header and footer sections will scale if a Shrink to fit scaling option (on the Print panel on the File tab or Scale to fit option on the Page Layout tab) is used to print the sheet.
Align with Page Margins	If checked, the content in the header or footer section is justified between the left and right margins, just like text in a word processing document.

Table 13-7 Options group options explained

Adding Content To The Header Or Footer Section

1. Open the Bigger Balance Sheet spreadsheet.

2. Insert tab ⇒ Text group ⇒ Header & Footer. Notice that the spreadsheet changes to the Page Layout view.

3. At the top of the spreadsheet you will see the header section. Click in the header section.

4. On the Design tab, click the File Name button, then press the space bar five times.

5. On the Design tab, click the Current Date button.

6. On the Design tab, click the Go To Footer button.

7. On the Design tab, click the Footer button, then select the Page 1 of ? option.

8. In print preview, the header section should look like the one shown in Figure 13-34. The footer section should look like the one shown in Figure 13-35. If you want to save the changes, save the spreadsheet with a new file name.

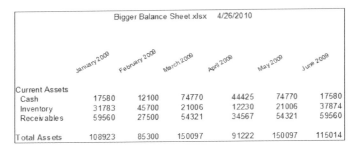

	January 2009	February 2009	March 2009	April 2009	May 2009	June 2009
Current Assets						
Cash	17580	12100	74770	44425	74770	17580
Inventory	31783	45700	21006	12230	21006	37874
Receivables	59560	27500	54321	34567	54321	59560
Total Assets	108923	85300	150097	91222	150097	115014

Figure 13-34 Header section

Toner	320	120	75	520	320	120
Electric	220	310	325	190	220	310
Paper	525	470	525	475	525	470
Total Expenses	170,610	174,200	163,075	167,110	170,515	172,200

Page 1 of 4

Figure 13-35 Footer section

THE PAGE LAYOUT TAB

Overview

This chapter covers the options on the Page Layout tab. You will learn about the following.

- ☑ Page Setup dialog box options
- ☑ Scale to fit options
- ☑ Creating print areas
- ☑ Page breaks

Overview

The options shown in Figure 14-1 are used to format the entire worksheet. The majority of the options are the same as those that are applied to individual cells in the worksheet.

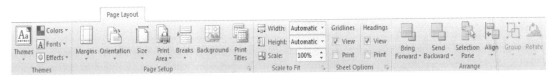

Figure 14-1 Page Layout tab

Themes Group

[See Chapter 7, Themes Group]

Printing Spreadsheets

Throughout the Excel chapters in this book, you have seen a variety of spreadsheets in terms of the number of rows and columns. Some of these spreadsheets can be printed just as they are without changing any of the print settings. Other spreadsheets like the Bigger Balance Sheet spreadsheet practice file would need to have some of the print settings discussed below changed, so that the spreadsheet would print in a layout that is easy to read.

Page Setup Group

The options in this group are used to change the margins, page orientation and print options, as explained in Table 14-1.

Option	Description
Margins	[See Chapter 7, Page Setup Group]
Orientation	[See Chapter 7, Page Setup Group]
Size	[See Chapter 7, Page Setup Group]
Print Area	Is used to select a specific section of the spreadsheet to print or clear an existing print area.
Breaks	Is used to add and remove page breaks.
Background	Is used to select an image file to use as the background for the entire spreadsheet.
Print Titles	Displays the Sheet tab on the Page Setup dialog box, which is used to select the rows and columns that need to be repeated on each printed page if the data will print on more than one page.
Dialog Box Launcher	Opens the Page tab on the Page Setup dialog box, as shown in Figure 14-2.

Table 14-1 Page Setup group options explained

Page Setup Dialog Box

The options on this dialog box are used to select printing options for the spreadsheet. It contains many of the options that are displayed on the Page Layout tab.

The options on the **PAGE** tab are used to select the orientation, scaling and paper size.

The options on the **MARGINS** tab shown in Figure 14-2 are used to select the margins for the spreadsheet and whether or not the spreadsheet should be centered on the page when printed.

The options on the **HEADER/FOOTER** tab are used to select pre-formatted options or create custom content for the header and footer sections. The Custom buttons open the dialog box shown in Figure 14-3.

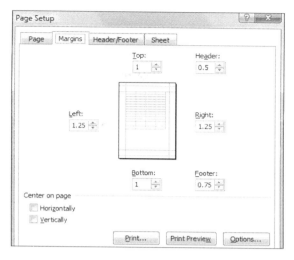

Figure 14-2 Page Setup dialog box

The options on the **SHEET** tab are used to create a print area, select cells for the print titles and non content items that will print with the spreadsheet.

Printing Gridlines
The gridlines that are displayed on the worksheet on the computer screen do not automatically print when the worksheet is printed. To print the gridlines, select the **GRIDLINES** option on the Sheet tab on the Page Setup dialog box.

The options on the Header dialog box are used to add content to the left, center or right section of the header or footer section.

These are the same options that are on the Header & Footer Tools Design tab.

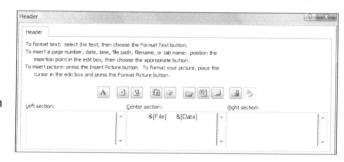

Figure 14-3 Header dialog box

Scale To Fit Group

The options in this group are used to reduce the print size of the spreadsheet to fit the paper size that you select. The options are explained in Table 14-2.

Option	Description
Width	Is used to shrink the width of the columns to fit better when printed.
Height	Is used to shrink the height of the spreadsheet when printed.
Scale	Is used to reduce or enlarge the size of the content when printed.
Dialog Box Launcher	Displays the Page tab on the Page Setup dialog box. The options in the scaling section are the same as the ones in the Scale to Fit group.

Table 14-2 Scale to Fit group options explained

Width And Height Options

The options in these drop-down lists are used to select the maximum number of pages that you want the columns to print on. Keep in mind that shrinking the column size means that the print will be smaller.

AUTOMATIC is the default option and will not reduce the width or height of the columns. The steps below illustrate how these options work.

1.   Open the Bigger Balance spreadsheet.

2.   File tab ⇒ Print panel. The display on the right is how the spreadsheet will look when printed.

3.   Display the spreadsheet in the Page Layout view. If you look in the status bar, you will see that the spreadsheet has four pages.

4.   Page Layout tab ⇒ Scale to Fit group ⇒ Change the width to one page. If you preview the spreadsheet you will see that the spreadsheet now fits on one page.

Sheet Options Group

The options in this group are used to select whether gridlines and headings (row numbers and column letters) are displayed in the spreadsheet or are printed. The Dialog box launcher displays the Sheet tab on the Page Setup dialog box, which contains more gridline and heading options.

Maybe it's just me, but the majority of spreadsheets that I print, I also print the gridlines. It would be nice if there was an option on the Excel Options dialog box that would let us set a default to print gridlines.

Arrange Group

The options in this group are the same as ones on the Picture Tools Format tab.
[See Chapter 6, Table 6-6]

Setting A Print Area

Some of the spreadsheets that you have modified are really large. Sometimes you may only need or want to print a certain part of the spreadsheet. To only print a certain part of the spreadsheet, you have to create what is known as a **PRINT AREA**. When a spreadsheet has a print area associated with it, only the portion of the spreadsheet that is in the print area will print. The steps below show you how to set up a print area.

1. Open the Bigger Balance spreadsheet.

2. Select the range A18 to M24. This is the range for the print area.

3. Page Layout tab $\Rightarrow$ Page Setup group $\Rightarrow$ Print Area $\Rightarrow$ Set Print Area.

4. If you look in the Name box, you will see the word Print_Area. If you click outside of the print area that you just created, you will see a border with dashes around the print area that you just created.

Add More Content To The Print Area

Print areas are not limited to one range of cells. The steps below show you how to add another range of cells to the print area.

1. Select the range A4 to M11.

2. Page Layout tab $\Rightarrow$ Page Setup group $\Rightarrow$ Print Area $\Rightarrow$ Add To Print Area.

3. Preview the spreadsheet and change the orientation to landscape.

As you preview the spreadsheet, notice that you see the first print range that you selected first, even though it is not at the top of the spreadsheet. Therefore, you have to select the print areas in the order that you want them to appear in when printed. If you want to keep the print area, save the document with a new file name. The print area stays in effect until you remove it.

If you wanted to use the Print Area option to print a portion of the spreadsheet once, you should not save the spreadsheet after you create the print area. If you saved the print area in this exercise, every time that you print this spreadsheet, only the portion of the spreadsheet that is defined in the print area will print, until you clear the print area option.

Adding Page Breaks

Page breaks are used to control how much of the spreadsheet prints on the page. Page breaks are added above the cell that the mouse pointer is in. For example, if you want the page break below row 11, click in row 12. To add a page break, follow the steps below.

1. Open the spreadsheet that you want to add the page break to.

2. Click in a cell in the row below the row that you want the page break added to.

3. Page Layout tab $\Rightarrow$ Page Setup group $\Rightarrow$ Breaks $\Rightarrow$ Insert Page Break.

Adding Print Titles To A Spreadsheet

The print titles option is used to select the rows or columns in the spreadsheet that will print on every page. This option is only necessary if the information on the spreadsheet will print on more than one page. The steps below show you how to use this option.

1. Open the Bigger Balance Sheet spreadsheet.

2. Page Layout tab $\Rightarrow$ Page Setup group $\Rightarrow$ Print Titles.

3. Click the button at the end of the **ROWS TO REPEAT AT TOP** field. If necessary, move the dialog box down past row 6.

4. Select row 4, then click the button on the dialog box.

5. Click the Print Preview button on the dialog box. You will see the months at the top of every page. Notice that from page 2 on, Column A does not appear.

6. Open the Page Setup dialog box from the Page Layout tab because the Page Setup link on the Print panel does not provide access to all of the options that are on the dialog box. On the Sheet tab, select Column A in the **COLUMNS TO REPEAT AT LEFT** field. Now when you preview the spreadsheet, you will see Column A on the appropriate pages.

Hiding Rows And Columns

Hiding rows and columns is another way to work with large spreadsheets. You can hide rows and columns that you do not need to see or do not want to print. Often, rows or columns that have confidential information like social security numbers are hidden when printed. To hide a row or column select the rows or columns that you want to hide, then right-click and select the **HIDE** option on the shortcut menu.

THE FORMULAS TAB

Overview

This chapter covers the options on the Formulas tab. You will learn about the following.

- ☑ Creating formulas
- ☑ Using Auto Fill
- ☑ Auto Sum
- ☑ Range names
- ☑ Functions

Formulas And Functions Overview

Formulas and functions are some of the most powerful features in Excel. Ironically, many people that are first learning Excel think that formulas and functions are one of the most dreaded features because there is math and logic involved <smile>. If you fall into this category, hopefully this chapter will help you overcome some of the fear. You have probably heard the phrase **NUMBER CRUNCHING**. Formulas and functions allow you to do number crunching. The options on the Formulas tab shown in Figure 15-1 are used to create formulas.

Figure 15-1 Formulas tab

What Is The Difference Between Formulas And Functions?

A **Formula** performs a calculation (like addition, subtraction or multiplication) on cells in the spreadsheet. You create formulas. The result of the formula is placed in a cell.

Functions are pre-built formulas that come with Excel. Functions are often more complex than formulas that you create. If there is a built-in function that meets your needs, use it because there is no point reinventing the wheel, as they say. Examples of functions include **NOW**, which returns the current date and time. **PV** is a function that calculates the present value of an annuity. There are over 300 functions that come with Excel. You can also use functions in your formulas.

 All formulas and functions must begin with an equal sign.

Function Library Group

The majority of options in this group are lists of some of the more popular functions. They are categorized by type. This makes finding functions easier. The options are explained in Table 15-1.

Option	Description
Insert Function	Opens the Insert Function dialog box which is used to search for and select a function to use.
Auto Sum	Is used to create a formula that adds the values in the cells adjacent to the cell that is selected.
Recently Used	Displays a list of the functions that you recently used. Selecting an option from this list adds the function to the selected cell.
Financial	These functions calculate things like investments, payment amounts and mortgage rates.
Logical	These functions create decision making and conditional formulas similar to the cell conditional formatting that you read about in Chapter 12.
Text	These functions are used for non numeric content.
Date & Time	These functions are used for date or time values.
Lookup & Reference	These functions are used find data in other cells.

Table 15-1 Function Library group options explained

Option	Description
Math & Trig	These are the basic functions like rounding, sum and truncate.
More Functions	The options on this drop-down list are more categories of functions.

Table 15-1 Function Library group options explained (Continued)

Defined Names Group

The options in this group are used to create and manage group names and use them in formulas. In Chapter 14 you created a (range) name when you created a print area. Names, or range names as I call them, are most often created when you need to use the same set of cells for more than one formula. Another reason range names are created is because it can make the formula easier to read. The options are explained in Table 15-2.

Option	Description
Name Manager	Opens the dialog box shown in Figure 15-2. The options on this dialog box are used to create, edit and delete range names. The **FILTER** button is used to narrow the number of range names that are displayed.
Define Name	The options are used to create a name or add an existing name to a formula.
Use In Formula	The options display the range names that are in the spreadsheet, as shown in Figure 15-3.
Create From Selection	Is used to create a range name automatically and use the text in cells near the range as the range name. Clicking this button opens the dialog box shown in Figure 15-4.

Table 15-2 Defined Names group options explained

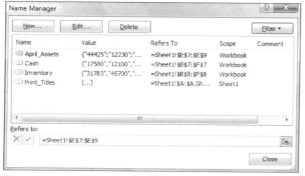

Figure 15-2 Name Manager dialog box

Figure 15-3 Use in Formula options

The options on this dialog box are used to select the cells that have the text that you want to use as the range name.

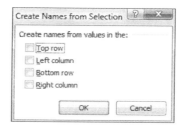

Figure 15-4 Create Names From Selection dialog box

Calculation Group

The options in this group are used to run the calculations in the worksheet. They are explained in Table 15-3.

Option	Description
Calculation Options	The options shown in Figure 15-5 are used to select when formulas are calculated.
Calculate Now	Calculates all of the formulas in the workbook.
Calculate Sheet	Calculates the formulas on the selected sheet.

Table 15-3 Calculation group options explained

Selecting the **MANUAL** option forces you to manually run the calculations.

Figure 15-5 Calculation Options

Insert Function Dialog Box

The options shown in Figure 15-6 are used to search for the function that you want to use.

This dialog box is primarily used when you do not know the name or category of the function that you want to use.

When you find the function that you want to use, click on it, then click OK.

You will then see the dialog box shown in Figure 15-7.

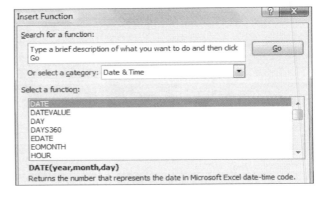

Figure 15-6 Insert Function dialog box

The options on this dialog box are used to select the cell or type in the data for each argument of the function.

Figure 15-7 Function Arguments dialog box

Creating Formulas Manually

The steps below show you how to create a formula to calculate the Total Assets for each month. The formula is Cash + Inventory + Receivables = Total Assets. The cells needed for this calculation are in rows 6 to 8 on the spreadsheet.

1. Save the Balance Sheet spreadsheet as Modified balance sheet.

2. Click in cell B10. Type = B6 + B7 + B8, then press Enter. Your spreadsheet should look like the one shown in Figure 15-8.

 You do not have to type spaces in the formula. I use spaces in this book to make the formulas easier for you to read. You do not have to type the cell letter as a capital letter. You can type them in lower case letters and they will automatically be converted to a capital letter once you press the Enter key.

The formula that you typed in is at the top of Figure 15-8.

If you need to modify the formula, press the F2 key. You can edit the formula in the cell or you can click in the **FORMULA BAR** and modify the formula there. You can also enter and edit non formula data in the Formula bar.

To the left of cell B10, you may see an exclamation mark, as shown in Figure 15-8. This indicates that the cell has a formula and the cell is not locked. If you click on this button, you will see the menu shown in Figure 15-9.

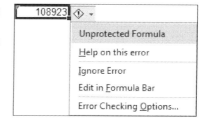

Figure 15-8 Formula entered in cell B10

The options on this menu are used to fix the error. When you fix the error, the green triangle in the cell will go away. Because this is not an error, you can select the **IGNORE ERROR** option, which will remove the green triangle.

You do not have to select anything. If you do not plan to lock cells in the spreadsheet, select the **ERROR CHECKING OPTIONS** on the drop-down list.

Figure 15-9 Error menu

Clear the check mark for the **UNLOCKED CELLS CONTAINING FORMULAS** option in the Error checking rules section on the Excel Options dialog box, then click OK. That will keep the warning from appearing on the spreadsheet.

3. Click in cell F13 and type = B6 + C6 + D6, then press Enter. This formula will calculate the amount of year to date cash that the company has. Save the changes.

Auto Fill

Auto Fill is another way to copy the value in a cell to other cells in the spreadsheet. If you are creating a personal income statement for the year you need to include your mortgage payment amount for each month, you could type the value in one cell and copy it 11 times to other cells or you could use Auto Fill.

1. Open a new workbook. In cell B3, type 2300, then press Enter.

2. Place the mouse pointer on the lower right corner of cell B3, as shown in Figure 15-10.

    Hold down the left mouse button and drag the mouse to cell F3. All of the cells should have 2300 in it.

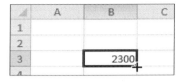

Figure 15-10 Mouse pointer in the Auto Fill position

3. With the cells still selected, change the format of the cells to comma, with no decimal places.

4. You can also fill down. Select cell E3.

    With the mouse pointer in the Auto Fill position, drag it down to cell E5.

    Cells E4 and E5 should now be filled in with the same number, as shown in Figure 15-11.

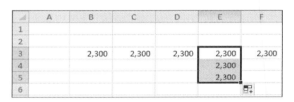

Figure 15-11 Cells filled in with the Auto Fill option

Auto Fill Options

As shown below and to the right of cell E5 in Figure 15-11, there is a button. This is the Auto Fill button. If you click on the button, you will see the options shown in Figure 15-12. The options are explained below.

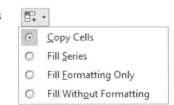

COPY CELLS Copies cells just as they are, including the formatting.
FILL SERIES Fills the selected cells in sequence.
FILL FORMATTING ONLY Only copies the formatting of the original cell.
FILL WITHOUT FORMATTING Fills the cells without the formatting of the original cell.

Figure 15-12 Auto Fill options

Figure 15-13 shows the (Auto) Fill options on the Home tab. (Home tab ⇒ Editing group ⇒ Fill) The options are explained below.

DOWN Fills the cells below the selected cell in increasing increments.
RIGHT Fills the cells to the right in increasing increments.
UP Fills the cells above the selected cell in decreasing increments.
LEFT Fills the cells left in decreasing increments.
ACROSS WORKSHEETS Opens the dialog box shown in Figure 15-14.
SERIES Opens the dialog box shown in Figure 15-15.
JUSTIFY Centers text between the margins.

Figure 15-13 Fill options

The options on this dialog box are used to select what is copied to the other selected worksheets.

ALL Copies contents and formats. The other options copy one, but not the other.

Figure 15-14 Fill Across Worksheets dialog box

The options on this dialog box are used to select the increment that will be used to fill the selected cells.

Figure 15-15 Series dialog box

Using Auto Fill To Fill In More Than One Column Or Row

You can use Auto Fill to fill in several columns or rows at the same time. Pay attention to the case (upper and lower) in step 1 below.

1. In cell A4 type `TEST1`. In cell B4 type `TestA`. In cell C4 type `Test3`.

2. Make cell A4 bold. Change the format color in cell B4 to red.

3. Add a **LINE STYLE** border to cell C4.

4. Select the range A4 to C4. Place the mouse pointer in the lower right corner of cell C4.

    Press the left mouse button and drag the mouse down to row 7. Your spreadsheet should look like the one shown in Figure 15-16. Notice that each column retained its formatting. Also notice that the numbers incremented in columns A and C.

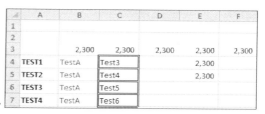

Figure 15-16 Auto Fill result for step 4

5. Change cell B6 to `Test4`, then highlight the range A6 to C6 and use the Auto Fill option to fill in cells D6 to G6. Notice that the numbers incremented, as shown in Figure 15-17.

⊿	A	B	C	D	E	F	G
2							
3		2,300	2,300	2,300	2,300	2,300	
4	TEST1	TestA	Test3		2,300		
5	TEST2	TestA	Test4		2,300		
6	TEST3	TEST4	TEST5	TEST6	TEST7	TEST8	TEST9
7	TEST4	TestA	Test6				

Figure 15-17 Auto Fill result for step 5

6. Save the changes. Type `Fun with auto fill` as the file name. Leave the spreadsheet open.

Fill Series

Fill Series is similar to Auto Fill because Fill Series fills in cells based on the criteria that you select. The difference is that Fill Series fills in cells with a pattern, similar to the pattern that was created with the Auto Fill example shown above in Figure 15-17.

Using The Fill Series Option With Days Of The Week

1. Type `Monday` in cell A8, then press Enter.

2. Click in cell A8. Drag the fill handle down to cell A12. You should see Monday through Friday in cells A8 to A12.

Using The Fill Series Option With Numeric Dates

1. Type `2/15/10` in cell B8, then press Enter.

2. Select the range B8 to B12. Open the Series dialog box. The value that you enter in the **STEP VALUE** field will increment the value in cell B8. If you leave the value at one, you will get dates in sequential order.

3. Change the Step value to 2, then click OK. The dates filled in, should be every other day.

Using The Fill Series Option With Months

1. Type `1/1/10` in cell C11, then press Enter. Select the range C11 to F11.

2. Home tab ⇒ Number group ⇒ Dialog box launcher.

3. Click on the Custom category. Type `mmmm` in the **TYPE** field, then click OK.

4. Open the Series dialog box, then select the **DATE** Type and **MONTH** Date Unit.

5. Change the Step value to 3, then click OK. The months April, July and October should have filled in the cells. Save the changes.

How To Copy Formulas Using The Auto Fill Command

The formula that you created in cell B10 in the Modified balance sheet spreadsheet is the same formula that is needed for columns C and D. The only difference is that the column letter has to be different. You could type the same formula in cell C10 and D10 or you could use the Fill Right command, which will copy the formula to cells C10 and D10.

1. Open the Modified balance sheet spreadsheet.

2. Cell in cell B10. Place the mouse pointer in the Auto Fill position and drag the mouse pointer to the right until cell D10 is selected.

    You may be thinking that the formula in cells C10 and D10 will be the same as the formula in cell B10.

    The **AUTO FILL** command copies the formula and automatically modifies it for the other columns that are selected. Excel is designed to think that you want the same formula that you used with the fill command, but that you want the formula to add the data in the cells in the column that is being filled. Therefore, it automatically changes the column letter in the formula.

3. Click in cell D10. Look at the formula in the Formula bar. You should see **=D6 + D7 + D8**.

    Your spreadsheet should look like the one shown in Figure 15-18.

	A	B	C	D	E
5	Current Assets				
6	Cash	17580	12100	74770	44425
7	Inventory	31783	45700	21006	12230
8	Receivables	59560	27500	54321	34567
9					
10	Total Assets	108923	85300	150097	

Figure 15-18 Formula copied to other cells

4. Save the changes and leave the spreadsheet open to complete the next exercise.

Auto Sum

The Auto Sum option on the Formulas tab is used to add the values in two or more adjacent cells. Auto Sum is most often used to add columns of data like cells B6 to B9 and place the result in B10. You can also use Auto Sum to add rows of data. The steps below show you how to use the Auto Sum option to calculate the YTD Receivables. (YTD stands for Year To Date).

1. Click in cell F15. Click the Auto Sum button on the Formulas tab, then select the Sum function. This is where you want the result placed. I find it easier to click in the cell where I want the formula placed before creating the formula.

The range F13 to F14 is automatically selected because Excel thinks that this is the range that you want to sum. The range that you really want to sum is B8 to M8. You can type the range that you want in the selected section of the formula in cell F15 or you can select the cells in the spreadsheet.

 Notice as you select the cells, that the cell range in the formula in cell F15 changes as you select more cells.

2. Select the cell range B8 to M8, as shown in Figure 15-19, then press Enter. The number **175948** should be in cell F15.

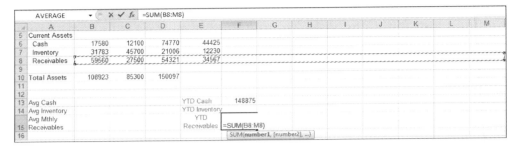

Figure 15-19 Range selected for the Auto Sum formula

3. Save the changes.

Range Names

Range names are used to identify a cell or a group of cells by a name of your choice, instead of the cell column letter and row number. If you needed to reference the Current Actual Sales for all regions, you would refer to it as B3:B8 in the Actual Sales vs Projects workbook. You could create a range name like Actual_Sales to reference these cells. Range names are used in formulas to make them easier to read.

Other Reasons To Use Range Names

① If you had a formula that subtracted Projected Sales from Actual Sales, the formula would be easier to read if it looked like this, **NORTH_SALES - PROJECTED_SALES** instead of **B5 - C5**.

② If you type the wrong cell address in a formula, you may not notice it as fast as you would if you were using range names in the formula.

 Range names can have a maximum of 15 characters and can include letters, numbers and the underscore. You cannot have spaces in a range name.

Creating Range Names

1. Save the Actual Sales vs Projected spreadsheet as Actual sales with range names.

2. Select the range B5 to B8.

   Formulas tab ⇒ Define Names group ⇒ Define Name ⇒ Define Name.

   You should see the dialog box shown in Figure 15-20.

   Type Actual_Sales in the Name field, then click OK.

Figure 15-20 New Name dialog box

3. Select the range C5 to C8, then open the New Name dialog box.
    Type `Projected_Sales` in the Name field, then click OK.

4. Select cell B7, then open the New Name dialog box. Type `East_Sales` in the Name field,
    then click OK.

5. On the Formulas tab, click the
    Name Manager button.

    Your dialog box should have all
    of the range names shown in
    Figure 15-21.

    Close the dialog box and save
    the changes.

Figure 15-21 Range names that you created

 Notice that the cell ranges are in the Refers To column. This is helpful if you do not
remember which cells the range name is referring to.

How To Create A Formula Using A Range Name

1. Open the Modified balance sheet spreadsheet.

2. Click in cell E10 and type `=Sum(April_Assets)`, then press Enter. The Range name
    April_Assets references cells E6 to E8.

This is not a range that you created. I created the April_Assets range among others and saved them
in the spreadsheet while writing this book. I'm telling you this because I don't want you to think that
you missed an exercise, or worse, that I left something out of the book.

Viewing Range Names On The Spreadsheet

If you create several range names in a spreadsheet you may want to see a list of them while you
are working, without having to open the Name Manager dialog box. To display range names on the
spreadsheet, follow the steps below.

1. Click in cell A18. Formulas tab ⇒ Defined Names group ⇒ Use in Formula ⇒ Paste Names.

2. Click the **PASTE LIST** button. Your spreadsheet should
    look like the one shown in Figure 15-22.

    If you had selected a portion of the spreadsheet
    that already had data in it, you would overwrite the
    data when the range name list was added to the
    spreadsheet. If this happens, click the Undo button,
    then select a portion of the spreadsheet where there
    is no data.

    When you are finished creating or editing a
    spreadsheet, you can delete the range name list
    from the spreadsheet unless you need it to stay
    on the spreadsheet.

Figure 15-22 Range name list added to
the spreadsheet in rows 18 to 20

If you create new range names after displaying the list on the spreadsheet, the new range names will not automatically be displayed in the spreadsheet. You will have to follow the steps above to re-display the Range name list.

Functions

Functions are built-in formulas that you can use to save time. The functions covered in the rest of this chapter are among the more popular functions. The Inventory spreadsheet that you will use keeps track of the quantity, cost, markup, sales price and profit per book, as well as, averages and the number of book titles that are on hand.

COUNT Function

This function will count the number of cells in the range. It does not add the values in the cells. If you need to know how many book titles are listed on a spreadsheet, you would use the Count function.

1. Save the Inventory spreadsheet as `Inventory with functions`.

2. Click in cell B13. Formulas tab ⇒ Function Library group ⇒ More functions ⇒ Statistical ⇒ Count.

3. The range B7 to B12 is filled in on the dialog box shown in Figure 15-23. Click OK.

This range is okay, even though cell B12 is empty. The Count function only counts cells that have a formula, text, number, the value N/A or ERR in it.

Because you selected cell B13 before you started to add the function to the spreadsheet, Excel remembered it.

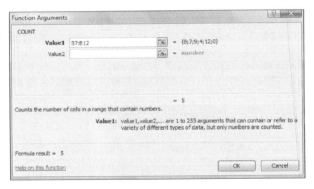

Figure 15-23 Function Arguments dialog box

Your spreadsheet should look like the one shown in Figure 15-24.

There are five book titles listed in the spreadsheet. Save the changes and leave the spreadsheet open.

	A	B	C	D
5	Name Of Book	Quantity	Cost	Markup %
6				
7	Learning Multimedia	8	$12.00	0.05
8	The New Way To Surf	7	$6.98	0.04
9	Excel Made Easy	9	$9.95	0.09
10	Learning Excel	4	$7.98	0.075
11	Surfing The Net	12	$5.95	0.03
12				
13	# Of Titles On Hand	5		

Figure 15-24 Count function illustrated

AVERAGE Function

The AVERAGE function calculates the average value of a range of numbers. The steps below show you how to calculate the average percent that books are marked up.

1. Click in cell D15. On the Formulas tab, click on the More Functions button.

2. Select the **STATISTICAL** option, then select the **AVERAGE** function.

3. Change the range to D7:D11, then click OK. The number **0.057** should be in cell D15.

MIN Function

The MIN function will evaluate all of the values in the range that you specify and find the lowest value in the range. In the Inventory spreadsheet, this function would be useful if you wanted to know which book had the least number of copies on hand or which book cost the least. The steps below show you how to use the MIN function to find the book that has the lowest markup percent.

1. Click in cell D16. On the Formulas tab, click on the More Functions button.

2. Select the Statistical option, then select the **MIN** function.

3. Change the range to D7:D11, then click OK. The number **0.03** should be in cell D16. If you look at the five values in the Markup % column you will see that 0.03 is the lowest value in the column.

Now that you have used a few of the functions you may be saying that you could do these calculations in your head. This is true for a spreadsheet that does not have a lot of data like the one that you are currently using. What if the Inventory spreadsheet had 500 or more books in it? It may not be so easy to determine which title had the least number of copies on hand or which book cost the least. If you wanted to keep the stats on your favorite sports team or if you coach a sports team, being able to easily maintain the players averages would save you a lot of time.

MAX Function

The MAX function will evaluate all of the values in the range that you specify and find the highest value in the range. The steps below show you how to use the MAX function to find the book that has the largest markup percent.

1. Click in cell D17. On the Formulas tab, click on the More Functions button.

2. Select the Statistical option, then select the **MAX** function.

3. Change the range to D7:D11, then click OK. The number **0.09** should be in cell D17.

STDEV.P Function

The Standard Deviation function (STDEV.P) calculates the mean (average) value in the range of cells selected and then calculates how far from the mean each value in the range of cells that you have selected is. The steps below show you how to calculate the standard deviation for the cost of the books.

1. Click in cell C19. On the Formulas tab, click on the More Functions button.

2. Select the Statistical option, then select the **STDEV.P** function.

3. Change the range to C7:C11, then click OK.

   The number **2.1637874** should be in cell C19.

   Your spreadsheet should look like the one shown in Figure 15-25.

   Save the changes.

	A	B	C	D
5	Name Of Book	Quantity	Cost	Markup %
6				
7	Learning Multimedia	8	$12.00	0.05
8	The New Way To Surf	7	$6.98	0.04
9	Excel Made Easy	9	$9.95	0.09
10	Learning Excel	4	$7.98	0.075
11	Surfing The Net	12	$5.95	0.03
12				
13	# Of Titles On Hand	5		
14				
15	Average Markup			0.057
16	Minimum Markup			0.03
17	Maximum Markup			0.09
18				
19	Cost Deviation		2.1637874	

Figure 15-25 Functions added to the spreadsheet

Calculate The Sale Price

The steps below show you how to create a formula manually to calculate the sale price of each book. The sale price equals the cost times the markup percent plus the cost.

1. Create a formula in cell E7 that calculates the sale price. You can use any method that you want. The number **12.60** should be in cell E7.

The first task that you need to complete is to calculate 5% of the cost. Multiplying C7 times D7 will give you the markup amount in dollars. Next you have to add the markup amount to the cost of the book. Therefore, the formula is =(C7*D7)+C7.

Using parenthesis in a formula determines the order of how the formula is calculated. The portion of a formula inside the parenthesis is calculated together. In the sale price formula that you just created, the value in cell C7 is multiplied by the value in cell D7. The sum of that calculation is added to the value in cell C7. The result is placed in cell E7.

2. Copy the formula in cell E7 to cells E8 to E11.

Calculate The Profit

The Book Profit column represents the profit for each book sold. The formula is Sale Price minus Cost.

1. Create a formula in cell F7 to calculate the book profit.

2. Copy this formula to cells F8 to F11.

Your spreadsheet should look like the one shown in Figure 15-26.

The formula is in the Formula bar.

	A	B	C	D	E	F
	F7		f_x =E7-C7			
5	Name Of Book	Quantity	Cost	Markup %	Sale Price	Book Profit
6						
7	Learning Multimedia	8	$12.00	0.05	12.60	0.60
8	The New Way To Surf	7	$6.98	0.04	7.26	0.28
9	Excel Made Easy	9	$9.95	0.09	10.85	0.90
10	Learning Excel	4	$7.98	0.075	8.58	0.60
11	Surfing The Net	12	$5.95	0.03	6.13	0.18
12						
13	# Of Titles On Hand	5				
14						
15	Average Markup			0.057		
16	Minimum Markup			0.03		
17	Maximum Markup			0.09		
18						
19	Cost Deviation		2.1637874			

Figure 15-26 Book profit formula added to the spreadsheet

3. Save the changes.

Using Functions In Tables

In Chapter 13 you learned how to create a basic table. Now that you have learned how to create formulas, you will learn how to add formulas to tables.

The **TOTAL ROW** option (on the Table Tools Design tab) is used to add a row at the bottom of the table that sums data in a column in the spreadsheet. When the Total Row option is enabled, a count of the number of records in the table is displayed by default, as shown in Figure 15-27.

You can change the count total to a different type of total by selecting one of the options shown in the drop-down list. If the function that you want to use is not in the list, select the **MORE FUNCTIONS** option, which opens the Insert Function dialog box.

	First Name	Last Name	Phone	Address	City	State	Zip Code	Category
18	Peter	Young	(718)505-4259	188 William	Bogota	NV	32881	Sports
19	Randi	Sherwood	(718)505-3388	777 Broad /	Ramsey	PA	19001	Computer
20	Carrie	Downing	(407)987-4563	63 Maple A	Glen Rock	NV	32888	Computer
21	Total							19
22								None
23								Average
24								Count
25								Count Numbers
26								Max
27								Min
28								Sum
29								StdDev
								Var
								More Functions...

Figure 15-27 Total row added to a table

Adding A Function To A Table

The steps below show you how to add a total row and function to a table.

1. Open the Table with totals spreadsheet.

2. Click in the table, then click on the Design tab. Check the Total Row option in the Table Style Options group. You should see the number 15 at the end of Column G. That is the number of records in the table.

3. Open the Total drop-down list shown above in Figure 15-27, then select Sum. You should see the amount $954.55, which is a total of the values in Column G.

4. In cell E17, type `Total Order Amount`.

5. Change cell A17 to `Total # of customers`.

6. Open the drop-down list in cell C17, then select Count. Row 17 should look like the one shown in Figure 15-28.

	First Name	Last Name	Address	City	State	Zip Code	Order Amount	
14	Peter	Young	188 William St	Bogota	NV	32881	$89.00	
15	Randi	Sherwood	777 Broad Ave	Ramsey	PA	19001	$71.25	
16	Carrie	Downing	63 Maple Ave	Glen Rock	NV	32888	$62.95	
17	Total # of customers		15			Total Order Amount	$954.55	

Figure 15-28 Total row added to the table

Using Other Worksheets

All of the formulas and functions that you have used so far have only referenced cells on the current worksheet. Formulas and functions can reference cells on another worksheet in the same workbook or in a different workbook.

I am not sure that referencing cells in a different workbook is a great idea in the workplace because it can be difficult to make sure that the workbooks are not moved to a different location on a server. At home, on your own computer, it should not be as much of a problem.

If you are using the Function Arguments dialog box to select cells on another sheet, click on the tab for the worksheet that has the cells that you want to use after you click the button at the end of the argument. After you select the cells, you will see the sheet name before the cells that you selected, as illustrated in Figure 15-29.

Figure 15-29 Syntax for a cell selected on another sheet in the workbook

The End!

If you are reading this paragraph, I hope it means that you have completed all of the exercises in this book. If so, congratulations because you have covered a lot of material. If some topics seem a little fuzzy right now, that is to be expected. Hopefully you have gained some valuable Word and Excel skills and techniques. As you have probably figured out, unless you are creating basic documents and spreadsheets, there are a lot of options and features at your disposal. I hope that you enjoyed the book.

INDEX

drop caps, 6-28
duplicate records, 8-13
Duplicate Values dialog box, 12-14

E

Edit Series dialog box, 13-12
editing group options (Excel), 12-16
editing group options (Word), 4-9
editing options, 4-2
embed font options, 2-26
embedded Excel spreadsheet, 9-14
embedding fonts, 3-26
envelopes, 8-19
Envelopes and Labels dialog box, 8-19, 8-23
eraser option, 9-8
error bars (chart), 10-11
error checking options (Excel), 11-13, 15-5
Excel Options dialog box, 11-10
Excel Starter 2010 vs Excel 2010, 11-3
Excel Starter help, 11-9
Excel Starter workspace, 11-4

F

F1 key, 1-15
F2 key, 11-27, 15-5
F4 key, 1-13
F7 key, 4-18
F8 key, 11-24
F9 key, 11-12
F11 key, 10-15
file format options (Excel), 11-19
file format options (Word), 3-2
File Locations dialog box, 2-32
File tab (Excel), 11-9
File tab (Word), 2-7
Fill Across Worksheets dialog box, 15-7
fill handle option, 11-16
fill series, 15-8
Fill-In dialog box, 8-6
Filter and Sort dialog box, 8-12
filter criteria, 8-14
filter data, 12-20
financial functions, 15-2
find & select options, 12-22
Find and Replace dialog box (Excel), 12-24
Find and Replace search options, 12-23
find command (Excel), 12-24
find command (Word), 4-9, 4-11
Find Duplicates dialog box, 8-13
Find Entry dialog box, 8-7
find in button, 4-11

Find Options dialog box, 4-15
finish group options, 8-7
floor (chart), 10-6, 10-11
Font dialog box (Word), 5-4
font group options (Excel), 12-7
font group options (Word), 5-2
fonts (Word), 5-4
Format Axis dialog box, 10-13
Format Cells dialog box, 11-26, 12-7, 12-11
Format Chart Area dialog box, 13-17
Format Chart Title dialog box, 10-9
Format Data Labels dialog box, 10-10
Format Data Series dialog box, 10-8, 13-10
Format Data Table dialog box, 10-10
Format Error Bars dialog box, 10-12
format options, 12-15
format painter, 4-7
Format Picture dialog box, 6-7
Format Shape dialog box, 6-17
Format Text Effects dialog box
   (Word), 5-7, 6-18
formatting text in a spreadsheet, 12-9
formula bar, 11-20
Formula dialog box, 9-13, 9-21
formulas, 9-20
formulas panel options, 11-12
Formulas tab, 15-2
Function Arguments dialog box, 15-4
function library group options, 15-2
functions, 15-2, 15-12
functions in tables, 15-15

G

galleries, 2-4
general panel options (Excel), 11-11
general panel options (Word), 2-21
globate template, 5-28
go to command, 4-13
Go To dialog box, 12-23
grammar shortcut menu, 1-10
greeting line field, 8-5
gridlines (chart), 10-6, 10-11
gridlines (Excel), 14-3
group options (Excel sparklines), 13-14
grouping sheets, 11-22
groups, 2-2

V

vertical axis, 10-5
vertical splitter bar, 11-4
view gridlines option (Word), 5-21, 9-9
view options (Excel), 11-5
view options (Word), 1-11

W

watermarks, 7-14
web layout view, 1-11
Web Options dialog box, 3-16
widow/orphan control options, 5-18
wildcard characters (Word), 4-10
word count, 1-9
Word Options dialog box, 2-21
Word Starter 2010 vs Word 2010, 1-6
Word Starter help, 1-14, 1-16
Word Starter workspace, 1-6
wordart styles group options (Word), 6-18
workbook defined, 11-2
Works database, 8-10
worksheet defined, 11-2
workspace (Excel), 11-4
workspace (Word), 1-6
wrap text (Word), 6-9, 6-10
wrap text in a cell, 12-10
wrapping style options (Word), 6-10
write & insert fields group options, 8-3
write group options (Word), 6-36

X

x axis, 10-5
XPS customization options, 3-28
XPS documents, 2-19, 3-27
xy scatter chart, 10-3

Y

y axis, 10-5
y axis scale, 13-6

Z

Zoom dialog box (Excel), 11-6
Zoom dialog box (Word), 1-11

No Stress Tech Guides

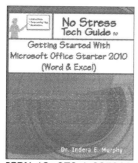

ISBN-13: 978-1-935208-14-3
ISBN-10: 1-935208-14-4

ISBN-13: 978-1-935208-09-9
ISBN-10: 1-935208-09-8

ISBN-13: 978-1-935208-10-5
ISBN-10: 1-935208-10-1

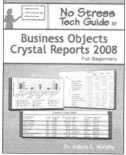

ISBN-13: 978-0-9773912-9-5
ISBN-10: 0-977391-29-9

ISBN-13: 978-1-935208-05-1
ISBN-10: 1-935208-05-5

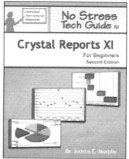

ISBN-13: 978-1-935208-00-6
ISBN-10: 1-935208-00-4

ISBN-13: 978-1-935208-08-2
ISBN-10: 1-935208-08-X

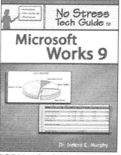

ISBN-13: 978-0-9773912-7-1
ISBN-10: 0-977391-27-2

ISBN-13: 978-0-9773912-8-8
ISBN-10: 0-977391-28-0

Other Titles	ISBN		ISBN
New In Crystal 2008	978-1-935208-01-3	Crystal Xcelsius 4.5	978-1-935208-02-0
Microsoft Works 8.5	978-0-9773912-1-9	OpenOffice.org Writer 2	978-0-9773912-4-0
ACT! 2009	978-1-935208-07-5	Crystal Reports for Visual Studio 2005	978-0-9773912-6-4

Visit us online to see the entire series www.tolanapublishing.com